Alice

P9-ECL-995

Skeletons from

the Opera Closet

Skeletons from the Opera Closet

David L. Groover
and Cecil C. Conner, Jr.

St. Martin's Press/New York
A Thomas Dunne Book

SKELETONS FROM THE OPERA CLOSET. *Copyright © 1986 by David L. Groover and C. C. Conner. All rights reserved. Printed in the United States of America. No part of this book may be used or reproduced in any manner whatsoever without written permission except in the case of brief quotations embodied in critical articles or reviews. For information, address St. Martin's Press, 175 Fifth Avenue, New York, N.Y. 10010.*

Library of Congress Cataloging in Publication Data

Groover, David.
Skeletons from the opera closet.

"A Thomas Dunne book."
1. Opera—Anecdotes, facetiae, satire, etc.
I. Conner, C. C. II. Title.
ML1700.G82 1986   782.1   86-13810
ISBN 0-312-72762-3

First Edition

10 9 8 7 6 5 4 3 2 1

Mr. Groover's Dedication:

When I was a boy growing up in Lebanon, Pennsylvania, I would go with my father to get my hair cut every other Saturday afternoon at Willard Bonawitz's barbershop. It was a very grown-up place to be, so I thought, for it had smells like no other, exotic magazines like Field and Stream, never any other boys getting their hair cut at that hour, and Mr. Bonawitz or one of his assistants always put some hot lather on my non-existent sideburns and shaved them off with a straight razor. It was a privileged, private little club.

A lanky man, with a magnificent sweep of pomaded hair, Mr. Bonawitz always had the radio turned on, played low so as not to disturb the men's conversation or the clicks of the scissors and the stropping of the razors. I had to strain forward to hear it. What came out of that white, clunky Philco was strange but beautiful music with people singing in an eerie language I had never heard. It was like music from the moons of Saturn.

While I was having my hair cut by Mr. Bonawitz—I had waited especially for him so I could be near the radio—I must have been bopping in the chair or tapping my fingers, probably both, when Mr. Bonawitz put his bony hand on my shoulder to quiet me.

"Do you like that music, Mr. Groover?"

To be called "Mr." by an adult when I wasn't being punished was the sincerest compliment. "I think so. What is it?"

"That is Opera, Mr. Groover. Isn't it . . . sublime!" He almost sang his praise.

By his smile and the way he flashed his scissors, and whatever that word meant, I knew he liked his Opera. Until his shop on Cumberland Street closed, I always went in on Saturday afternoon to have my hair cut to those soft, sublime sounds coming from his radio.

To you, Mr. Bonawitz, the Barber of Lebanon, who introduced me to this strange and grand new world, I happily dedicate this book.

Mr. Conner's Dedication:

To my mother, who knows little about opera, but who'll buy this book anyway.

Contents

Skeletons from

the Opera Closet

Prelude

You're sweating through another excruciating set of push-ups at Paris Island boot camp when your favorite melody, *The Marine Hymn,* swirls through your brain. You smile and start to hum, oblivious to the evil eye of your drill sergeant.

"Hey, dog face, who told you to sing Offenbach?"

"But, Sarge, it's our own song. You know, 'From the Halls of Montezuma . . .'"

"Yeah, well you can call it anything you like, but it's Offenbach and from *Geneviève of Brabant.* Now drop and gimme twenty more! And next time you wanta sing opera, get your composer straight!"

Such is the way of opera: expect something and be assured you'll probably get something completely different. Go to a performance wanting to hear the famed soprano and leave singing the praises of the scenery and the comprimario.

Opera never ceases to amaze, assuring itself of perpetual youth and vigor. Certifiably one of the grandest of the arts, the longevity of this hybrid is testament to its greatness, if not to its stubbornness. Some of western civilization's highest moments are to be discovered and savored upon the opera boards. Majestic, sublime, unparalleled, and ofttimes silly beyond its own words and music, opera has a potent magic for banishing tension, relaxing the fevered brow, or driving one mad.

The beauty that opera inherently possesses has been praised in a score of books, her majesty acclaimed in even more tomes, and her spellbinding allure amply conjured for over 400 years, an object of absolute veneration are her flaws. Even goddesses have their faults. Often it's their human frailties that are their best, true qualities. And, believe us, the pimple right on the end of her nose keeps the pedestal low enough so we can worship the statue. *Skeletons from the Opera Closet* is an appreciation and dissection, albeit humorous and light-hearted, of this most lively art's weaknesses, faux pas, trumperies, unusual and uncommon manners, overlooked glories, and weird and funny occurrences. In short, a catalog of some of the worst it has to offer, as well as some of its least-appreciated bests.

Though a serious subject, opera can and should be fun, and, the gods know, there's much here in this dizzying world to be made fun of. As the wonderful art that it is, though, opera needs an irreverent approach from a fresh perspective to keep the dust out. We hope *Skeletons from the Opera Closet* will be one such new broom.

So, curl up with our book and eat some pêche Melba, or tournedos à la Rossini, or just some Risë Stevens' fudge, and enjoy.

How to Build
a Chinese Opera House

*O*n a synthesizer, the *Magic Fire Music* fades in. You've
finally made it. National television. Prime time.
"Name that Aria!" Your dream chance at Valhalla's Treasure
Chest awaits. Your host R. W. beams. R. W.'s breast-plated
assistant, her own treasure chest sheathed in Las Vegas battle
gear, caresses the bumper of the red Ferrari, paws through the
Harry Winston goodies, sprays herself with Jungle Gardenia.
Furs, cars, jewels, yachts—your fame and fortune—are behind
one of the doors.

Your heart pounds. R. W., intense, reads the question like
a sermon: "What is the first opera?" He repeats the question.
Murmurs rumble through the audience.

You're shocked. Could it be this easy? You've known the answer all your life. Everybody knows it. Instinctively, you blurt out, "Peri's *Dafne*. 1597. In Florence!"

The audience's collective groan nearly knocks you over. R. W. is crushed. Slowly, sadly, but with that TV twinkle in his eyes, he addresses the camera. "Oh, I'm *so* sorry. That was the first opera in the *Western* world. You've overlooked the Chinese."

Your consolation prize for making a fool out of yourself is two weeks' worth of orchestra seats to the next Jean-Pierre Ponnelle horror in Tallahassee. No furs, no cars, no jewels, no yachts—and you're ineligible for another game show for two years. Under your breath, you curse the Chinese. Technically, of course, R. W. is correct, but even he didn't venture a guess as to the first opera. Who knows? Who cares? It might just as well have been the *Triumph of Horus* at the Teatro Luxor, Ancient Egypt. After all, that rite was also a drama with music—the original *Singspiel*, only with funnier costumes and a hippopotamus. Suffice it to say, we'll never know.

However, we do know that the medieval Yuan Dynasty of the Mongols, c. 1280–1368, had as rich a bardic tradition as any of the West's ancient empires. Resembling their European theatrical contemporaries in their pageant wagons, these Chinese musical troupes traveled about the countryside, performing in temporary theaters erected by the townsfolk. In rural areas near Hong Kong, these traditions persist. At least once a year, to commemorate an ancient goddess or a special anniversary, a village will rent an opera company and built a theater. For all you swells out there who harbor dreams of being an impresario, we gladly supply the blueprints on how to build your own Chinese opera house. Procuring the divas is up to you.

1. If you're the type of person who only eats grass and twigs, or else swears by "no preservatives, no additives," you had better plan your opera house at least two years in advance, since—"naturally"—you'll want to grow your own bamboo, and the tropical grass takes up to twenty-four months to mature into stalks thick enough for good theater material. You

[4]

more practical people out there can order the plants from your neighborhood horticulturist or Korean greengrocer.

2. If you've followed the planting instructions, you should be the proud owner of a fine canebreak, with stalks that range in diameter from four to ten inches. The four-inch stems are used for the frame, the ten-inchers for the base poles. *Arundinaria* is frighteningly resilient and will prevail against the harshest weather. So, if you're going to build your opera house in Hurricane Alley, don't fret; just nail your singers to the floor.

3. Buy stacking metal chairs. The cheaper the better. Remember this is a Chinese theater. Think take-out.

4. The coastal fishing villages abutting the South China Sea build their transient structures over the water. It would be a most picturesque setting should you schedule *Holländer, Otello, Gioconda, Billy Budd, Rheingold, Troyens,* or *Aida.* If you decide on *Tosca,* however, give your diva an inner tube.

5. Gather together all former Cub Scouts and Brownies and teach them the "Bamboo Hitch." This consists of a single strip of bamboo, pulled taut around the post, twisted in the front, with the ends tucked under the turns. A double hitch will lash the large posts. The framework is a trellis of horizontal and vertical bamboo woven onto the exterior larger frame. All this is set out and lined through by eye, please. No calipers, no set square, no rod and chain. This is a temporary theater, not the Pyramids.

6. Don't forget to build a box for the "ancestors" high in the rafters. Furnish it with a red lamp and burning incense, and the invisible old-timers will be most serene and bless your operatic endeavors.

7. If you've prayed to all the right gods, your completed theater should be approximately 125 feet long, 81 feet wide, and 81 feet from floor to roof edge. A three-foot wide catwalk should encircle the building to ensure a proper promenade during intermissions.

8. Admission must be a set price for all, except the bleachers, with seats numbered and drawn for. *Fa pai* shrines, decorated with paper flowers and offerings of sweet cakes should

[5]

grace the entranceway. These sweets are to be eaten by children since the gods have already consumed the essence of the food. Very practical, these Chinese. Vendors of cotton candy must also be hired to spin out one of the villagers' favorite delicacies.

And there you have it. Your own opera house built by your very own hands. Aren't you proud? Gatti-Casazza would weep from envy. Now all you have to do is fill it! Even the gods have their fingers crossed.

Unlike our newly constructed Chinese theater, opera houses in the West were never built in a day, though due to the ravages of fire many lasted no longer. The European opera house was intended for spectacle with a capital S and required princely resources to stage the musical extravaganzas. The section allotted for the audience was equally elaborate. This is, today, of great relief to the viewer, especially when what's taking place on stage fails to please. To relieve boredom, look around; count the putti or the crystal drops in the chandeliers.

In the nineteenth century it was common for young gentlemen to gather in the aisles to see the performance and, of course, to be seen. In England this area became known as "Fops' Alley." Benjamin Lumley, the era's preeminent opera impresario and manager of London's Italian Opera House, described the circus proceedings: "It was the practice of the day for all the more exquisite and fashionable of the male operatic patrons to quit their boxes or their scanty stalls during various portions of the performance, and to fill the vacant spaces in the center and sides of the pit, where they could laugh, lounge, chatter, eye the boxes from convenient vantage points, and likewise criticize and applaud in common. The meetings and greetings that took place were looked upon as an essential portion of the evening's entertainment." Today, unfortunately, such activity is only socially accepted during the intermissions, except for those oblivious, ravenous few who habitually unwrap their ten-decible candy wrappers during the pianissimo passages.

In Venice in 1637, the first "public" opera house opened, the

[6]

Teatro San Cassiano. Horror of horrors, the attendees, no longer guests at a private court's entertainment, had to purchase their tickets. Public theater impresarios couldn't afford the extravagant productions that so enamored the nobles, such as complete naval battles in the flooded main floor of the theaters that were reminiscent of ancient Rome, and music began to predominate. The Italian predilection for the human voice didn't hurt either. To show off the human voice to best advantage, the opera house became as compact as a Yugo. Two magnificent examples of these intimate theaters are still extant: Sweden's Drottningholm and Munich's Cuvilliès.

The exquisite Swedish theater is in the royal palace eight miles from Stockholm. Drottningholm's heyday was the late eighteenth century under Gustavus III, a great operaphile who wrote librettos and whose life and dramatic assassination at a masquerade at the Stockholm Opera House has been the subject of two operas. In Sweden, Verdi's *Un Ballo in Maschera* wasn't permitted, even with the traditional change in locale to Boston, until the 1920's. When it was finally performed, the Swedish public derided the historically inaccurate story since even their children were well aware that Gustavus's sexual preference would never have been for Amelia and that his assassin was never his friend.

As was common with the ubiquitous wooden theaters of the time, the first Drottningholm, built in 1744, soon burned down. During a performance, the fire was clamorously announced by a member of the audience who rushed on stage and was mistaken for a member of the cast, giving a new dramatic twist to the action. With Gustavus's untimely demise, Swedish opera languished. Fortunately, Drottningholm was spared the wrecker's ball and only closed up. Like a Sleeping Beauty it was reawakened in 1921 by an assistant in the royal library who went looking for a painting thought to be in storage somewhere in the haunted, musty theater. He found the painting, more dust than inside a phalanx of Hoover vacuum cleaners, thirty complete sets of scenery, and the antique stage machinery quite intact and only in need of new ropes to make it

[7]

all operable. There's no better way to be transported into the fairy tale charm of the eighteenth century than with a summer performance at Drottningholm. The ushers in perukes and knee breeches escort you into the raked-bench auditorium, which seats only 350, where you can relive the sweet discomfort of unupholstered eighteenth-century seating.

Although it doesn't offer quite the pristine experience of Drottningholm, the 437-seat Cuvilliès Theater, built between 1751–53 as the Residenztheater, was designed by the court jester. François de Cuvilliès's modern counterparts in scenic design and direction can barely boast better credentials. No Sleeping Beauty, this theater would have been lost during World War II had not local foresight led to its being transported, box by box, to a secure place away from the threat of Allied bombing. Some say it was actually Hitler who had it dismantled after a premonition that it would be bombed. The story may be apocryphal, but, in fact, bombs did destroy the actual spot in the Residenz where the theater had stood before its removal.

The eighteenth century was the age of private theaters. Prince Esterhazy, the patron of Haydn, built a 400-seat house at Eszterhaza Castle, his isolated "lodge" in the Hungarian marshes. Remote even from Eisenstadt, the traditional summer retreat from Vienna, Eszterhaza was nevertheless a great palace, second only to Versailles in its splendor, and blessed by the music of Haydn. Some lodge! Eszterhaza also possessed a grotto-like marionette theater where that peculiar form of puppet-theater opera was much beloved by the court. Except for his first, lost work, all of Haydn's incomparable operas were written for this secluded palace. "I could make experiments and be as bold as I pleased," Papa wrote; "I was cut off from the world, there was no one to confuse or torment me, and I was forced to become original."

In Caserta, a hill town east of Naples, another princely theater was constructed in the never-completed palace complex of Carlo di Borbone, the King of Naples and son of Spain's Philip V. Carlo planned to move his capital to neighboring

Caserta, where he could consolidate his power and out-Versailles Versailles. Everybody wanted to be a Sun King. Designed by Luigi Vanvitelli, the grandiose palace had a 500-seat theater, the Chapel of Apollo, with a rear stage wall that could dramatically slide open to reveal the palace grounds for a most spectacular, realistic garden vista. Frescoes and sculptures were all based on motifs from classical antiquity, since Carlo was the foremost collector of ancient art as the excavator of Pompeii and Herculaneum. When his mad half-brother Ferdinand died, Carlo rushed back to Spain to become Charles III, and Caserta was abandoned. He had never even spent a night there nor seen a performance in his own private theater.

Although private theaters were the preserve of the eighteenth-century nobility, the "new" nobility has been known to indulge themselves. The famous diva Adelina Patti built an elegant little theater in her Welsh castle, Craig-y-Nos. Its opening on 12 August 1891 had Patti singing the first act from *Traviata* and the garden scene from *Faust.* The theater, a Bayreuth in miniature, had a single gallery at the rear, no side boxes, and stalls that sloped down to the nearly invisible orchestra. Nearing the end of her career, the old trouper built the theater to continue her singing on the stage—any stage, even her own—and to amuse a few choice friends (G. B. Shaw, the Prince of Wales, et al.) with dramatic presentations. Royal vanity productions know no age.

Although the first opera house in Parma, the Teatro Farnese, still extant, is the second oldest theater of modern Italy, the infamous Parma reputation began at the Ducale, built in 1688. When Federici's *Zaira* appeared there in 1816 with the tenor Alberico Curioni in the title role, it was greeted with boos and catcalls. In retaliation, the tenor shouted obscenities at the audience. The police were called in to quell the uproar, arresting the singer. In revenge, at a later performance, Curioni advanced to the footlights and whistled at the audience—a most audacious insult. Again, riot ensued. Curioni was arrested, jailed for eight days, and then unceremoniously banished from Parma. Two years after this incident, Ducale's impresario was

[9]

jailed after the failure of the season's opening night for "offending the public's sensibilities."

With the fall of Napoleon, his second wife, Marie Louise, refused to go into exile with him. Could you blame her? Granted a divorce, she was made the Duchess of Parma and, to show her magnanimous gratitude, built a new opera house for the city. In 1828, the "new" 1500-seat Ducale (the present Regio) opened with another *Zaira*, this one by Bellini, which created as great a fiasco as did the earlier one. Bellini had rejected the libretto, written by one of the theater's directors, thus insulting the Parma public. At the opening they showed their indignation not with their usual whistles or caterwauls, but with deadly silence. His opera was never performed again in Parma.

The Parma "panthers," those inhabitants of the Regio's top balcony, show their critical disdain and opinion with prolonged throat clearing, murmurs and sighs for slight slips of pitch, perhaps the famous "Parma groan" for more serious mistakes, or with total verbal abuse for the worst debacles. Sometimes, the panthers attack with all of them. Numerous stories are recorded of an audience member yelling out, "This is how it goes," or giving even ruder instructions to the performers, or hurling chairs onto the stage at the hapless singer. On countless occasions, the demonstration continues in the streets of Parma. More than one artist has been reported as rushing out of town in costume and makeup, followed by an irate contingent of opera fanatics.

Parma may still be known as the place for singers' trials by fire, but unruly audiences are scarcely limited to the regional theaters in Italy. The country's greatest theater, Milan's La Scala, is a hotbed of scandal, both on and off the stage. As the largest and grandest lyric theater of Italy, La Scala represents the paradigm of Italian opera house development; however, its audiences can sometimes be positively prehistoric.

Taking its name from the church that had previously stood on its site, the Santa Maria della Scala, La Scala opened on 3 August 1778 with Salieri's *L'Europa Riconosouta*. The grand

[10]

auditorium had 260 boxes, each with its own anteroom that could be bought by individual subscribers and decorated to their own liking. With their servants in attendance, boxholders often played cards and dined during performances. La Scala also had the added inducement of gambling, which reputedly supported the theater until the Austrians put an end to such sybaritic practices in 1815. Though deprived of its added lucre, La Scala quickly became the center of Italian opera, and by the 1830's was one of the principal opera houses in Europe, with forty premieres in that decade alone, culminating with Verdi's first opera, *Oberto, Conte di San Bonifacio,* on 17 November 1839.

In the second half of the twentieth century, La Scala has been so beset by controversy that one never knows what's going to occur on stage, or for that matter if the performance will take place at all. There's bound to be an audience fight between rival factions—be it Callas vs. Tebaldi or, more recently, Scotto vs. Freni—or there'll be a temperamental artist threatening to withdraw, or strikes, or some political crisis, or all of the above. It's more demolition derby than grand opera.

The 1964–65 *Traviata* was a new production directed by Zeffirelli, conducted by von Karajan, and starring Mirella Freni. Renata Scotto reported that she wasn't chosen for the plum role because Zeffirelli said she didn't "look" the part. Well, that was the last straw for the Scotto fans. Needless to say, a sizeable portion of audience arrived at the theater bearing verbal tomatoes. The disturbance began even before the music, and when Freni didn't sing the high E flat at the end of the first act, it was all over. Naturally some partisans claimed Freni didn't sing the E flat because she doesn't have one.

Labor strikes postponed the December 1970 production of *Trovatore,* and the later revival of *I Puritani* was a comedy of errors. It was reported that nothing like it had happened at La Scala in recent memory. The Milanese have remarkably short memories. After unsuccessful dress rehearsals, both Freni and Pavarotti conveniently came down with "acute tonsillitis," and the opening was canceled a few hours before the curtain went up. Postponed for ten days, it finally opened with a new so-

[11]

prano, tenor, baritone, and conductor. By this time the stage director, Franco Enriquez, felt compelled to announce to the press that he was "no longer responsible for what occurred on stage," having never met the three new singers nor the conductor. The audience was not pleased. Parma came to Milan.

As recently as the closing week of the 1984–85 season, La Scala was running true to form. Its final production, *Andrea Chénier,* was beset by a strike that—what else—almost canceled its performances. As a result, most of the first night principals were no longer in town when the opera resumed in the final week. So be warned: if you plan a visit to La Scala, don't count on anything. You might just get it!

La Scala isn't the only great opera house that is scandal prone. The Vienna State Opera is, if anything, worse, it's just that the manners of its audience are so impeccable. In Vienna, the opera is the city's crown jewel, and the Viennese put music before all else, except perhaps Sacher torte. Operatic gossip is the life blood of the city, and the intrigues behind the scenes are discussed by everyone from the highest government minister to the streetcar fare collector, and it would take an eraser the size of an Austrian Alp to remove the latest *Opernskandal* from the headlines.

Just a year before Karajan and Zeffirelli were creating such a stir with their La Scala *Traviata,* they were doing the same in Vienna with their production of *Bohème.* The 1963–64 season began with Karajan's return as co-director, after having resigned his manager's position the previous year. As soon as the season got underway, the war with his co-director began. With the entire Viennese aristocracy present in full dress, the premiere of *Bohème* was canceled. Karajan insisted on having an Italian prompter, but the theater's staff would have none of that and "promptly" went on strike. Viennese compromise prevailed by the next performance: the Austrian prompter was paid to stay out of the prompter's box, while Karajan conducted and prompted without extra compensation.

While the location of the Vienna State Opera reflects its place in its city's life—right on the Ringstrasse, it couldn't be

[12]

more prominent—the Teatro la Fenice in Venice, on the other hand, is hidden away on a tiny skewed plot, wedged between minor canals and alleys, as if gerrymandered by a blind gondolier. The site is so irregular that the lobby's stuck on one side of the building and leads into the right rear corner of the auditorium. However, it does have the distinct, romantic advantage of being the only opera house in the world with a front entrance for arriving gondolas. The current structure, built in 1836, replaced the original 1792 theater that was—guess what —destroyed by fire. Named "The Phoenix" because the 1792 house had replaced the burned-down Teatro San Benedetto, La Fenice was planned by a syndicate of Venetian merchants, citizens, and nobles, and was designed by Gianantonio Selva, who inscribed the word "Societas" on the facade to commemorate the patronage. Before the last letter was chiseled, the Venetians had already coined their own acrostic: Sine Ordine Cum Irregularitate Erexit Theatrum Antonius Selva (Without order, with irregularity, this theater was built by Antonio Selva).

Despite its problematic setting and looking like a gondolier's idea of heaven with all its gold cherubs, La Fenice was, nevertheless, one of the most important theaters in the development of Italian opera, being the premiere home of Rossini's *Tancredi* and *Semiramide,* Bellini's *I Capuleti e i Montecchi* and *Beatrice di Tenda,* Donizetti's *Belisario* and *Maria di Rudenz* (now that's a pair of distinguished first nights), and Verdi's *Ernani, Attila, Rigoletto, Traviata,* and *Simon Boccanegra.* It also bestowed free tickets to the gondoliers, probably to insure a water-bound Hit Parade for the tourists. Maria Malibran was not enchanted when she arrived to sing in Venice. She was depressed by the place, especially the black gondolas, which made her feel as if she were "going to her own funeral"; hence, she commissioned her own personal gondola of dove gray, with blue curtains, a scarlet and gold interior, punted by gondoliers in blue trousers, red and black jackets, and yellow hats with black velvet bands. Even Malibran had her own vision of heaven.

La Fenice also has the peculiar tradition of sending a cat

[13]

down the aisle before each performance begins. For those who might be more than superstitious, the Drury Lane in London is the theater, though, to avoid. In 1848, a remodeling crew working on the theater found a hollow wall. Knocking open a hole, they found a small room. Inside, a skeleton was slumped over a table, a dagger stuck in its ribs. The identity of the dead man has never been discovered, but from as early as 1750 there have been haunting reports of The Man in Grey emerging from the room in which the secret chamber was found. He can still be seen to this day, wearing a grey riding coat, strolling spectrally along the upper circle of the theater and then disappearing through the wall. He's even been seen in the greenroom, greeting frightened operagoers. The management reveres their macabre mascot and has stoutly rejected any offers at exorcism.

A much grislier ghost has appeared at London's Lyceum Theater, site of such English premieres as *Freischütz, Ballo,* and *Otello.* Mr. W. H. Pollock reported in the 1884 Christmas issue of the *Illustrated Sporting and Dramatic News* (which sounds like an opera publication from Parma) that he and a friend saw a lady sitting in the stalls during a performance with the decapitated head of a man in her lap. She appeared to take no notice of the head even when the lights were turned up at intermission. Was she a critic? Was the head?

No less an institution than the Paris Opera, the most ornate example of the traditional Italianate opera house, has had at least one such ghostly curse. Halévy's *Charles VI* was well received at its premiere in 1843, but the resemblance between the eponymous character (France's insane monarch who thought he was made of glass) and the reigning French monarch, Louis Philippe, was too close for comfort and the work was banned until the Bourbon abdicated in 1848. When the opera was revived, it had three performances, and at each, just as the aria *Oh God, Kill Him* was sung, someone in the theater dropped dead: first a box-holder, then a stagehand, and finally the conductor. The French tried it once more, but the Emperor's coach was attacked on the way to the theater, and Halévy's opera flew out of the repertoire faster than a poltergeist.

[14]

In direct reaction to the design of the Italian baroque theater (with its gold telamons and enough curves to make Dolly Parton look like a yardstick), Richard Wagner wanted something different. When in doubt, build your own. Though Wagner is given credit for the idea of the covered orchestra pit—the "mystic abyss"—which coalesced and balanced the larger, more brilliant orchestral sound, the French architect Claude-Nicolas Ledoux had already designed a theater at Besançon in 1778 with just such a sunken, concealed orchestra; and the Schauspielhaus in Berlin, built in 1818–21, also foreshadowed Bayreuth. In the early opera houses, the problem was inadequate orchestral sound, with the musicians placed on the audience's level so they could be heard. Turin's Teatro Regio had a semicylindrical trough below the orchestra's wooden floor to reflect and reinforce the sound; while in some theaters, the acoustical trough extended under the audience and was covered with an open grill. At the Teatro Argentina in Rome, this reflecting trough was filled with water, on the principle that water was an efficient sound reflector. Bayreuth's "abyss," coupled with the hall's wooden floor, unpadded seats, and lightweight wooden ceiling, affords exceptional acoustics. Nothing is perfect, though; the singers may not have to strain to be heard, but they ofttimes have to strain to hear Wagner's ethereal orchestra.

If you want unhurried, elegant surroundings for your opera, try Glyndebourne, England. The theater is nothing to write home about: the acoustics are harsh and over-resonant; it surely has the plainest of interiors, resembling a small town's movie house; but the setting and ambience of the place more than compensate. The art of the picnic has reached its apogee at Glyndebourne. With their servants laden with hampers, lawn chairs, and fine china, ladies in evening gowns and men in black tie dine in the fields with the other ruminants. Glyndebourne has the distinct reputation of being the only opera house where the cows aren't on the stage.

There's one drawback to this sylvan scene if you're not a chiropterist or beloved by a suave, mysterious gentleman from

Transylvania: bats. They made their debut the very opening night, appropriately in the evening garden scene of *Figaro*. When a public health officer was called in the following day to deal with the pests, John Christie, the founder, sent him packing, and the bats and their descendants are there to this day, performing admirably in the dungeon scene of *Fidelio*, the midsummer night in *Falstaff*, and costumed as swallows for the sun-filled *L'Elisir d'Amore*.

Old New York had an early, grand passion for opera. The John Street Theater opened in 1767, followed shortly by the Park, partly owned by John Jacob Astor, where *Figaro* and *Barbiere* had their American premieres. The Park was the home of America's version of Fops' Alley, with the young attendees wearing uncomfortably high collars, white cravats, and the oh-so-modern "Brutus Crop," a lock brushed high off the forehead, when they appeared for their twice-weekly fix of opera sung in English.

There was one New Yorker who dreamed of Italian opera sung in its original language—none other than Lorenzo Da Ponte, the former librettist for *Don Giovanni, Figaro,* and *Così*. The toothless, dandified Italian had arrived in New York in 1805 and unsuccessfully pursued such various non-theatrical professions as book seller, greengrocer, liquor broker, and distiller by the time Manuel Garcia and his illustrious singing family came to New York to present Rossini's *Barbiere* in 1825. Da Ponte teamed up with the French tenor Montressor in 1832 in the Richmond Hill Theater, the converted former home of Aaron Burr, for a brief enterprise that lasted exactly thirty-five nights. Next, he convinced Chevalier Rivafinoli to finance a new building at Church and Leonard Streets where subscribers could buy their own boxes for $6,000 and decorate them as lavishly as they desired. Da Ponte's La Scala-like venture fared no better, opening on 19 November 1833 with Rossini's *La Gazza Ladra*. After sixty performances, the endeavor was finished. Da Ponte washed his hands of opera, but ended his final days teaching Italian at Columbia.

New Orleans was one of America's first cultural centers after

La Spectacle de la Rue St. Pierre was built in 1791. It was condemned as unsafe in 1804. So much for culture. The Theatre d'Orléans, home of such American premieres as *L'Elisir d'Amore, La Juive,* and *Le Prophète,* opened in 1809, burned down in 1813, and was rebuilt by 1816. At a subsequent vaudeville, the audience was amused with a loud cracking sound they thought part of the ingenious stage effects until they noticed the second and third galleries break away from the wall and slowly settle orchestra-ward. Thirty years later in 1885, when Adelina Patti sang *Traviata* in the rebuilt French Opera House, the audience was so unrestrained in its enthusiasm that their clamorous ovations caused the plaster ceiling to collapse. Not to be outdone, the re-rebuilt theater presented the American premiere of Gounod's *Reine de Saba* in 1899. The opera's third act features the sculptor Adoniram in his workroom, complete with roaring furnace and vats of molten metal. At the climax of the forging scene when the mold is made, the furnace exploded and engulfed the stage in flames. They never attempted *Benvenuto Cellini.* We wouldn't recommend *Samson et Dalila* either.

Even the wild, wild west didn't want for opera. Houses were everywhere, including Dawson City, Alaska. The prototype of all mining town theaters was Piper's Opera House in Virginia City, Nevada, bought in 1868 by the enterprising John Piper. Rough, tough miners could shell out $10 for an upper box or $.50 for the back lounge, affectionately known as the "pig pen," where spitting was allowed, if not required. Like every opera/vaudeville house, the programs varied from Patti to Shakespeare, from Lola Montez to unattended temperance lectures. Twice, Piper's burned down, and twice was rebuilt. In 1883, the year of the Met's inauguration, Piper's boasted a raked stage, cantilevered balconies, a cloakroom for personal firearms, a stage floor on springs, and its own orchestra. Quite spiffy, but who's gonna clean up that pig pen?

Who'd have ever thought that the bicycle would build an opera house? Stranger things have happened. The "bicyclette moderne" of the French engineer G. Juzan and the "safety" bicycle of the Englishman J. F. Starley, both patented in 1885, both using two wheels of equal size, and both with a chain-driven rear wheel, peddled into spectacular popularity. When the veterinary surgeon John B. Dunlop, using rubber sheeting and strips of linen from his wife's old dresses, patented the pneumatic tire to cushion his son's tricycle rides over the cobbled streets of Belfast, the bicycle craze whirled into a mania.

Meanwhile, one thousand miles up the Amazon, in one of the most uninhabitable regions on earth, the steamy outpost of Manaus languished in a perpetual siesta. As late as 1870, this way station at the confluence of the muddy Amazon and the ebony-tinged Rio Negro was populated by only a few thousand. By 1910, because of the rubber bonanza, the "Pearl of the Amazon" boasted electric lights, a trolley system, piped gas and water, an artificial harbor with a floating tidal pier, a cast-iron fish market designed by the renowned Eiffel, palatial homes of Carrara marble, direct steamship connections to New York and Liverpool, telephone lines, an $8 million diamond trade, boulevards tessellated in Portuguese tile, the highest per capita income in the world, and a $10 million opera house—the Teatro Amazonas. Cafe society rivaled that on the Champs Élysées. The rubber barons sent their children to Eton, their wives to shop in Paris, and their dirty laundry to London.

Inaugurated on 31 December 1896, after seventeen years of construction, the Teatro Amazonas was an Art Nouveau dream in pink and white. Designed by the Lisbon School of Engineering, lavishly embellished with the finest building materials of the time, and equipped with state-of-the-art lighting and backstage machinery, the theater rivaled any in the world. The rubber barons wanted respectability; with their sumptuous opera house, they got it in spades. Nothing was too expensive: Italian marble sheared from the same cliffs out of which had come Michelangelo's masterpieces, gold leaf mined in Brazil and wrought in England, Portuguese stone work, French cast iron, Alsatian glass tiles, Venetian crystal, hardwood inlays of mahogany and walnut from the surrounding forests. The auditorium's ceiling was adorned with paintings derived from the

[18]

operas of Antonio Carlos Gomes, Brazil's foremost composer, whose *Il Guarany*, a heady mix of Indian rhythms and Verdian melodrama, was offered opening night. Its world premiere had occurred at La Scala in 1870.

The civilized, cultured life in this amazing place seemed too good to last. It didn't. By 1910, the over-inflated tire was leaking badly; by 1915, it was flat. From seeds of the *Hevea Braziliensis* tree, smuggled out of Brazil by the English explorer Henry Wickham in 1876 and transplanted to Britain's Asian protectorates, huge tracts of the rubber trees sprouted and dominated the world supply. Now, the demand was even greater, for the automobile industry's insatiable need for tires far outweighed the humble two-wheeler's. With plentiful labor cheaper in the East Indies, with virtually none of the notorious Brazilian red tape or export taxes, with leaf blight unknown, and with unobstructed transport from the plantations to the ports, Asian raw rubber bounced right over the Brazilian product and rolled out in front. In Manaus, banks failed, jewelry was pawned, great steamships were auctioned, children returned from private schools, the suicide rate increased, and quite a few parcels of shirts went unclaimed at the London laundries.

By 1921, Brazil nuts were the chief export of the Amazon region. After such a heady decade, Manaus swooned into a jungle lethargy. Today, with tourism steadily increasing, Manaus has witnessed a resurgence. Renovated and spruced up in 1974, the Teatro Amazonas remains Brazil's unparalleled opera house, if not the world's. Its audiences may not be as glittering as they once were during the city's Belle *Époque*, but the grand house on the river is a testament to a people's resiliency between flush times and folly. It must have come from all that rubber.

· *Intermezzo* ·

The Drag-nation of Faust

Suppose you were taking the evening air along the picturesque banks of the Arno in Florence in mid-April in 1831 and happened to pass a couturiere's salon. The dresses in the window look inviting; you have a few extra lire in your handbag, and a new bonnet would be just the proper thing to put you in a spring mood. You enter the cozy store and, in the dressing area in the back, who should be standing there being fitted in a fetching maid's outfit—dress, hat, green veil, and the rest—but Hector Berlioz! You're taken aback, to say the least. What do you say to the young Prix de Rome winner? "Hector it's *you.*" or "The veil is lovely, but do you think green goes with your sideburns?" Ah, these French musicians, so *au courant,* so chic.

Well, for the fashionable Monsieur Berlioz, this was a serious affair, indeed. The masquerade was part of his elaborate scheme to return to Paris and shoot not only his fiancee, Camille Moke, who had just sent him a "Dear Hector" letter, but also her nettlesome mother and Monsieur Pleyel, his replacement for Mme. Moke's affections. In the guise of a certain lady's personal maid conveying an urgent message for the family, Hector would enter the house at 9 P.M., when the happy trio would be gathered for supper. He would be shown into the drawing room. While the bogus letter was being read, he would draw his double-barreled pistols and blow their brains out. He would then pay his respects to himself in similar manner, or drink the two vials of laudanum and strychnine that he had brought along for that very purpose.

However, his plans went comically awry. Discreetly hiding

his distaff attire in the door pocket of the mail coach bearing him out of Florence, he forgot to take the parcel with him when he changed coaches at Pietrasanta for Genoa. Once in Genoa, he had but a few hours before the next departure to Turin. Frantically, he ran around to find a servant who could speak both French and Italian, and hiring a liberal fellow set off yet again to procure some lovely Genoese travesty. What his bilingual cicerone thought of this odd Frenchman's taste in clothes is unfortunately unrecorded; but knowing how fastidious Hector was, it is beyond doubt that he looked ravishing.

While Berlioz was straightening his seams, the Sardinian police, on the lookout for suspicious Parisians who might be cohorts of the Carbonari, those instigators of the July 1830 Revolution who advocated the overthrow of Austrian and Papal rule in Italy, cast a raised eyebrow in Berlioz's direction and refused him a visa for Turin. Instead, they ordered him to detour south toward Nice and Saint-Tropez, obviously mistaking him for one of the infamous *Cagelles*.

In the coach on the way to Nice, and now re-equipped with fresh handmaiden's mufti, Berlioz had second thoughts about killing himself. Although he fervently desired to send that nymphomaniacal concert pianist, Mme. Moke, off to Hades, he realized that he had music inside him, important music, aching to be written. The sea and the balmy breezes of Nice brought him to his senses. He returned to Italy to complete the studies granted him for winning the Prix de Rome and put Mme. Moke out of his mind. Great music lay ahead. And just when he had mastered how to walk in heels.

Beckmesser's Revenge

$\mathcal{B}$eing a music critic is no easy task. Musical tastes change faster and with no more discernible reason than a punk's hair color. What, on first hearing, may be construed as too old-fashioned, or too modern, or just too mundane, oftentimes becomes after a second hearing like the bed of Goldilocks's: just right. The works that we now take for granted as standard items in the repertoire were, in more cases than not, usually viewed as abominations, anomalies, downright disasters, or trash.

Time has seen to it that the great works have been vindicated, and there is exquisite pleasure to be had in Monday morning quarterbacking. What follows includes a critical potpourri, in no particular order—chronological or preferential—of what the first night critics had to say. Their observations, right or wrong, certainly are a chronicle of past fashions, manners, and conventions, in the world of opera. Some are trenchant, some are wry, and some veer toward pumpernickel.

La Bohème (Giacomo Puccini)
1 February 1896. Turin. World Premiere.

Amazing as it may seem, this much-beloved and favorite staple of every opera house in the world was neither much beloved nor appreciated at its first performance at the Teatro Regio. Even the incandescent conducting of the twenty-nine-year-old maestro, Arturo Toscanini, could not secure a solid hit.

With its "clouds of melody," its evergreen sweetness, its youthful exuberance, and its contemporary harmonies, Puccini's fourth opera rather bored the audience. It wasn't until the Palermo production on 13 April 1896, conducted by Leopoldo Mugnone, and with Ada Giachetti (Caruso's common-law wife) as Mimi, that La Bohème riveted their attention. We have taken this masterpiece to our hearts for almost a century. Its freshness refuses to age.

> Music which can delight but rarely move. Even the finale of the opera, so intensely dramatic in situation, seems to me deficient in musical form and color. La Bohème, even as it leaves little impression on the minds of the audience, will leave no great trace upon the history of our lyric theater, and it will be well if the composer will return to the straight road of art, persuading himself that this has been a brief deviation.
> Stampa. 2 February 1896.

> The music of La Bohème is real music, made for immediate pleasure—intuitive music. And it is precisely for this that we must praise and condemn it.
> Gazzetta di Torino. 2 February 1896.

We wonder what could have started Puccini towards the degradation of this *Bohème*. The question is a bitter one, and we do not ask it without a pang, we who applauded and shall continue to applaud *Manon*, in which was revealed a composer who could combine masterly orchestration with a conception in keeping with the best spirit of Italy.

You are young and strong, Puccini; you have talent, culture, and imaginative ability such as few possess; you have today conceived the whim of forcing the public to applaud you where and when you will. That is all very well for once, but for once only. For the future, turn back to the great and difficult battles of art.

Gazzetta del Popolo. 2 February 1896.

Let us await better things from the strong endowment of this composer, when he will find a subject less pressing.

Corriere della Sera. 2 February 1896.

22 April 1897. Manchester. First production in England.

Signor Puccini's new opera, about which so much interest has been excited, was produced last night before a large and brilliant audience, and we have not often had to record so successful a first performance.

The construction of the opera allows for very few opportunities for responsive cheers in the course of an act, but more than once loud applause interfered with the continuity of the music, and once the audience insisted on the repetition of the elaborate concerted piece.

At the end of every act, however, there were ringing cheers from all parts of the house, and the composer was compelled to make his bow more than a dozen times.

Manchester Guardian. 23 April 1897.

26 December 1900. New York. Metropolitan Opera Premiere.

La Bohème is foul in subject, and fulminant but futile in its music. Its heroine is a twin sister of the woman of the camellias, whose melodious death puts such a delightfully soothing balm upon our senses that we forget to weep in Verdi's opera. But Mimi is fouler than Camille, and Puccini has not been able to administer the palliative which lies in Verdi's music.

The stage of degradation to which dramatic music has been reduced in *La Bohème* is that occupied by the art in Massenet's *Navarraise.* Sometimes it is for a moment the vehicle of passionate expression, but oftener it is the vehicle of noise and sometimes not the vehicle but the sonorous disturbance itself.

In his proclamation of passion Puccini is more successful so soon as he can become strenuous; but even here the expression is superficial and depends upon strident phrases pounded out by hitting each note a blow on the head as it escapes from the mouths of the singers of the accompanying instruments.

Altogether the performance was exceedingly spirited and the stage furnishings and management adequate.

New York Tribune. 27 December 1900.

Cavalleria Rusticana (Pietro Mascagni)
19 October 1891. London Premiere.

Of the music of *Cavalleria,* I have already intimated that it is only what might reasonably be expected from a clever and spirited member of a generation which has Wagner, Gounod, and Verdi at its fingers' ends, and which can demand, and obtain, larger instrumental resources for a ballet than Mozart had at his disposal for his greatest operas and symphonies. Far more important than that it has a public trained to endure, and even expect, continuous and passionate melody, instead of the lively little allegros of the old school, which were no more than classically titivated jigs and hornpipes; and to relish the most poignant discords without making a wry face, as their fathers, coddled on the chromatic confectionery of Spohr and his contemporaries, used to do when even a dominant seventh visited their ears too harshly.

Mascagni has set *Cavalleria Rusticana* to expressive and vigorous music.

Music in London. G. B. Shaw. 28 October 1891.

Les Troyens à Carthage (Hector Berlioz)
4 November 1863. Paris. World Premiere.

If anyone had the right to suffer from ulcers it was Berlioz. The "in" place to be was the Paris Opera, that unconquerable bastion of French musical taste and theory, where careers were made and broken, and Monsieur Berlioz literally made himself ill over his abortive sieges to storm that snobbish citadel. Armed with the Prix de Rome, the *Symphonie Fantastique, Harold en Italie,* and his *Requiem,* he was begrudgingly allowed entrée through the great gates with *Benvenuto Cellini* (10 September 1838). With its resounding defeat—four performances to half-filled houses—Berlioz was cashiered with a most dishonorable discharge. The Opera's doors were slammed in his face and forever bolted.

Outside the walls, Berlioz had to watch while the "routineers, academics, and the deaf" such as Halévy, Meyerbeer, Saint-Jullien, Thalberg, David, Dejazet, Maillard, Cadux, Grisar, and Villeblanche were feted, lauded, and, worse, performed. Here were the Second Empire's musical equivalents to our own Jackie Collins, Sidney Sheldon, and Danielle Steele—successful hacks. The situation would have given ulcers to an entire platoon.

For twenty-five years, Berlioz was excluded from the French operatic circles. Having completed his masterpiece *Les Troyens* in 1858, he resigned himself with bitter irony to having produced a work of art that was destined never to be produced in its entirety while he lived. When Carvalho dangled the chance of a production at his Theatre Lyrique, Berlioz, heedful of the inadequacy of the small house to mount such a "grand and powerful" work, nevertheless acquiesced.

Recalling those horrid visions of his early anatomy studies in the gore-encrusted room of the Hospice de la Pitié with its "swarms of sparrows wrangling over scraps of lung" and "rats gnawing the bleeding vertebrae," Berlioz hacked his creation in two pieces and suffered it to be further butchered by the "craven stupidity" of director Carvalho. He wanted a performance, even an "irrelevant and positively ridiculous" one. Out of his own pocket he augmented the orchestra with more players, he cut the orchestration "to fit the resources available," he was driven mad by Carvalho's niggling criticisms and sloppy staging, and he had to contend with mediocre singers and an incompetent chorus and ballet.

With an orchestral introduction and a prologue added to compensate for the dumping of the original Part I, *La Prise de Troie,* and with a truncated Part II, *Les Troyens à Carthage* premiered 4 November 1863. The excisions included: (numbered from the full score published in 1969) the entries of the builders, sailors, and farmers (#20, 21, 22), Narbal and Anna's duet (#30), the second ballet at Dido's court (#33), Iopas's aria (#34), Hylas's aria (#38), and the final duet between Aeneas and Dido (#44). When the inept stagehands couldn't manage the scene change after the *Hunt and Storm,* causing a 55-minute pause before the opera could resume, even this famous interlude (#29) was removed for the remainder of the run. In his *Memoirs,* Berlioz recalled that first night:

There was one solitary, rather subdued boo at the end, when I was called for, and that was all. The gentleman in question clearly regarded it as his duty to keep up the good work throughout the weeks that followed, for he came back with a colleague and booed at precisely the same point at the third, fifth, seventh, and tenth performances. Five papers were crudely insulting, but more than fifty articles of appreciative criticism, written with genuine enthusiasm and uncommon perception, appeared during the following fortnight and filled me with happiness such as I had not known for a long time.

Les Troyens à Carthage ran for twenty-one performances. Receiving double royalties as librettist and composer and by selling the vocal score in Paris and London, Berlioz received a handsome recompense for this torso of an opera and could now

[28]

resign his secure and lucrative, yet frustrating, post as critic of the prestigious *Journal des Débats*. Later, he was commissioned to write a comic opera for Baden's Theatre der Stadt, his graceful and lyric *Béatrice et Bénédict* (1862), which received glowing notices and earned for Berlioz—with his concert performances— the Cross of the Order of Hohenzollern.

When I see what certain people mean by love and what they look for in the creations of art, I am reminded involuntarily of pigs snuffling and rooting in the earth with their great coarse snouts at the foot of mighty oaks and among the loveliest flowers, in search of their favorite truffles.

Berlioz didn't do so badly for himself. After all, he is remembered, not the hacks he so detested. Perhaps, had he lived in a different musical atmosphere than Paris, the city he loved to hate, he wouldn't have had to endure so many headaches from butting his head against the establishment; but had circumstances been easier for him, perhaps he wouldn't have followed his own idiomatic, glorious musical visions. For all of that, we wouldn't have wanted Monsieur Berlioz to alter one single note. We still don't.

"Non-symphonic Interlude"
"Well, what about this Royal Hunt? And the virgin forest? And the cave? The stream? The naiads? The satyrs? The nymphs? The storm? etc., etc."
"In the waste-paper basket."
"Oh, M. Berlioz—but that was why I came! Didn't the public like it then? What a dangerous admission! On that principle your waste-paper basket would very soon be full."
Journal Amusant. 28 November 1863.

I do not mean to pretend that *Les Troyens* is a work without fault. It contains real, nay, considerable faults. The recitatives and the airs are too often confounded together in it; in both, the accompaniment is sometimes overloaded; the abruptness and

harshness of some modulations may be noticed; we may point out a phraseology which is sometimes laborious and inverted. We could desire more simplicity in an antique subject. But at the same time what accents! what constant elevation! what respect for truth! what beautiful lyric declamation! and what an admirable orchestration! Alternately brilliant, profound, colored, varied, impetuous, poetical and always sonorous, while remaining sober and discreet!
Evening Gazette. 9 January 1864.

At the new and beautiful Theatre Lyrique, erected in the recently improved part of Paris, Hector Berlioz's opera of *Les Troyens* is in full tide of success. Deeming it necessary, perhaps, when ancient Troy was the theme, to impart to his work a local and appropriate coloring of vagueness, Monsieur Berlioz has, in my estimation, succeeded in producing the wildest and most disappointing music. Still, large audiences grace nightly the elegant salle of the Theatre Lyrique, and listen to *Les Troyens* with their air of complacent superiority assumed by those who make a conscientious duty of admiring what they do not in the least understand.
Dwight's Journal of Music. 20 February 1864.

Jenůfa (Leoš Janáček)
6 December 1924. New York. American Premiere.

A more complete collection of undesirables and incredibles has never previously appeared in opera.

To [the] crude story, Janáček has written music that is obviously the work of a man who, however many works he may have to his credit, is only a cut above the amateur. The best things in the score are the national songs and dances, which are charming. For the bigger moments he has mostly nothing but conventional operatic formulae. It is a little puzzling, to the non-Czech listener, to find cheerful national dance rhythms running through the most tragic scenes. Apparently in these Central European countries, you do everything to these rhythms: you shave yourself to a Krakoviak, cut a man's throat to a Mazurka, and bury him to a Czardas.

The company labored hard to make absurd stage figures

credible. The opera was charmingly staged, and the costumes were a delight to the eye.

Evening Post. December 1924.

Il Barbiere di Siviglia (Gioacchino Rossini)
20 February 1816. Rome. World Premiere.

Rossini's sparkling *opera buffa* masterpiece was planned, composed, rehearsed, and staged within three and a half weeks. On hearing this, Donizetti, no slouch himself when it came to churning out the latest operatic commodity, replied, "Well, he always was lazy."

With contract in hand for (1) an opera to be written from any libretto given him, (2) his adaptation of the music to fit the singers, (3) his supervision of said opera, (4) his conducting of same for the first three performances, and (5) the incredibly low fee of 400 *scudi* (the prima donna was to be paid 500 *scudi!*), Rossini, financially secure and still glowing from the Venetian successes of *Tancredi* and *L'Italiana in Algeri,* set about his work with his usual celerity, wit, and dazzle.

Even blessed with Cesare Sterbini's peerless adaptation of Beaumarchais's comedy (1777), Rossini was prudent enough to change his opera's title to *Almaviva, or the Useless Precautions,* and even had printed in the libretto a "Notice to the Public," wherein he stated his "respect and veneration for the immortal composer who preceded him." He thought this would deflect untoward criticism and comparisons against his use of the same play that Giovanni Paisiello, the grand old man of *opera buffa,* had used as the basis for his immensely successful *Barbiere* of 1782. Rossini was wrong.

The partisans of Paisiello were out in force at the Teatro Argentina, having no intentions of placidly accepting this parvenu's slap to the Italian Master. To make matters worse, the patrons of the Teatro Valle, the *opera buffa*'s regular home, were not at all pleased to see comic opera staged at the rival *opera seria* house, the Argentina. They were also abundantly, and vociferously, present. The evening careened toward disaster.

Entering the orchestra to take the conductor's place at the harpsichord, Rossini was greeted with howls of laughter. It wasn't so much the musician who was jeered, as it was the musician's outfit. Domenico Barbaja, the operatic impresario of Naples who launched the careers of Rossini, Bellini, Donizetti, the glorious dancer Fanny Elssler, and the phenomenal singer Giuditta Pasta, had given Rossini a Spanish-styled ensemble for the premiere. The fashionable Romans thought this was quite the silliest thing they had ever seen a grown man wear.

Throughout the evening, the production was plagued, almost cursed, with one mishap after another. The operatic cognoscenti easily recognized the overture as the same one, slightly modified, that Rossini had previously used for *Aureliano in Palmira* (1813) and also *Elisabetta, Regina d'Inghilterra* (1815). Familiar duets and arias cropped up intermittently, to which the audience vocally showed its disapproval. Why the patrons should have been slighted by this standard practice of the Bel Canto age can only be attributed to the vicious cabal organized against the young composer. And anyway, if a musician's going to plagiarize anybody, better he should steal from himself so he won't be sued. Rossini said it best: "I had the right to remove from my fiascos those pieces which seemed best, to rescue them from shipwreck by placing them in new works."

Manuel Garcia, the Almaviva, having persuaded Rossini during rehearsals to allow him to substitute a Spanish tune for his *serenade* to Rosina and to actually accompany himself on the guitar (Garcia was an accomplished musician), forgot to tune it before going onstage. The tuning, itself, produced whistles; when a string broke, pandemonium. When Figaro entered, carrying another guitar, the audience went wild. They jeered at Signora Righetti-Georgi's entrance as Rosina, and had a field day when Bartolo accidentally tripped over the trapdoor and continued his aria desperately trying to stop his nose from bleeding.

During the First Act finale, a cat suspiciously appeared onstage to the consternation of the cast and the great merriment of the audience. Righetti-Georgi had this to say: "The excellent Figaro, Zamboni, chased it off one side; it returned from the other, and hurled itself into the arms of Bartolo; the charitable audience called out to it, imitated its meowing, and encouraged it by voice and gesture to proceed with its improvised role."

And the Second Act was even noisier! Castil-Blaze, the critic for the prestigious Parisian *Journal des Débats,* reported that "all the whistlers in Italy seem to have given themselves a rendez-vous for this performance." At the end of the act, in defense of his artists, Rossini rose to applaud them. He was greeted with the evening's loudest shouts of disapprobation. (He should have removed that ridiculous coat.)

Conflicting reports follow as to what happened next. Some say that Rossini, depressed (who wouldn't be!), took to his bed; others, that he took to his bed unconcerned about the rude Romans. He did refuse to conduct the second performance, though, and stayed home. However, operatic miracles being what they so often are—unpredictable and totally off the wall —the performance was a smash. The audience clamored for Rossini. When he didn't show himself, they marched to his house and gave him an alfresco ovation. Rossini probably greeted them wearing that silly coat.

10 March 1818. London Premiere.

The music is by Rossini, a young composer of extraordinary merit, now living, who enjoys great celebrity in all parts of the continent. This opera is the first specimen of his compositions which has been submitted to the judgement of an English audience.

Taken as a whole, perhaps, it bears marks of haste, and still more of extravagance; but we are persuaded that all persons who have carried the study of music to the last degree of refinement must have been delighted and astonished by the occasional touches of genius, the variety, and originality of his style.

The general character of Rossini's music is extreme ornament, the perfect reverse of what is called the simple style: but his resources in that line and the fertility of his invention seem

almost unlimited. It is possible that its effect may lessen by frequent repetition: the first impression, however, is delightful.
The Times. 11 March 1818.

A more perfect representation *in all its parts* we have never witnessed: the music combining enchanting melodies, scientific harmonies, and at the same time truly dramatic: the variety and novelty of the modulations, the fire and sprightliness infused into all the accompaniments, are truly rapturous to the ear, and stamp him, as a musician, a perfect master of nature and of his art. The Finale to the first act and the quintets in the second are beyond all praise.
The Observer. 11 March 1818.

His style is less remarkable for its variety than for the prodigality of ornament which rather characterizes than adorns it. There is no originality about it, either in passion or fancy.

In the *new Barber of Seville* we therefore looked with some eagerness for some touches of genius or nature—some wildness of fancy at once graceful and original, which should justify the boldness of an attempt for which no other excuse could be invented—but we were disappointed.

Indeed, with three or four exceptions, the music of the opera is considerably more flat and commonplace than anything we recollect lately to have heard: and its whole surface is labored into an artificial richness by an accumulation of a thousand small graces, which would scarcely have been used by any musician of moderate taste—even if he possessed no splendor of imagination.
The News. 15 March 1818.

29 November 1825. New York Premiere.

In what language shall we speak of an entertainment so novel in this country, but which has so long ranked as the most elegant and refined among the amusements of the higher classes of the old world? All have obtained a general idea of the opera from report. But report can give but a faint idea of it. Until it is seen, it will never be believed that a play can be conducted in recitative or singing and yet appear nearly as natural as the ordinary drama.

New York Evening Post. 30 November 1825.

Faust (Charles Gounod)
19 March 1859. Paris. World Premiere.

"Abbé" Gounod's ooh-la-la treatment of Goethe's Romantic archetype did not set Paris on fire when it first pulled into the Theatre Lyrique, but it did produce enough heat to keep it running for fifty-nine showings. Chugging along like the proverbial "little engine," it gradually picked up momentum and fame, until it literally seemed to career out of control, becoming one of the most produced operas in the world. At the Paris Opera alone, between 1869 and 1894, *Faust* had a *second* run of 500 performances; it was a personal favorite of Queen Victoria's; and was staged so often at the Metropolitan that W. J. Henderson of the *New York Times* dubbed the theater the "Faustspielhaus."

Unfortunately for Gounod, the profits to be had for his labor did not run into the black until late in his life. With its slow start, only one music publisher in Paris showed interest. Gounod sold his French rights to Antoine de Choudens for 6666 francs and 66 centimes; the remaining third being paid to the machinelike, libretto assembly line team of Barbier and Carré. Not a man who appreciated music, Choudens only liked what made money. He was soon infatuated with *Faust*. The sheet music, alone, made him fabulously wealthy. He showed little interest in the opera itself; and whenever his children misbehaved he threatened them, if they didn't shape up, to take them to see it.

Although *Mireille* (1864) might have more drama and *Roméo et Juliette* (1867) was more of an instant success, Gounod spent the remainder of his creative life trying to recapture that elusive quality that had made *Faust* such a "limited special." Somewhere along the line he had mislaid his schedules. He just couldn't run fast enough to catch up.

[35]

The *new Faust*—Monsieur Gounod's five-act opera on this known subject was produced on Saturday last, under circumstances of uncommon excitement and expectation.

As regards choice of subject, however, and the manner in which the story has been treated by MM. Barbier and Carré, in professed imitation of Goethe's drama, first and last thought must be one: the tale is unfit for the musical stage. Neither the German dramatist's Faust nor Méphistophélès can be rendered by concords or discords, by sweet *cantabile* or bitter staccato movements. In the new opera Faust becomes a washed-out *Robert le Diable,* Méphistophélès a tame *Bertram.* Only one of the three principal characters, Margaret, has been strong enough to keep anything like its original form or color. Many of the persons and scenes which give significance and variety to Goethe's play have been left out; others have been awkwardly jumbled together, leaving an outline to be filled up.

Possibly the very qualities which, as a theme for opera, should have repelled, may have beckoned to M. Gounod. That which has hitherto hindered the complete success of his genius on the stage has been his over-anxiety to produce chameleon colors, passing lights, half shades—all that is comprehended in the untranslatable word "nuance."

How large, how frank, how noble M. Gounod can be in his melodies and their treatment *Faust* shows abundantly in its choruses, and in most of its great situations; but his *Faust,* also, contains too many charming passages, which never may be valued as they deserve, owing to their evanescent brevity. Crowding and change are faults as well as meagerness and monotony.

Athenaeum. 26 March 1859.

11 June 1863. London Premiere.

It is seldom that public opinion so surely expressed itself, and in terms which leave so little room for suspicion or mistrust. The audience "went" for the music from the first note to the last, and the future popularity of this opera can hardly be a matter of question.

Gounod's forms of melody are various, and not at all times

pleasing, but in his warm and felicitatious instrumentation, in which there is sufficient fullness without actual depth, or even any feature of remarkable originality, there is an obvious and abiding charm. Nor is the art of strongly and emphatically individualizing the personages of the drama absent.

The Observer. 14 June 1863.

Norma (Vincenzo Bellini)
20 June 1833. London Premiere.

We cannot however award any high praise to this opera of Bellini's. It is lamentably deficient in original ideas (Rossini, as usual, being the source principally drawn upon) and but for a certain dramatic character discernible in its musical world, unusually short as it is, put the patience of the audience to a somewhat severe test.

The admirers however of the singing and acting of Pasta will do well to see her in this opera. The ballet of *La Sylphide* with Taglioni followed. The house was crowded.

Morning Post. 24 June 1833.

On Thursday the 20th of June, a new opera was actually produced—the first attempt of this kind this season! The occasion was Mme. Pasta's benefit: the name of the piece, *Norma,* a tragic opera in two acts, composed by Signor Bellini, and got up under his personal direction.

That this is an imitation of *Medea* is evident, and, as in that opera, Mme. Pasta is the life and soul of this. Her acting alone saves it here, as it did in Milan, where it was first produced last year.

Considered as a whole, the music, though not censurable in regard to the rules of composition, possesses the most fatal of all faults—it is deplorably uninteresting. Except the motivo of the duet, *Deh! con te li prendi,* and aria, *Norma! che fu?,* and the finale, not a piece has the slightest pretense to originality, or produces the least effect. The overture and introduzione stun one with all kinds of noisy instruments, and half, or more, of the first act is accompanied by the same intolerable din.

[37]

The music of the last scene, and the acting of Pasta, but especially the latter, will keep the opera on the stage while she remains to fill the part; without her, or her equal, if such should ever be found; it has no chance of being listened to in London; and even with her, it is with a half reluctance permitted. *London Harmonicon.* June 1833.

Paging Maria Callas!

Tristan und Isolde (Richard Wagner)
20 June 1882. London Premiere.

The most wearying thing we've sat out for some considerable time. Rather a long, dull sermon in a stuffy church on an August afternoon, than one act of *Tristan.*

Taken as a whole, it is the embodiment of stupendous boredom, must be the verdict of all English opera-goers who delight in the operas of Rossini, Mozart, Meyerbeer, Gounod, Verdi, Balfe, Wallace, Bizet and, we are not afraid to add, even in these days of aesthetic mysticism, art-vagueness, and high cultchaw —Bellini.

This sort of music can never, in our lifetime, at least, thank goodness, become popular with the British public.

We don't mind hearing occasionally *The Flying Dutchman, Meistersinger* (abbreviated), and selections from *Tannhäuser* and *Lohengrin.* Richard Wagner's operas will be remembered when the *Barbiere* and a few more trifles are forgotten, but not till then. *Punch.* June 1882.

To those persons who were not previously saturated with the spirit of the Wagnerian lyric-drama, last night's performance came as a revelation of all that is tawdry, artificial, and unnatural in art; while to the disciples of the master it appealed with the force of a revelation of the highest conceivable beauty.

There assuredly is some power in the elaborate love-duet in the second act, and the closing scene is not devoid of pathos; but against these isolated points of merit must be cited interminable quantities of tiresome declamation, and an insufferable amount of noise, turbulence, and striving after effect. *Standard.* 21 June 1882.

[38]

Rinaldo (George Frederick Handel)
24 February 1711. London. World Premiere.

The timing of the "Orpheus of our century," like much of his music, was exquisite. Handel arrived in London during the autumn of 1710, flush and with pockets full from the Venetian success of *Agrippina* (26 December 1709) and his German appointment as *Kapellmeister* (16 June 1710) to the Elector of Hanover, who would soon reign in England as George I. (Having friends in the highest places never hurts.)

Like the current rage for the post-modern, minimalist movement that is omnipresent in all the arts ("Is that a Keith Harring, or just plain ugly?"), London was plagued with the phenomenon of Italian opera and its peculiar interpreters, the castrati ("Is that a man, or just an Italian?"). Disregarding dire predictions of national ruination, societal upheaval, and personal abandonment of good sense, spirit, and virtue, Londoners embraced this "Italian squalling" with all the frenzied urgency of Pavarotti straining for a high C.

The new Queen's Theatre in the Haymarket was given over entirely to opera, but the expense in mounting this novel art form quickly began to run the ledgers into the red—and still does to this day! They needed help, and who should appear with a blast from his own trumpet but the "sweet Saxon" himself. Supplied with a libretto from one of the Haymarket's managers, Aaron Hill, Handel deftly re-cycled his previous works and composed the first commissioned Italian opera for England in two weeks. *Rinaldo*, sung by a magnificent cast which included the extraordinarily gifted male contralto Nicolini as the hero, was a smash.

Rehearsals were frantic, and the newly refurbished stage machinery remained obstinate, denying the Saracen Aragante his entrance on a horse-drawn chariot and comically scrambling together the sea sets and the forest drops, revealing a stagehand "in full-bottom'd wig without any visible concern taking snuff." The incontinent sparrows and finches, let loose for the "Garden" scene in Act I, confused the audience's white-powdered heads for appropriate targets, thereby becoming opera's first avian critics; while Nicolini was "exposed to a tempest in robes of ermine, and sailed in an open boat upon a sea of pasteboard."

All this mattered not. The Haymarket had its savior, the music lovers of London were ecstatic, and the *Kapellmeister* of Hanover remained in England and became richer, more famous, more English, and fatter than ever.

[*Cara Sposa* is] one of the best airs in that style that was ever composed by himself or any other master, and by many degrees the most pathetic song, and with the richest accompaniment, which had then been heard in England.

The Opera of *Rinaldo* is filled with thunder and lightning, illuminations and fireworks; which the audience may look upon without catching cold, and indeed without much danger of being burnt; for there are several engines filled with water, and ready to play at a minute's warning, in case any such accident should happen. However, as I have a very great friendship for the owner of this theater, I hope that he has been wise enough to *insure* his house before he would let this opera be acted in it.
The Spectator. June 1710.

Falstaff (Giuseppe Verdi)
19 May 1894. London Premiere.

It remains to be seen whether the subscribers and the fashionable world in public care for an opera which, since it contains no dull moments, allows no opportunities for comfortable conversation during the music.
The Times. 20 May 1894.

Turandot (Giacomo Puccini)
25 April 1926. Milan, Italy. World Premiere.

How extraordinary is the power of evocation possessed by music which bears in itself the clear imprint of the composer's personality! Last night at the Scala Puccini was with us. The exotic colors and the unfamiliar setting lessened in no degree the sense of his presence felt from the first notes of *Turandot.*

The artist was among us yesterday with the sadness of his own tragedy. The opera stopped yesterday at the point where Puccini had had to leave it. The performance, punctuated by frequent applause, ended with a moment of silence, when the little mangled body of Liù disappeared behind the scenes followed by the procession of the mourning populace, and a shrill E-flat from the piccolo seemed to tell once more of the fleeting soul and of the far-off and forever impenetrable mystery to which alike great passions and obscure loves like little Liù come at last and are lost. Then from where he stood as conductor, Toscanini announced in a low voice full of emotion that at that point Puccini had left the composition of the opera. And the curtain was slowly lowered on *Turandot.*

This moment of intense emotion will not be repeated. For at the second performance the opera will be given with the addition of the last duet and the short final scene of which Puccini had merely outlined the music.

Corriere della Sera. 26 April 1926.

Samson et Dalila (Camille Saint-Saëns)
25 September 1893. London premiere. Performed as an oratorio because of a stage ban on biblical subjects.

> I cannot imagine why the Paris Grand Opera should fascinate English impresarios as it does. Here is Mr. Farley Sinkins putting himself out of his way and charging double prices to produce a concert recital of *Samson et Dalila.* Who wants to hear *Samson et Dalila?* I respectfully suggest, Nobody. In Paris that is not a reason for not producing it, because Saint-Saëns is an illustrious French composer, and the Opera a national institution; consequently Saint-Saëns must occasionally compose an opera, and the director produce it, for the satisfaction of the taxpayers. No doubt Saint-Saëns had to copy Meyerbeer, just as poor Meyerbeer had to copy himself from the day when he made a specialty of religious fanaticism in *Les Huguenots.*
>
> If Saint-Saëns were to be commissioned to write a new "historical opera" entitled "Ulster," we should have the zealous Protestants of that region devoting the Pope to perdition in

[41]

a Rataplan chorus, and confining themselves to ascetic accompaniments of double bass and piccolo; whilst their opponents would pay the same compliment to King William of glorious, pious, and immortal memory, in crisp waltzes and galops, whipped along into movements of popular fury by flicks on the side-drum, strettos, sham fugatos, and pas redoublés, with a grand climax of all the national airs of Ireland worked in double counter-point with suitable extracts from the Church music of the rivals' creeds, played simultaneously on several military bands and a pair of organs.

This is the sort of thing a French composer dreams of as the summit of operatic achievement. I long ago gave up Paris as impossible from the artistic point of view.
George Bernard Shaw. *Music in London.* 4 October 1893.

Die Entführung aus dem Serail (Wolfgang Amadeus Mozart)
16 July 1782. Vienna. World Premiere.

"Too beautiful for our ears and a great many notes, my dear Mozart."
Austrian Emperor Joseph II.
"Exactly as many as are necessary, Your Majesty."
W. A. Mozart.

Madama Butterfly (Giacomo Puccini)
17 February 1904. Milan. World Premiere.

Poor Butterfly. Had she been a real insect, she would not have suffered any less torment than what she endured at La Scala on her opening night. Nets in hand, the lepidopterists swarmed around her, neatly chloroformed her, impaled her on the specimen board, and gleefully tore off her wings. Her tortured flight lasted but one performance. That Italian audience is a mean one!

Although *Manon Lescaut* (1893), *La Bohème* (1896) and *Tosca* (1900) were only mildly received at their premieres, it did not take them long to sweep into the standard repertoire. Puccini was now rich, famous, and feared. His mentor and early patron, Giulio Ricordi, scion of the powerful Italian musical publishing house, was equally rich, famous, and feared. Controlling the rights to Verdi's operas, the "Don" had a velvet stranglehold over the international operatic world; if you wanted to perform Verdi, you also had to choose something from his other clients: preferably Puccini, the "crown prince" to Verdi's king.

Mascagni and Leoncavallo, though successful with their phenomenal efforts of *Cavalleria Rusticana* (1890) and *I Pagliacci* (1892), were still trying to match their good fortunes and didn't take kindly to Ricordi's temperate treatment of them. Their partisans saw Puccini's rapid ascent as a deliberate effort to use Mascagni and Leoncavallo as stepping stones. Leoncavallo, also, never forgave Puccini for usurping his idea of using Murger's novel *Scènes de la Vie de Bohème* as an apt subject for an opera; his *La Bohème* (1897), later retitled *Mimi Pinson,* was obliterated by Puccini's juggernaut.

In hopes of creating suspense and of giving *Butterfly* the patina of a "special event," Ricordi closed the rehearsals to the press and didn't offer them a special preview. What he inadvertently created was a packed gallery filled with angry newspapermen. He also misjudged the incredible hostility the Scala-ites still harbored against Toscanini, who had resigned with a characteristic, autocratic flourish during the last performance of the season, Verdi's *Un Ballo in Maschera,* when the audience demanded an encore of the "laughing quintet," *E scherzo od é follia.* In his usual manner, Toscanini pressed ahead with the performance; pandemonium ensued, and the Maestro walked out. Since he was no longer available for abuse, the audience would vent their spleen on his current honey, Rosina Storchio, Madama Butterfly herself.

Puccini's inimitable sense of timing also left him at the mercy of the claque. In the month before the premiere, on 3 January 1904, Puccini finally married the woman with whom he had been living for years, Elvira Gemignani, whose husband had just died. His eighteen-year-old son, Antonio, was, at last, legitimate.

All of the above turned that first night of *Madama Butterfly* into a shambles. When the audience wasn't sitting on their hands, defying Puccini to amaze them, they were whistling or shouting their loathing. Cries of *"Bohème"* repeatedly greeted certain sections that sounded familiar; others were met with funereal silence; Butterfly's vigil echoed with imitation bird and animal calls; and when her kimono billowed out, Signora Storchio bravely faced howls of laughter and incredibly boorish shouts of "Butterfly is pregnant" and "Yes, with Toscanini's baby!" Regrettably, for Mrs. Toscanini, the gallery's jibes turned out to be true.

The morning newspaper headlines varied from "Puccini Hissed" to "Butterfly, Diabetic Opera, Result of an Accident." The piano scores that Ricordi had placed in the music shops had all disappeared, and Puccini wisely withdrew his opera and repaid the theater his fee for the production rights.

Being a most practical man of the theater, Puccini realized that his music was not the primary cause of the disaster. However, he did streamline the ailing creature, aerodynamically dividing the long third act into two, and excising some of the ballast in Act One.

When *Madama Butterfly* made her next appearance, only three months later at the Teatro Grande in Brescia, Italy, 28 May 1904, her new wings lifted her into the operatic empyrean. She hasn't touched ground yet.

First performance of *Madama Butterfly*. Growls, shouts, groans, laughter, giggling, the usual single cries of *bis*, designed specially to excite the audience still more: these sum up the reception given by the public of the Scala to Giacomo Puccini's new work. After the pandemonium, throughout which practically nothing could be heard, the public left the theatre as pleased as Punch. And one had never before seen so many happy, or such joyously satisfied, faces—satisfied as if by a triumph in which all had shared. . . . This is a true account of the evening, after which the authors, Puccini, Giacosa, and Illica, with the approval of the publishing house, withdrew *Madama Butterfly* and returned the fee for rights of performance to the management

of the theatre, notwithstanding the earnest requests of the latter for permission to produce the opera again.
Musica e Musicisti. 17 February 1904.

10 July 1905. London Premiere.

Madama Butterfly is not an epoch-making work. But its magic is full of that suavity and passion which Puccini most of all among the brethren of Italy has at his command, and for such a favor in these barren operatic days we may well be grateful. *Tosca,* with its ugly and unmusical subject, will never be among the cherished things of the lyric stage, but *Butterfly* has the old qualities in profusion, and with them, we think, a further and deeper power of expression, and even more skillful mastery over the orchestra, and a heightened sense of what is beautiful in phrase, cadence, and harmony.

It is mainly in the restraint and finish of his music that Puccini puts such as Mascagni and Leoncavallo to shame.
Daily Telegraph. 11 July 1905.

Whether *Madama Butterfly* is destined to be equally successful it is as yet too early to say. That it is extremely interesting and individual there can however be no question.

At the same time there is a refreshing unconventionality about Signor Puccini's harmonic methods which cannot but appeal to one. In this respect he is, indeed, a master to himself. It must be added that over a richly embroidered harmonic "parterre," brightened up by a variegated orchestral coloring, he has scattered some of those choice flowers of melody that only blossom under an Italian sun.
Morning Post. 11 July 1905.

12 November 1906. New York Premiere.

Puccini's *Madame Butterfly,* which was given for the first time in New York last evening at the Garden Theater, was heard by a very large audience. It was given in English.

The music is more variegated in its substance, more paragraphic, it might be called, even, than that of *Tosca.* With this deliberately accepted handicap, the composer has, nevertheless, made his music of strange and enamoring beauty. He uses a large number of representative themes; and though he develops them in a broadly symphonic style at hardly any point, they make a very characteristic musical background.

But in the purely pictorial effects suggestive of the time and place and the succession of incident and emotion he has written charmingly and in a vein that, if not strikingly original, is at least more purely personal and individual. His orchestration is more refined, more pointed and delicately colored than ever. He has ventured far into new and adventurous harmonies and some of his effects in this direction are captivating.

It may be that all this does not reach very far nor go very deep. *Madame Butterfly* may not be destined for so long a life as others of Puccini's works. The musical substance is probably slighter; it is not easy to judge certainly of its value on the first hearing. But it has abounding charm and ingratiating refinement, and they made their effect on the audience last evening. *New York Times.* 13 November 1906.

We leave this chapter with the critical words of Richard Wagner from the *Gazette Musicale* of 18 October 1840:

"To be continued in the next world!"

· *Intermezzo* ·

The Audience

Carl Maria von Weber said about audiences: "Individually, every one of them is an ass, but as a whole they are the Voice of God."

That voice was heard loud and clear by a tenor named Gabrielli, a brother of the famed eighteenth-century soprano, Caterina Gabrielli. After he had sung only the first few bars at the Teatro Argentina in Rome, the godly voices cried, "Get away, you cursed raven! Get off, you goat." The tenor interrupted his execrable croaking to address his accusers. "You fancy you are mortifying me, by hooting me; you are grossly deceived. On the contrary, I applaud your judgment, for I solemnly declare to you that I never appeared on any stage without receiving the same treatment, and sometimes much worse." Despite the amusement created by the speech, the godly voices were obeyed. Gabrielli never sang there again.

Two centuries later in Rome, the tenor Gilbert Py addressed the Rome Opera opening night audience from the stage, not with words but with obscene gestures. The voices had hissed him in no uncertain way, and this Lohengrin was insulted. He was also mistaken. The booing was directed at his Elsa, Maria Grazia Palmitessa. Learning the truth, Py apologized to the offended viewers, declaring he had suffered a crisis of nerves. Once Py had recovered, a different crisis struck the conductor, Giuseppe Patane, who smashed the door of his dressing room in a deranged fit during the first intermission and collapsed on the podium early in the second act. The voices of God were by then justifiably an assemblage of braying asses, and an hour passed before heavenly calm was restored with a new conductor.

Eyes are used by performers to communicate with the audience, intentionally for artistic purposes. Elisabeth Söderström, the Swedish soprano, however, found to her dismay that eye contact can be a dangerous thing. For years among the fan letters she received, there had been numerous romantic cards with printed verses decorated with flowers and birds, signed Frank Carson. There being no return address, she could not respond to this admirer. Then one morning the door bell rang at her home, and there stood the mysterious Frank. He had given up his job and hired himself onto various ships, gradually working his way to Sweden, following the call of the singer, whom he had seen many years before at a concert in San Francisco. She had been singing just for him, he knew it by the way she looked him straight in the eyes, over and over again. And at the reception after the concert, when he introduced himself to her, she pressed his hand hard for a long time. Söderström fortunately remembered that she had a rehearsal at the opera and gave Frank a ride into town. He did not show up at her house again. She received only one more letter from him four years later saying, "I saw a movie with Marlene Dietrich. She was cruel to men but you are not. You told me to forget you, but I cannot." As von Weber said, individually . . .

I Bombieri
(Opera's Greatest Duds)

The Spanish conquest of New Spain and inevitable annihilation of its two great civilizations, Aztec and Maya, would seem to be a ripe subject for operatic treatment. It has everything: culture shock, revenge, larger-than-life protagonists, titanic spectacle, barbaric rites, Cyclopean sets, bizarre costumes, Christianity triumphant, incredibly dramatic confrontations, gore, chocolate, and enough tension for a dozen Hitchcock movies. And it's all true.

By last count, there were more than a score of operas on this grand, tragic theme. As early as 1733, Vivaldi wrote a *Montezuma* for Venice. In 1755, Frederick the Great, amateur musician and patron of the arts, wrote a French prose text *Montezuma* whose Italian translation was set to music by Karl Heinrich Graun. "Old Fritz" must have had a good publicity agent; his work was revived in Germany in 1936. Rossini's nemesis, Paisiello, composed his *Montezuma* for Naples in 1772; and Sacchini composed his for London in 1775. The professional amateur, Sir Henry Bishop, in his perpetual, fruitless endeavors to become rich and famous in the English operatic world, tried his hand and came up with his clunker of 1823: *Cortez, or the Conquest of Mexico.* Always attempting to outdo someone else's previous success, "Wrong Way" Henry unwisely thought he could better Gasparo Spontini, who had achieved an unprecedented triumph in Paris with his *Fernand Cortez* (1809). As usual, Sir Henry was mistaken, but as director of Covent Garden he did succeed in keeping Spontini's opera out of London until his own work was produced. When it proved itself a dud, Spontini's was allowed entrée.

Spontini's *Fernand Cortez, ou la Conquête du Mexique,* a magnificent historical pageant, ushered in the era of Grand Opera. This Meyerbeerian precursor was filled to the flies with spectacular tableaux, which included a cavalry charge, the burning of the Spanish fleet in the harbor of Veracruz, the drowning of the heroine in Tenochtitlán's artificial lake, an integrated ballet, and the use of the chorus as a central character. Since the plot revolved around Cortez's love for Montezuma's daughter, the drama was a comic merry-go-round but a stunning eyeful in the theater. With its anti-Spain bias, it was Napoleon's favorite opera. The Emperor needed all the propaganda he could muster in his frustrating Peninsular War against his neighbor.

When Spontini's opera came to the Metropolitan on 6 January 1888, it was an international potpourri: an Italian composer, a French librettist, a Mexican story, Spanish conquerors, a German text, sung by Germans, in an American city. H. E. Krehbiel wrote of the production in the *New York Tribune*: "The people employed in the representation rivaled in numbers those who constituted the veritable Cortez's army, while the horses came within three of the number that the Spaniards took into Mexico."

The subject of New Spain was shelved for nearly a century until the musical world buzzed with the news that *Montezuma* would be set by America's "Grand old man" of music—no, not Aaron Copland—Roger Sessions. Uh, oh! This iconoclastic composer, this "composer's composer," this scion of Schoenberg's 12-tone system, this venerated teacher, this "authentic genius" whose works once made Ernest Bloch weep himself to sleep, was no Verdi. When this musical maverick decided to write for a venue as downright commercial as the opera house, we kissed *Montezuma* goodbye. Composer's composers are not known for their lilting melodies, their singing lines, their dramatic intuitions, or their ability to fill an auditorium. Acolytes, students, and other composer's composers were sure to be there, but the public would run screaming from the house before you could say *Moses und Aaron.* As Verdi advised Gatti-Casazza upon his succession to La Scala's directorship, the only reliable barometer of an opera's success is the cashbox. "The theater is intended to be full and not empty. That is something you must always remember." Would that these modern composers heeded such wise counsel.

Contemporary 12-tone music makes Berg sound like Puccini. Yes, it's complex, rhythmically harsh, thick, dense as good Irish oatmeal; and yes, sometimes it can indeed be beautiful, eerie, and affecting; but it usually seems designed to dare you to like it. It has an inbred arrogance to it. It's music with attitude. For use in drama, its attempts to express character and emotion—other than psychotic—are feeble. How can even a simple love duet be stated when the tune sounds like an example from Bedlam. It's madman's music.

Therefore, Sessions's *Montezuma,* musically speaking, was just what was expected. Convoluted and "intelligent," it encompassed a catholicism of musical styles. In its own distinct way it made masterly use of the Schoenberg 12-tone serial technique: with long sweeping spans in the musical line like a demented twenty-first century Bellini, fractured vocal intervals, intricate interweavings of weighty song and heavy orchestration without pause for breath, but with an exciting, barbaric rhythmic complexity. Needless to say, except for an air sung by a drunken conquistador, Montezuma's lyric final monologue, and the invisible Cloud chorus at the closing scene, this wasn't pretty to hear. But then again, *Elektra, Wozzeck*, and, yes, even *Rigoletto*, in their time were branded as ugly and unplayable. This type of music just isn't for us. If it must be serial, give us shredded wheat.

However . . . much as we dislike this type of music for opera, it is not Sessions's diligent composition that pushed this work into *I Bombieri*; it is its execrable libretto. Without qualification, this has to be the worst damned opera libretto ever written!

Prolix, pompous, unintelligible, historically as inaccurate as Spontini's, and incomprehensibly undramatic, Giuseppe Borgese's treatment, to be charitable, is a mess. Like the Inquisition's own Torquemada, Borgese has tortured the English language, racked it unmercifully, and quartered the syntax with a sadist's glee. Spared from negotiating Sessions's gymnastic vocal leaps, wrap your tongue around, "Not forbidden to the slave, whose ravine-torn path her woe-drunken will shall pave," or, "No expert Circe she, nor yearning Ariadne, haughty Medea, for all her fleeces and Minotaur, a girl with a girlish idea, that th'earth, less round than goes the story, bears just her country on its pear-nipple, where Eden, risen from the searipple, *must* make each morning a morning-glory." And this said by a conquistador! How about this: "I saw the hungerers in Tlaxcala with not a sprinkle of salt on the poultice of their lamar dish"; or, "Us enchants he, but eke frightens." Compared to this, Chaucer's middle English reads like the *New York Post*.

Everyone from the emperor of the Aztecs to the coarse, hairy Spaniards talks like this throughout. When it's sung, you can't understand it because of the thick orchestral textures; when it's read you can't understand it at all. It's so full of itself, and so haughty, you want to slap Signor Borgese for his gall and disdain of our language. Even if Sessions's music were beloved, this opera would have no chance of success because of such wretched excess in its book.

Stodgy and static, the opera is a series of tableaux, wherein great philosophizing and proselytizing occur from both camps, usually at the same time. The highly respected author of *Freedom and Discipline in a Vital Democracy* and *Foundations of the World Republic*, Borgese should have been the last in line to write a drama whose actual precept is: where is the gold and when do we get it. The historical conquistadors did not give a Hail Mary for the rights of man, modern progress, or the causes of Fascism; nor did Montezuma, an extremely superstitious despot, pine away for universal peace and brotherly love. It was never like that.

When *Montezuma* had its 1976 American premiere in Boston under Sarah Caldwell's direction, Mr. Sessions had already been honored with a special citation from the Pulitzer Prize Committee for his distinguished career; in 1982, a few months after the work's New York premiere, he received a Pulitzer for his *Concerto for Orchestra*. Posthumously, for the disastrous *Montezuma*, he is now the proud owner of Opera's Golden Turkey.

The terrible and horrific true tale of the mighty Aztec's fall at the hands of a few scruffy soldiers of fortune has yet to be made into a satisfying opera. All the elements for an exciting evening in the theater are there in history, waiting to be recast. All it needs is a libretto and some music.

What do Lina Cavalieri, Maria Caniglia, Gina Cigna, Claudia Muzio, Rosa Ponselle, Magda Olivero, Renata Tebaldi, Joan Sutherland, Monserrat Caballé, and Renata Scotto have in common? They all sought a vehicle and found the same one: *Adriana Lecouvreur*. No Rolls Royce this. If the lemon laws had existed sooner, this mediocre *Tosca* would have been recalled right off the assembly line. Francesco Cilèa's poor excuse for transportation is opera's Edsel. Its only justification is that it showcases a prima donna playing prima donna. With its one, routine melody continuously repeated throughout like the most banal Broadway score, there is no sufficient reason for this opera's continued existence.

The irony of this work is that its title character is an actress who was credited with introducing a natural style of acting—"la déclamation simple, noble et naturelle"—at a time when French tragedy was characterized by an extremely formal, almost oratorical delivery. To hear Monserrat Caballé vocalizing the score in a language resembling oatmeal or to watch her stolidly plod through this role of a legendary actress is lamentably laughable. Entertaining as theatrical comedy it may be, but operatic theater or theatrical opera it is not. Even with Magda Olivero, a true verismo actress and a real ham from the old school, or with Renata Scotto, probably the best singing actress of today's leading ladies, *Adriana* is little more than an example of what bad opera was like in the proverbial good old days: campy and trash.

Fortunately for all of us, Francesco Cilèa had a slight career as a composer and his output is mercifully forgotten. Born in 1866 in Parmi, Calabria, he devoted himself to music from his earliest years. He didn't receive any formal training until Francesco Florimo, a friend of Verdi's and librarian at the Conservatory of Naples, encouraged the family to send the ten year old to the "liceo-convitto" in Naples. At fifteen he entered the Conservatory and began to study composition. While there, his first opera, *Gina*, was successfully produced, and that brought him a commission from the ever-present publisher Sonzogno. *La Tilda*, given its premiere at the Teatro Pagliano in Florence, was equally successful.

Cilèa slouched ahead, composing some piano pieces and a cello sonata, before the opera world was cursed in 1897 with *L'Arlesiana*, a poorly constructed work, unsuccessfully produced at the Teatro Lirico in Milan. Its sole claim to fame is that it provided Caruso with his first major success. Then came *Adriana Lecouvreur*, premiered at the Teatro Lirico 6 November 1902, also with Caruso. His last opera, *Gloria*, had a modest success at La Scala in 1907, and thereafter Cilèa quit composing and devoted himself to teaching, reputedly because he disliked "self-obsessed tenors and prima donnas." The irony being that only through the efforts of these singers is his work remembered.

Occasionally Cilèa became involved in productions of his self-beloved *Adriana*. He lured Magda Olivero out of retirement in 1950 for a new production of the work, and she sang it for years. *Adriana Lecouvreur* really should be banned. Or shot. Sopranos are always screaming that it be mounted for them. Sometimes a manager has the good sense not to indulge them; sometimes this backfires. Edward Johnson refused to revive it for Rosa Ponselle, and she left the Metropolitan for good.

The critic Amintore Galli once wrote that "Cilèa is the most talented of them all because the divine gift of impassioned inspiration is his alone." We shudder to think what the rest of "them" must have composed. *Adriana* is a very pretty work at times, but it has about as much dramatic tension as a Diet Pepsi commercial. Even its one leitmotif is something Puccini would have written with both hands tied behind his back and then discarded. You'd think a story set backstage at the historic Comédie Française with all its inherent rivalries, sordid jealousies, thwarted love affairs, attempted poisonings with "love lozenges," hectic activities à la *Noises Off*, lascivious duchesses, homosexual abbés, and both Voltaire and Louis XIV could have been turned out with a little more finesse and interest than this sentimental, soiled lace valentine.

The real Adrienne Le Couvreur, whose life is a thousand times more exciting than the flat and false one depicted in the Scribe play and the Colautti adaptation, deserves to be commemorated with a better opera than this flabby, routine thing. When she died of dysentery in 1730, her corpse, excommunicated like all actors at that time, was unceremoniously dumped into an unmarked lime pit. When Voltaire's *Candide* goes to the theater, he inquires as to the treatment of actresses in France. He's told that they are "adored when they are beautiful and thrown into the gutter when they are dead." Cilèa, watch out!

The New York City Opera must be given great credit for offering a harbor to contemporary American opera. Many would never have found their way to New York City or even seen the light of day without this venerable institution's chart. Promoted under Julius Rudel with the worthiest of intentions, this policy only alienated a large portion of the house's audience. Beverly Sills has retreated from that goal somewhat with popular revivals of Broadway shows, but still offers a safe haven for new works. Recently, Dominick Argento's beguiling comedy *Casanova* gracefully sailed in for its New York premiere. But many of the new operas have not been as seaworthy.

Barnacle-encrusted, Leon Kirchner's first opera, *Lily,* based on Saul Bellow's *Henderson the Rain King,* had its world premiere 14 April 1977. Within twenty minutes the audience began jumping overboard. This wasn't as disastrous as New York City Opera's prior year's production of *Ashmedai* by Joseph Tal, which appropriately had its American premiere on April Fool's Day, 1976. Giving them a convenient excuse for a hasty exit, Mr. Tal prodded half the audience to run away at intermission. Learning a valuable lesson, Kirchner wisely wrote his opera in one act.

Writing his own libretto, Mr. Kirchner reportedly spent seventeen years bringing his opera to fruition. His *Music for Orchestra,* composed for the New York Philharmonic in 1969, was fashioned with the opera in mind, and a 1973 concert piece, *Lily,* was billed as "a segment, self-contained, but part of a larger piece based on Saul Bellow's novel." As the work progressed, both Rudel and Kurt Herbert Adler, director of the San Francisco Opera, expressed interest in it. Kirchner worked out a deal with the New York City Opera that allowed him a sabbatical from teaching at Harvard, and he went to the American Academy in Rome as composer in residence to finish the work, living in the same studio where Samuel Barber had written *Vanessa* fifteen years earlier. He should have had the foresight to insert a few leftover manuscript pages of Mr. Barber's in his own score.

The director for *Lily* was Tom O'Horgan, Broadway's then "enfant terrible," and director of the fashionably with-it productions of *Hair, Lenny,* and *Jesus Christ Superstar.* After staging *Hair,* he had been asked by the Santa Fe Opera to direct *Salome* for them because they had found a singer willing to strip completely for the sake of art. O'Horgan, insulted that putting nudity on stage was his only talent they recognized, turned down Santa Fe saying he would prefer to direct a Mozart opera and have the orchestra naked. Opera companies should not be museums doing potboilers, he said. "There has to be an interest in doing new opera. That's the only reason I'm doing *Lily.* It will be a theatrical and musical experience." That was an understatement. As is his style, O'Horgan pulled out all the stops, as he had done in Vienna for *Les Troyens* to great criticism from the conservative press. In *Lily* he used anthropological film footage culled from Harvard's archives, projections, streamers, skeletal huts, and cardboard cut-outs, to great criticism from New York's liberal press.

Cutting Bellow's novel, Kirchner compressed the book's first third to emphasize Gene Henderson's wrong-headedness in attempting to bring American civilization to the natives of Africa. With his wife Lily, Henderson lives with the Arnewi tribe, thinking they have a deeper connection to the mysteries of life than the sophisticated, jaded West. By bringing them civilization, Henderson makes their life worse. He blows up their water supply to destroy a pestilence of frogs, represented in the opera by dozens of giant rubber frogs dropping from the flies. Kirchner's comments on ugly-American imperialism confronting Rousseau-like primitive naiveté worked no better than Bellow's.

The text worked no better than the plot. "In an age of madness to expect to be untouched by madness is a form of madness. But the pursuit of sanity is a form of madness too." With dialogue like this, it required a musical talent greater than Kirchner's to make it singable. As a pupil of Sessions's, Kirchner composed in a well crafted post-Schoenbergian style, but Kirchner's serial technique lacks dynamic variety, even with his use of pre-recorded tape juxtaposed with live voices and orchestra. Rudderless, it was a bore.

At the other end of the musical scale, minimalism, sails flapping, swept into the City Opera 4 November 1984 with the production of *Akhnaten* by Philip Glass, contemporary music's current god. Enormously successful, popular not only with a vociferous segment of the younger generation of the classical music audience, but also as a leading composer for the "post-modern" choreographers for the last two decades, Glass is the quintessential cross-over artist. He has achieved unprecedented international renown and financial success in his own lifetime, selling records in numbers that no twentieth-century classical composer could have dreamed possible for "serious music."

Akhnaten was presented at the State Theater in 1984, in a co-production with the Houston Grand Opera after its world premiere in Stuttgart, West Germany, on 24 April 1984. It is the third opera in Glass's trilogy of portrait operas about Science, Politics and Religion, consisting of *Einstein on the Beach* (Albert Einstein), *Satyagraha* (M. K. Gandhi), and *Akhnaten,* the ultra-conservative Egyptian pharaoh who espoused a twisted form of monotheism.

The text of the opera uses ancient poems, decrees, and temple inscriptions, sung in their original languages of Biblical Hebrew, Egyptian, and Akkadian, to tell this bizarre true story of ancient Egypt's "heretic king." Upon his father's death, Amenhotep IV ascended to the throne and, for reasons beclouded by millennia, instituted radical, hostile reforms to Egypt's already ageless religion. With a surgeon's precision, but a butcher's mentality, he excised every god in Egypt's extensive pantheon except two: the Aten and himself. There were to be no other gods before him. It was a staggering blow to the superstitious *fellahin,* an economic hardship for the pseudo-middle class of artisans and craftsmen dependent on Egypt's well-greased industry of religion, and it was anathema to the priests, who lost their jobs. Temples were abandoned, idols were smashed, and any godly inscriptions were chiseled off walls. Amenhotep IV, despised yet feared, changed his name to Akhnaten (Spirit of the Aten), moved Egypt's capital north from Luxor to an uninhabited region on the Nile, and built a new home to house his megalomania, Akhet-aten, "Horizon of the Aten." At some point in his twenty-year reign, he banished his ravishing wife, Nefertiti, had an affair with his son-in-law (or maybe half-brother) Smenkhkare who ruled with him as co-regent, and paid scant attention to Egypt's alarming decline in foreign affairs. His history is sketchy to say the least, but Akhnaten died from a worsening encephalic disorder or was assassinated in a coup d'etat. His name, his city, his religion were systematically obliterated by succeeding rulers. From the brutal thoroughness of it all, we can assume he was murdered.

Not much of this was evident in the opera. The Great Ones skipped about foolishly, while the mediocre pageant wasn't up to a bus-and-truck tour of *Aida*. However, like the previous German run, the City Opera's production was a sell out, but not unanimously loved. Dumbfounded, many wondered what the hell was going on. It looked like the emperor's new clothes to us.

A three-foot wide pool of water ran across the entire width of the stage apron, with sand stretching back to a wrinkled sky-blue scrim—the land of Egypt. At the river's edge a man made bricks of mud and straw, upstage a group of men in loincloths fought in slow motion, while upstage left a couple with wooden rakes and a pile of wheat separated the grain from the chaff—the eternity of Egypt. These three activities continued the entire evening, undisturbed and oblivious to the minimal opera taking place. The eternity of it all, indeed! Actually, the wheat-threshing couple created a pleasurable diversion to the monotony of the music and the stage action, with its mushroom-like cloud of wheat slowly floating back to earth like thousands of pieces of confetti, sparkling in the backlight. The sand served a double purpose. Throughout the second act, an intricate sandcastle city was constructed by the performers that eventually covered the entire stage and represented Akhnaten's new world. It was a marvelous image that kept our concentration focused as the music droned on. However, since we knew from the story that his city would be razed, we immediately realized that this set construction had nowhere to go dramatically. In the third act, the enemy faction stomped on the miniature city like petulant children at the playground.

Unlike serial music, Glass's minimalism is a whole other bag and the complete antithesis of its older brother. Wildly popular and ubiquitous, it pervades our culture and is as difficult to get rid of as those magazine scratch-and-sniff perfume ads. We may not like the end result, but with serial music we know where we stand. It is, if nothing else, grown-up music, intelligent and thought out. Glass's minimalism, however, is childlike music. Basic triad arpeggios repeat with a vengeance, like a crazed Czerny at a Xerox machine. It's music for druggies—an endless wash of non-threatening sound, blissful Musak for getting stoned. You can be mesmerized and go soft by Glass's trance-like noise. With minimal progression, drama, and conflict in this stuff, it's perfect background music, the ultimate "easy listening" for the 80's. It won't interfere in the least with your thinking. As music for theater, Glass's music is contradictory and ornery. Lacking tension and character, it's useless for the stage. The purpose of drama isn't to put your audience to sleep or turn them into zombies. It's torture to be trapped in a theater seat, especially when what's happening on stage is as endlessly repetitious as the music.

Besides the pleasure of anticipating the next aerial flight of wheat, it was interesting to figure out what the conductor's two-fingered "victory sign" meant to the orchestra. Was he telling the violins how many more times they had to repeat this boring phrase, or was it a code for a marking in the score, or would he rather have been conducting Beethoven's *Fifth?* There was also a vivid lesson in how a singer's diaphragm works. Akhnaten, bare chested but breasted like a hermaphrodite, stood center stage in the second act intoning "ah, ah, ah, uh-ah, uh-ah, uh-ah, ah, ah," etc. etc. etc. With every single syllable

the diaphragm pushed upward once, with every double syllable, it pushed up twice. These are not the elements of great
theater, but in the face of hours of tedium, anything of interest
is a blessing, even stomach toning by Philip Glass.

Writing thirty-three hundred years ago, Akhnaten himself
put his finger on this opera's problem. We take a line from his
Hymn to the Aten. "How efficient are your designs, Lord of Eternity." Efficient? Hell, no. Lord of Eternity? Hell, yes!

Until he hit his stride with *Rigoletto* (1851), Giuseppe Verdi,
a.k.a. "Mister Opera," had more highs and lows than a
meteorologist's map of Hurricane Hazel. With the promising
start of *Oberto, Conte di San Boniface* (1839), Verdi took a disastrous nose dive with his second effort, the *opera buffa Un Giorno
di Regno* (1840). Miraculously, he survived the one-night-only
performance. With prodding from La Scala's manager Merelli,
who had more faith in the composer than the composer did in
himself, he soared with his first two unqualified successes:
Nabucco (1842) and *I Lombardi alla Prima Crociata* (1843). While
international fame through *Ernani* (1844) puffed him up, he
leveled off with *I Due Foscari* (1844), *Giovanna d'Arco* (1845),
Alzira (1845), a love tragedy between an Inca princess and a
conquistador that had about as much to do with New Spain as
José Greco, and the coarse and brutal *Attila* (1846). *Macbeth*
(1847) shows Verdi flying very high indeed; but turbulence in
the form of *I Masnadieri* (1847), commissioned for London's Her
Majesty's Theater for Jenny Lind, *Jerusalem* (1847), *Il Corsaro*
(1848), and *La Battaglia di Legnano* (1849) forced him into idle and
a perilous position near to stalling. Once again, he stabilized
with *Luisa Miller* (1849), but banked wildly with *Stiffelio* (1850).
After this last, embarrassing novice performance, he revved
engines, went full throttle, and zoomed high and wide to become the operatic ace we all know and love.

Verdi called this period his "years as a galley slave," and we
are hard pressed to choose one turkey over another. But, if a
musical parody à la Verdi were to be written, it would probably
sound much like *Giovanna d'Arco.* All of the maestro's annoying

[61]

mannerisms are present, as well as some good ones that fore-shadow the greater things to come; but the limited amount and quality of the finer passages only forces the pedestrian ones to stand out in greater relief, making them sound worse. Verdi can't quite pull it together to give the cardboard characters and situations any musical life.

In this operatic pastiche, we find the usual early Verdian characteristics: barrel organ tunes with their um-pah-pah accompaniments, patriotic choruses, a "grand" triumphal march, a plot that hinges upon a baritone father and his soprano daughter, two required love duets, happy peasant music, a storm scene, a noisy prelude, naive orchestration, a perfunctory shrug toward empty emotionalism, and a vigor and excitement mismatched to the drab dramatics. Giovanna's cavatina in the Prologue, her father's two set-pieces in Act I, and Giovanna and Carlo's love duet, also in Act I, are the best things in the score, but they're still journeyman's tunes. Granted, Verdi's conventional music can be more interesting than most, but here it can't redeem the sparse action, the fragmentary nature of the scenes, or its own skewed logic. When Joan is tormented by an offstage chorus of evil spirits, their music sounds every note as heavenly, if faster, as does the angels' music. The devilkins are no more threatening than the toothless witches in *Macbeth*, whose bouncy music is anything but frightening. The music doesn't differentiate. Everyone sounds alike. You can't tell who is who or what they're thinking. Only in his later works would Verdi be able to musically distinguish emotions and characters.

We sound like a nineteenth-century critic when we carp about the plot and its utter disregard for historical accuracy, but only music from the pen of a much-wiser Verdi could keep us intrigued in a love affair between Joan of Arc and Charles VII! And then there's that small matter of the ending. The Maid's true story has more conflict, intrigue, and passion than a season of "Dynasty"; it would have been an ideal Verdian subject. However, the librettist, Temistocle Solera, without protest from Verdi, concocted his own true horror. No longer is Joan abandoned by the King she helped crown, tried by the French ecclesiastics, or turned over to the English for execution. She does not go up in a blaze of glory on her martyr's stake. That's much too operatic for Signor Solera. His solution is simplicity, or stupidity, if you will, itself.

Joan is imprisoned in the English encampment awaiting her doom. Hearing battle cries outside the walls, she imagines the melee and asks God to forgive her for her impure love for Charles. Blithely walking through the enemy lines, who should enter and overhear her pleas for salvation but dear old Dad, who has been denouncing her as a witch ever since Act I. By ranting in the French court, he has succeeded in turning everybody against her. Well, quicker than you can say Joan of Orleans, he realizes that she is a good and honest girl, even though she's more of a man than the entire French army; and that, maybe, he was a little too hasty. So she hears voices, is that so bad? After all, he talks to himself. Instantaneously repentant, he frees her. Not only do the English let him walk about, but they also give him keys! He sings, Forgive me. She sings, OK, but I need your sword. Rushing out full of divine inspiration, she is mortally wounded. Borne in by the soldiers, she has enough saintly breath left in her to sing her *Addio terra* before succumbing. An unearthly light fills the stage. The angels sing, "Return, exultant sister." The bad little demons sing, "The triumph of Heaven is our torment." Hmmmph.

Everything in this opera—except its ridiculous premise—reminds us of something that Verdi would write later, and better. Tantalizing fragments of *Aida, Rigoletto,* a lot of *Macbeth,* some *Ballo* and *Trovatore* pop in and out, prick us awake, then vanish like those bad little demons. Maybe, just maybe, it might be conceivable to save this opera, if you pretend it's not the story of Joan of Arc. Perhaps that's why the title was changed for the Rome premiere to *Orietta di Lesbo.* You figure that out.

Whoever Verdi was writing for in *Giovanna,* it wasn't posterity. There's not much here to remember or need hear again. It's routine stuff, flaccid and colorless. The music is nineteenth century; only in the works to come would it sing in that time-less Verdian voice. We're left with some warm, lyric snatches, but not nearly enough heat to bring this dry, brittle work to combustion. This is the type of opera where Joan has to carry her own matches.

"Possibly the greatest social event since the Nativity," so did one blasé matron sum up the expectations of a watching world. Shana Alexander in *Life* dubbed it "the single biggest theatrical event in all of human history." With such demands for great-ness, how could Samuel Barber's *Antony and Cleopatra* hope to succeed? It couldn't and it didn't. It was the greatest and costli-est operatic bomb of all times.

Composed to inaugurate the new Metropolitan Opera House in Lincoln Center on 16 September 1966, *Antony and Cleopatra* was intended as an all-American event. Conducted by Thomas Schippers, it starred Leontyne Price, Jess Thomas, Jus-tine Diaz, Rosalind Elias, Ezio Flagello, and Mary Ellen Pracht. The one foreign exception was Franco Zeffirelli, who designed and directed the production and also wrote the libretto. With the perspective of hindsight, it seems unthinkable that the Italian director would have been asked to adapt Shakespeare's play, but, in fact, the libretto was not Zeffirelli's greatest blun-der. As usual, he didn't trust the music and consequently over-produced everything.

Antony and Cleopatra was supposed to represent Zeffirelli's operatic apogee; it turned out to be his perigee. He couldn't decide what he wanted and kept the hoards standing around doing nothing, while he stroked his chin and tried to figure out how to use all the Met's marvelous new machinery.

The Egyptian costumes were woefully inaccurate, overdone, glitzy as Las Vegas and so heavy and massive, especially those for Price, that movement was virtually impossible. She was forced to float around the stage much like the giant Sphinx, which was the centerpiece of his design concept. The Sphinx was planned for the new turntable stage, but Zeffirelli so over-weighted the turntable with sets, people, and animals that it broke down and couldn't be fixed until the following summer. As a result, the Sphinx was refurbished and made movable. It aimlessly wandered all over the stage—antiquity's *Runaway Train*. The horizontal metal pipes, used to create room-like spaces that matched a metallic, multi-leveled floor of stairs, simply looked like a stageful of Venetian blinds from flies to floor. Amidst the clutter of Levelors and a complete menagerie, desperately trying to escape from the manic Sphinx, there was also a miniature pyramid that opened up to disgorge Romans. Price got stuck in it during rehearsals. The entire production was one of comically overblown chaos and confusion.

The audience was just as glitzy and hardly in the mood to appreciate a Barber opera. The Met's new house was being celebrated, as well as those who had paid dearly to be celebrated with it: Lady Bird Johnson, Ferdinand and Imelda Marcos (remember them?), the Vice Chancellor of West Germany, UN Secretary-General U Thant, numerous foreign ambassadors, consuls, and domestic government officials, the old rich, the new rich, the not-so-rich, the social climbers, the press, and a few true opera lovers, who were relegated to the top of the house or the standing room. The gossip columnist Suzy Knickerbocker said the conflux of humanity had "all the goodies of the world of the rich, the celebrated and the social . . . dressed, jewelled and coiffed to the teeth." One such lady, Mrs. Laura Johnson, the widow of a department store tycoon, was escorted by an officer from Cartier who spent most of the evening keeping careful watch over the jewels the store had lent her. She admitted that she had pinned her own emerald-and-diamond earrings to her silk "underpanties" in case of a fainting spell. Jess Thomas's wife was covered with dozens of gold chains, causing Rudolf Bing to exclaim, "My God, she thinks she's an Egyptian empress." The *New York Times'* Harold Schonberg called the event "Big, grand, impressive, vulgar; a Swinburnean mélange of sad, bad, mad, glad . . . with the enthusiasm of a group of children around an Erector set."

Musically, Samuel Barber deserved no better. Much of the opera sounds like a rejected score from a Maria Montez movie.

Only Cleopatra's final aria has any tragedy or grandeur, witnessed by Leontyne Price's subsequent recording. The rest consists of choppy phrases, lacking dramatic impulse, a lot of offstage trumpet fanfares, and no melody. It's a definite hybrid, falling somewhere between the cracks of Montemezzi and 1930's modernism. Even Barber's recension with new libretto from Menotti, unveiled at a Juilliard performance, although tighter and a bit more dramatically muscular, is not much better. We're stuck with *Aida*. Too bad.

Price summed up the debacle nicely when asked later about doing a new Zeffirelli production of *Trovatore*. "Zeffirelli's a genius, but I don't want him to be a genius for me twice in my operatic career."

Symphony #8 was not the only work Schubert left unfinished. His *Quartettsatz*, nine piano sonatas, one other symphony, two string quartets, the Easter Cantata *Lazarus*, and four operas were abandoned mid-staff. He should have had the good sense to forsake his other operas, too. For a musician who is indisputably the nineteenth century's "King of Lieder," who could spin out songs in his sleep, Schubert is a disaster as an opera composer. *Alfonso und Estrella*, composed in 1821–22, is his only true opera since it contains no spoken dialogue. If only it did!

This undramatic work was Schubert's favorite. A few beautiful passages are hidden within it, but it's as unnaturally padded and stuffed as a French goose. Blame for this mediocrity has always fallen upon the librettist, Schubert's friend Franz von Schober, a Viennese poet-manqué whose texts were set by Schubert in over thirty songs. He rightly deserves every clump of mud thrown at him, but so does Schubert.

We don't go to an opera to appreciate its libretto. Even if we did, we probably couldn't understand the words anyway. We desire beautiful singing, gorgeous music, dramatic situations with characters we can care about, and, we hope, some believable acting. We do not want concert arias in costume. A stupid libretto has never sunk a good opera. The poor composer must

[66]

bail like mad, but if he knows what he's doing his music will buoy up almost any amount of verbal tonnage. In *Alfonso und Estrella,* however, the over-blown poetry and the weak dramatic focus and the timing of its scenes has already swamped the work before Schubert even has a chance to get out his musical bucket. The book is a meandering collection of *opera seria* set-pieces, without flow or grace, or any semblance of dramatic structure. Whole paragraphs are endlessly repeated and repeated. We're drowsy during Troila's second-scene aria and, by the time his son Alfonso enters in the fourth, asleep. Out of thirty-four pieces, only one—the most beautiful in the score, Troila's lovely Act II *Song to the Cloud Maiden*—does not repeat itself. It's such a satisfying, complete little drama that Schubert recast it as the *Tauschung* in his *Winterreise,* five years later.

What hope is there for any dramatic tension when everything stops for a nice airy song that is thrice repeated. At its conclusion, another pleasant ditty, also repeated, takes its place. The pace of this waterlogged scow is *Reverse.* The drama stops completely in the last scene of Act II. King Mauregato, usurper of the throne, bemoans the disappearance of his beloved daughter. She has absent-mindedly wandered into the neighboring valley ruled by the usurped former king and has fallen in love—at first sight, of course—with the tenor, the heir apparent. As much as she'd like to stay and play, she knows her father must be worried. We know she means this because she says it six times. Guided by her new sweetheart, she's off to Dad. We await her entrance in the throne room, but, Sweet Schubert, does she take her time!

First, the chorus sights her, "The princess has appeared!" The king asks "The princess?" The chorus confirms, "The princess." The king asks twice, "Has she appeared?" The chorus answers, "Yes, she has appeared. She is approaching the palace." While the king says, "She is coming here," the chorus reassures him, "She is approaching the palace. She is coming here." The king is happy, "Bitter grief depart, joy shines again." He repeats this, then asks, "Where can she be so long?"

The vigilant chorus pipes in, "I see her hurrying. I see her hurrying." The king questions yet again, "Where can she be so long? All wounds will heal when I see my beloved." Not to be rushed, the chorus replies, "She is near now." The king reiterates his "healing wounds" three more times. Not to be outdone, the chorus repeats their lines. And then, in a concerted passage, they all sing it again!! Thanks, Herr Schober, but we got it twice the first time! Apollo collaborating with every Muse on Parnassus couldn't move this jalopy.

Schubert doesn't even try. His music is blindly inappropriate. If Schober's book is tepid drama at best, it's not helped by Schubert's pretty tunes. Troila's sad laments sound just as peppy as the happy peasants' music; the love duet is passionless; and what should be rousing war chants and malevolent "vengeance" choruses are pseudo-galops and effete airs. It's too controlled and confined, reined in and prim.

It's certainly no surprise that all the theaters in Vienna turned thumbs-down on this work. Its questionable theme boldly advocated a rebellious overthrowing of a monarch and was, therefore, every bit as censurable as were the amateurish libretto and the pedestrian music. More of a surprise is that, undaunted, Schubert plowed ahead with other operas in hopes of success. His operatic struggle with fame and fortune was a ten-years' war, wherein he lost every battle. He filled more sheets of music with operatic scribbling than he used for any other works in his prodigious output. Why he was so blind to his theatrical shortcomings is one of opera's great mysteries. Perhaps he was just to busy bailing.

If its composer had not later become one of opera's incomparable composers, *Mitridate, Rè di Ponto* and its creator would have been relegated to the footnotes of opera history. Commissioned for the sum of one hundred gold gulden by the Viennese Governor General of Lombardy, Count Karl Joseph von Firmian, from a fourteen-year-old prodigy named Mozart, *Mitridate* was a considerable success at its premiere on 26 December 1770 in Milan and had twenty-two performances to full houses before it was retired from the repertory. It vanished thereafter. Bombs do not always explode on first impact.

After all, Mozart's first operatic attempt, *Die Schuldigkeit des Ersten Gebots* ("The Obligation of the First Commandment"), was composed when he was only eleven, and between that work and *Mitridate* came the musical intermezzo *Apollo et Hyacinthus*, the *opera buffa La Finta Semplice* and the *singspiel Bastien und Bastienne*, an unambitious single-act curtain raiser, occasionally performed today when a novelty is sought for repertory purposes. Mozart would also give the world a pastoral two-act opera *Ascanio in Alba*, a dramatic one-act serenade *Il Sogno di Scipione*, another *opera seria, Lucio Silla*, another *opera buffa, La Finta Giardiniera*, and the forgettable *Il Rè Pastore* and *Thamos, König in Ägypten*, and the incomplete *Zaide*, before he created *Idomeneo, Rè di Creta* at the age of twenty-four. From that point until the end of his life, Mozart wrote a string of indelible masterpieces, except for the unfinished works *L'Oca del Cairo* and *Lo Sposo Deluso* and the one-act *Der Schauspieldirektor* ("The Impresario") which, delightful comedy though it is, cannot compare with his other mature works.

The International Mozarteum Foundation organized the first "Mozart Week" in Salzburg in 1956, on the bicentenary of the composer's birth, to concentrate exclusively on the works prior to *Idomeneo* that Mozart scholars claimed to have been unaccountably neglected. As a result, in January 1970 a little explosive device, long lying fallow, discharged its lethal force in the form of a concert performance of *Mitridate, Rè di Ponto*. If we aren't careful we'll be subjected to staged performances of this endless bird warbling; there being a constant search by opera houses for "new" works since little's composed today that holds the audience for even a single season. Josef II's comment about too many notes is truly apt here. *Mitridate* is Philip Glass in coloratura.

Mozart's commission for *Mitridate* specified the libretto and the singers, requiring the work to be tailored to them—"made to measure clothing," as the young man called it. Coupled with the composer's youth and inexperience, these problems jammed the operatic sewing machine. It would be many years before Mozart gained the facility to stitch together a seamless garment out of such a patchwork. The story is based on Racine's tragedy *Mithridate*, the historical king of Pontus who caused Rome such headaches with his constant belligerence in the first century B.C. The play was translated into Italian by Giuseppe Parini and thus lost whatever small amount of overblown poetry and passion Racine had given it.

King Mitridate, a tenor, is engaged to the young Aspasia, a soprano, though both of his sons, the good Sifare, a castrato soprano, and the bad Farnace, a castrato alto, are also in love with Aspasia. Early on, the report of Mitridate's death sets both brothers into pursuit of Aspasia. Mitridate returns, explains his death ruse was intended to confound his enemies, and commands his son Farnace to marry a Parthian princess, Ismene, another soprano, though he suspects both sons love Aspasia and intends to discover the truth. He questions his governor Arbate, yet another castrato soprano, who admits Farnace loves Aspasia and covets the crown. Mitridate then questions Aspasia, who confirms Arbate's suspicions but plays dumb to all else. She then confesses her love for Sifare when she is put in his protection. Mitridate, meanwhile, goes off to do battle with his son Farnace, who tells him of the affair between Sifare and Aspasia. Is that all perfectly clear?

In the third act there are condemnations for betrayal, imprisonments, pleadings for the lives of young lovers, suicide threats, prison escapes, suicide preventions, and a final battle with the Romans. Mitridate is mortally wounded, but lives long enough to forgive everyone and to bless the union between his son Sifare and his almost-to-be stepmother Aspasia and the union between his other son Farnace and his previously rejected Ismene. The curtain falls with the question remaining—who gets the crown?

As if that plot weren't enough trouble, Mozart had to contend with two sopranos, two male sopranos, one alto castrato, and two tenors. Trying to satisfy that many egos is the job of Bellevue, not a fourteen-year-old. The singers expressed a similar opinion, threatening to insert arias by their favorite composers. Although Leopold Mozart complained that his son had accommodated the singers with so many alterations that he had actually written two operas, the young Mozart did in fact greatly please his exacting singers with his musical clothing store. However, with so many similar voices all expressing virtuosic, coloratura arias, the effect is numbing, like a whole stage full of Lakmés. There's no relief; it's just unvaried alterations of recitatives and bravura arias, no choral scenes and virtually no ensembles. Today, we're lucky to hear one competent coloratura singer; there's no way five can be scheduled for the same performance.

Mitridate might conceivably be enjoyable as a succession of brilliant arias sung in costume, but we certainly don't have to revive unworthy Mozart to get that. Like the Met's 1985 *Tosca,* any performance starring Luciano Pavarotti and Monserrat Caballé offers the grandest of costumed, static pageants.

Mithridate VI, the King of Pontus, survives in spite of Mozart or Racine. Thinking he was a clever guy, he immunized himself against the threat of enemy poisoning by taking small daily doses. It worked like a charm. However, when he faced the Roman legions of Pompey, aware of the treacherous revolt of his own son, and wanting to spare himself a humiliating capture and triumph through Rome, Mithridate tried to kill himself. The poison didn't work. Hale and hearty, the once-mighty king had to stab himself. Slow and messy. He didn't like it one bit. Mozart's mithridating works exactly in reverse. No matter how many times we hear it, we'll never get used to it. We don't like it either, not one bit.

What can we say to such a thing like *Mona* except, "Fetch!" Judged from a field of twenty-five entries, this dog of an opera won the coveted $10,000 prize offered by the Metropolitan Opera in their much-ballyhooed new American opera competition announced on 15 December 1908. The rules stated that (1) the composer must be a "native born citizen of the United States, no matter where he lived," (2) the libretto must be in

[71]

English, (3) the performance length, including intermissions, was not to exceed three hours and a quarter, (4) all scores were to be anonymous, "containing a mark of identification corresponding with an identical mark on a sealed envelope containing the names of the composer and librettist," (5) the jury was to comprise "recognized authorities selected by the board of directors," (6) the agreement of at least two-thirds of the jury was necessary for a decision, and (7) the winning opera would be staged by the Metropolitan the season following the award.

On 1 May 1911, the unanimous decision of the jury was announced to a breathless press. Alfred Hertz, Walter Damrosch, George W. Chadwick, and Charles Martin Loeffler had chosen Dr. Parker and Mr. Brian Hooker, his librettist, as the fortunate recipients. It seemed of little matter that both Mr. Chadwick and Mr. Loeffler were intimate friends of this eminent Bostonian composer who was the head of the Yale music department. Even without his name affixed, they could have smelled his style a thousand miles away. If *Mona* was the pick of the litter, what in hell could the remaining little runts have sounded like?

It's unfortunate that Gatti-Casazza, whose bright idea started all this trouble, wasn't a juror. Knowing full well what worked on the opera stage, he immediately spotted the main problem of this "cold and arid thing," as he familiarly called it. "Parker was a learned man, but not a man of the theater. He did possess creative power, and, moreover, had a libretto that was certainly too grey and only faintly interesting. He was not an artist, deep down in his soul. He was simply a cerebral, a pedagogue."

As a composer and respected teacher, Dr. Parker was gifted, but hardly unique. His hymns, songs, chorales, and fairly successful oratorio *Hora Novissima* (1893), although bombastic and Victorian, suited the pre-war sentimentality of the era. As a dramatist, though, he was a flop. Saddled with Hooker's static, marmoreal prose, Parker lurched forward, disregarding the flow of the text or the shape of the melodic line.

In its plot, *Mona* is a third-rate knockoff of *Norma,* but lack-

ing its classical shape and effective dramaturgy; in its music, ^
Mona is a mediocre mélange of impressionistic Wagner, but
lacking his lyric genius. If you recorded *Tristan*, spliced out
every third and fourth measure, and played it in reverse, that's
Mona. It has an annoying case of the "blind staggers," like a
crab on LSD. Scuttling about in tight, pinched circles, it never
gets anywhere. Great opportunities for thrilling theatrical climaxes go untapped. Mona's blessing of the swords, the *Tristan*-
aping love duet, the *Götterdämmerung* parroting of Mona's final
aria are cast aside with an indifferent shrug while Parker's
hesitating phrasing makes a mush out of the dramatic structure's existing gruel.

Parker's idiosyncratic use of different harmonic keys to represent various characters and emotions, certainly a novel use
of Wagnerian *leitmotif*, was not, in itself, such a bad idea, but
layering it upon the already thick impasto of the orchestration
was an aural blunder. In one section, this dizzying acoustic
amalgam consists of Mona's womanliness expressed in E flat
major, while her masculinity as predestined leader of the Britons is heard in E flat minor; her lover Gwynn is in B flat, and,
therefore, their love duet swirls around in G flat major, "the
legitimate offspring of the keys of B major and E flat minor,"
as Parker pontificated in an address to the MacDowell Club.

What would a musical turkey be without an equal helping
of textual stuffing. Mr. Hooker, a colleague of Parker's at Yale
where he taught English, would later attain respect as a librettist for Rudolf Friml's operetta *The Vagabond King* (1925) and as
the translator of Rostand's *Cyrano de Bergerac*, a triumph on
Broadway with Walter Hampden (1923). With *Mona*, however,
inspiration failed. In an interview for the *New York Tribune* in
1911, Hooker stated that he wrote *Mona* "to express the idea
that I had long desired to express—that woman derives her
strength from her womanliness and not from usurping the
functions that belong to man. Mona, instead of being feminine,
has spent her life in dreaming and in the idea that she has a
mission. It is this idea that in the end defeats her own cause
and kills her lover, whereas she might have accomplished her

[73]

purpose and saved her lover had she had recourse to other methods. So you see, though I have set my story in ancient Britain it possesses a story of which the appeal in imminent." And out of date at the same time.

Tightly woven as a "protest against the 'new' woman," Hooker's plot restricts the characters' actions and binds them in an unalterable pattern of behavior; the lifeless puppets execute unnatural gymnastic contortions and pretzel twists to conform to his convoluted thesis. In the penultimate scene, Mona loves Gwynn, but must kill him because of the mechanical exigencies of the plot; Gwynn, a Roman brought up by the Britons, reveals his heritage to the wrathful Mona at the inopportune moment and then doesn't tell her of his secret peace mission to the Romans, which would save his life; the Roman Governor, Gwynn's father, doesn't inform the Britons how easy peace could be achieved by the marriage between Mona and his son; while Nial, the Puckish simpleton, dances around with his shadow and propounds philosophically on the nature of man. All very Druidic.

At the time, probably out of deference to the idea of a commissioned American opera making its world premiere at the Metropolitan, the critics treated *Mona* with cool respect. She lacked drama, her musical flow was peculiarly choppy, she was imbued with a sanctimonious gloom, they all agreed; but no one blasted the girl for her damned dreary, plain-Jane ordinariness. And, she was a bore. The most telling comments came from the *New York Morning Telegraph:*

Mr. Parker, however, won the prize and there has been universal rejoicing among the Parkerites. Having achieved so important a victory he naturally proceeds to give his valuable estimate of other and less fortunate composers. He has begun with Verdi, of whom he entertains a strange opinion. "With the exception of *Falstaff* and *Otello,"* says Mr. Parker, "the rest of Verdi is worthless, while *Rigoletto* is funny." About *Rigoletto,* Mr. Parker was particularly emphatic. He had recently seen it—at New Haven.

[74]

It will be noted that Mr. Parker includes among the worthless music of Verdi the *Manzoni Requiem, Aida,* all of *Traviata,* and the melodic wonders of *Trovatore.* Opera-goers will be able to form a fairly correct idea of Mr. Parker's delicate and correct taste in music and in drama when they hear that he considers the last act of *Aida* "absurd." Plain folk, however, may be permitted to express the devout wish that Mr. Parker has written in *Mona* half a dozen scenes just as "absurd" as the final episodes of *Aida.*

These opinions come very strangely from a man who, before *Mona,* had never written an opera and who even now has still to prove that he has written one. Nor is there anything in this world quite so graceless at the attack of an academician upon a genius.

Premiering 14 March 1912, this string of fragments called *Mona* had a grand run at the Metropolitan of four performances. She popped up again in New York in 1935 and 1961 for two concert performances of extracts and then, like Erda, disappeared forever. In 1935, Paul Rosenfeld, the critic for *The New Republic,* carried a dim torch for this priestess-warrior and compared this operatic Mona-tony to both *Pelléas* and *Elektra!* The only resemblance among these works, Mr. Rosenfeld, is that they're named for the main character. We already have a first-class *Norma, Tristan, Pelléas,* and *Elektra,* why bother with a steerage-quality *Mona.*

Uncrushable, Dr. Parker and Mr. Hooker garnered another $10,000 prize, this from the National Federation of Women's Clubs, for their next atrocity *Fairyland* (1915), which premiered in Los Angeles and which had even fewer performances than *Mona.*

A month after *Mona*'s world, and final, premiere, the *Titanic* sank. *Mona* should have been on board. "Norma, Tristan, into the lifeboats! Ummm . . . Mona, you wait by the rail. We'll be right back. We promise. Bye!"

It's in the Stars

ARIES. The Ram. 21 March through 19 April.
Ruling Planet: Mars.
Element: Fire.
Sign: Masculine.
Quality: Cardinal.

   Assertive. Lively. Committed to idealistic causes. Brash and aggressive in speech. Self is foremost. Enormous fount of energy. Disarming naiveté. Pioneering spirit. Fearless. Annoyingly straightforward. Accident prone. Self-absorbed concentration. Yelling and screaming to get his/her way. Supreme ego and self-confidence. Frank and disarmingly honest. Explosive flash-fire temper. Total involvement with the moment. Heedless attitude toward love. Eternally youthful.

   ARTURO TOSCANINI. MONSERRAT CABALLÉ. FRANCO CORELLI. HERBERT VON KARAJAN. MARIA EWING. CATHERINE MALFITANO. CAFFARELLI.

TAURUS. The Bull. 20 April through 20 May.
Ruling Planet: Venus.
Element: Earth.
Sign: Feminine.
Quality: Fixed.

   Possessive. Practical. Strong, silent type. Solid, steady. Reliable and incredibly patient. Stubborn. Slow to anger, but, when aroused, displays destructive fury. Stoic. Conservative.

Passive. Endurance of the Pyramids. Love of luxury. Love of home and hearth. Obsessed with routine. Trustworthy. Creature of the physical. Easy-going. Greedy. Stable.

BIRGIT NILSSON. ZINKA MILANOV. NELLIE MELBA.
MAGDA OLIVERO. ELISABETH SÖDERSTRÖM. FIORENZA COSSOTTO.

GEMINI. The Twins. 21 May through 21 June.
Ruling Planet: Mercury.
Element: Air.
Sign: Masculine.
Quality: Mutable.

Versatile. Adaptable. Two-faced. Inconsistent. Sensitive. Nervous and high-strung. Superficial. Busy. Lively. Flair for communications and writing. Many lovers. Restless. Ageless appearance. Resentful of monotony and drudgery. Demanding of change and challenge. Facility of doing two things at the same time. Up-to-date. A gossip. Interest in new ideas. Brilliant con artist. Contradictory views held simultaneously. Charming and witty. Gregarious.

RICHARD WAGNER. BEVERLY SILLS. TERESA STRATAS.
RICHARD STRAUSS. FREDERICA VON STADE. ILEANA COTRUBAS.
EVA MARTON.

CANCER. The Crab. 22 June through 22 July.
Ruling Planet: The Moon.
Element: Water.
Sign: Feminine.
Quality: Cardinal.

Sensitive. Sympathetic. Emotional roller-coaster. Moody. Great worrier. Sentimental streak. Urge to protect. Excellent memory. Shrewd. Harsh and bad-tempered. Tenacious. Retreat in face of sadness. Reverence for the past. Highly intuitive. Ability to side-step to achieve goals. Conservative outer shell, soft interior. Prone to ulcers. Secretive. Love of home and family. Natural reticence and timidity. Excellent memory. Thrifty to a fault. Sex life tinged with sensationalism.

JAMES LEVINE. PETER PEARS. KIRSTEN FLAGSTAD. GUSTAV MAHLER. LUISA TETRAZZINI.

LEO. The Lion. 23 July through 22 August.
Ruling Planet: The Sun.
Element: Fire.
Sign: Masculine.
Quality: Fixed.

Magnanimous. Showy. Natural exuberance. Enthusiasm for life. Dogmatic. Pompous. Innate dignity. Commanding air. Extravagant. Flair for drama. Supreme organizer. Transparent vulnerability. Condescending manner. Fiery pride. Egotistic. Affectionate. Optimistic. Neat and clean. Stoic dignity. Susceptible to flattery. Hard working, hard playing, but lazy when it suits them. Fiercely loyal. Creative and original. Vain. Large-scale vision. Brutally frank and tactless, yet warm-hearted and well-meaning. Astute. Generous. Royalty incarnate.

RICCARDO MUTI. JANET BAKER. PETER HOFMANN. RITA HUNTER. LEO SLEZAK. GIUSEPPE DI STEFANO. KATHLEEN BATTLE.

VIRGO. The Virgin. 23 August through 22 September.
Ruling Planet: Mercury.
Element: Earth.
Sign: Feminine.
Quality: Mutable.

Analytical. Modest. Overly fastidious. Inner anxieties. Worriers. Fussy. Flair for detail. Extremely practical. Desires to serve. Precise and neat. Sincere. Dependable. Ruled by habit. Love of routine. Lacking breadth of vision, but with an amazing ability to assimilate facts. Shrewd and logical. Visibly restless. Prudent and conservative. Independent. Selfish. Punctual. Always seeing the flaws. Purity of thought. Devotion to family and friends. Love of work, duty, and discipline. Sharp intellect. Clean.

JESSYE NORMAN. ANTONIN DVOŘÁK. LEONARD BERNSTEIN. PAUL PLISHKA.

LIBRA. The Scales. 23 September through 23 October.
Ruling Planet: Venus.
Element: Air.
Sign: Masculine.
Quality: Cardinal.

Striving for balance. Indecisive. Easy-going. Gullible. "It's not fair." Works best in tandem. Cheerful, natural optimism. Amazing instincts. Inconsistent. Moody. Extreme activity balanced by periods of rest and leisure. Philosophical. Logical. Gentle. Argumentative. Careful weighing of all possibilities. Scrupulously honest. Love of books. Loathing exaggeration. Strong sense of justice. Anxious to share. Sharp sense of humor. Confusion makes Librans nervous. Flair for design. Over-extravagant. Natural tact and diplomacy.

GIUSEPPE VERDI. LUCIANO PAVAROTTI. RICHARD BONYNGE. ALFREDO KRAUS. GEORG SOLTI. BENITA VALENTE.

SCORPIO. The Scorpion. 24 October through 21 November.
Ruling Planet: Pluto.
Element: Water.
Sign: Feminine.
Quality: Fixed.

Powerful intensity. Passionate. Total ego. Resentful. Obstinate. Intractable. Highly imaginative. Strong sense of purpose in life. Jealous. Sadomasochists. Great endurance. Adaptable. Responsive to discipline. Good sex. Brutally honest. Strong intuitive knowledge. High analytical perceptions. Personal magnetism. Mysterious and fascinating. Supreme self-sacrifice. Proud and confident. Will always get even. Never forgets an injury. Fiercely possessive. Sensualist. Rigid control of emotions. Mean and violent. Dabbler in arcane knowledge, ancient mysteries.

LEONIE RYSANEK. JOAN SUTHERLAND. BENJAMIN BRITTEN. AGNES BALTSA. JON VICKERS. GWYNETH JONES.

SAGITTARIUS. The Centaur. 22 November through 21 December.
Ruling Planet: Jupiter.
Element: Fire.
Sign: Masculine.
Quality: Mutable.

Must have freedom. Restless. Sincere and frank. Free of malice. Love of animals. Attracted to danger. Capricious. Boisterous. Scrupulous. Dependable. Formidable intellectual capacity. Affinity for languages. Claustrophobic. Randy sex life. Pleasure of exploration. Warm and generous. Extrovert. Irresponsible. Blind optimism. Need for constant challenge. Reckless abandon. Violent temper. Can analyze old problems in new ways. Clever wit. Cannot tell a lie successfully. Naive trust. Constant traveling. Says what he/she thinks. Acts how he/she feels.

MARIA CALLAS. JOSÉ CARRERAS. ELIZABETH SCHWARZKOPF. HECTOR BERLIOZ.

CAPRICORN. The Goat. 22 December through 19 January.
Ruling Planet: Saturn.
Element: Earth.
Sign: Feminine.
Quality: Cardinal.

Prudent. Reliable. Conventional. Persevering. Ambitious. Splendid business sense. Social climber. Conscious camouflage. Calm, deliberate. Serious. Relentless. Rational mind. Cool and calculating. Prone to depression. Great musical ability. Creature of habit. Shyness in intimacy. Miserly. Needing security. Respectful of authority. Melancholic. Traditional. Controlled passions. Sober and temperate. Heading always toward career goals and prestige. Disciplined. Iron determination. Artistic talent. Dry wit. Conservative appearance.

SHERRILL MILNES. GIACOMO PUCCINI. GRACE BUMBRY. PLACIDO DOMINGO. MARILYN HORNE. KATIA RICCIARELLI. JEAN DE RESZKE. ANNA RUSSELL.

AQUARIUS. The Water Bearer. 20 January through 18 February.
Ruling Planet: Uranus.
Element: Air.
Sign: Masculine.
Quality: Fixed.

Humanitarianism. Independent. Eccentric. Rebellious. Progressive outlook. Original. Fixed. Kind and tranquil. Refusal to conform. Coolly impersonal. Rational, clinical in thinking. Intensely analytical. "I want to be alone." Aloof glamour. Typically vague. Saturated with friends, but not many intimates. Ahead of his/her time. Genius or madman. Love of mankind. Abhors prejudice. Frank, but respectful of individuality. Obsessed with the new and modern, or the ancient and revered. Power of concentration. Knowledge by osmosis. Psychic precognition. Will not lie or cheat. Firmly opinionated. Secretive, yet yearning for truth. Revolutionary, but will leave fighting to others.

LEONTYNE PRICE. RENATA TEBALDI. HILDEGARD BEHRENS. JUSSI BJÖRLING. MOZART. FARINELLI.

PISCES. The Fish. 19 February through 20 March.
Ruling Planet: Neptune.
Element: Water.
Sign: Feminine.
Quality: Mutable.

Dreamer. Humble. Compassionate. Vague. Impressionable. Indecisive. Unworldly. Adaptable. Easily confused. Extremely sensitive. Impractical. Eager to escape from reality. Great compassion. Need of the arts to channel fantasy life. Torrent of emotion. Unable to cope with routine and conformity. Genuine softness and gentle charm. Sentimental. Creative and artistic. Tendency to go with the flow, rather than challenge. Natural timidity. Fantastic memory. Flair for the romantic. Deep wisdom. Most susceptible to drugs and alcohol. Need to identify. Must have inspiration to succeed.

ENRICO CARUSO. KIRI TE KANAWA. RENATA SCOTTO. ROSSINI. JEAN-PIERRE PONNELLE. LAURITZ MELCHIOR. REGINE CRESPIN. CHRISTA LUDWIG. GERALDINE FARRAR.

Hey, Huh! or,
What the Maestros Said
About Each Other

In 1859, Charles Gounod was hastily scribbling down the last act of *Faust*, sending Marguerite off to Heaven to provide the despotic prima donna Madame Carvalho with yet another show-stopper, when a knock at the door disturbed his concentration. The maid, not being able to bear hearing one more *Salve*, had fled earlier, shrieking obscenities. Thinking it was a decree from Madame Carvalho, Gounod rushed downstairs and opened the door. It was the postboy with a letter. Gounod tipped him a sou.

The envelope was plain, with no return address. Not Madame's style at all. Curious, he thought. He tore it open. A single page, printed like a miniature handbill, was folded inside.

MUSICIANS GOOD LUCK LETTER
DO NOT BREAK THE CHAIN! MISFORTUNE WILL FOLLOW!

Copy this missive, add your name to the bottom, and send it to the next composer on the list. Tell them what you think of their work. Good luck will be yours. Send no money. DO NOT THROW THIS AWAY! Good luck will be yours always. Send this today!!

Gounod was an easy mark. *Faust* was scheduled to open in less than two months. He needed all the luck he could get. Rushing to his piano, he threw Madame Carvalho's aria aside and penned his letter to the next composer on the list. The rest is history . . .

GOUNOD on BERLIOZ:

His *Les Troyens*, which he had foreseen as being the source of all his sorrows, truly finished him. It can be said of him, as of his heroic namesake, Hector, that he perished under the walls of Troy.

With Berlioz all impressions, all sensations—whether joyful or sad—are expressed in extremes, at the point of delirium. As he himself says, he is a "volcano."

The great geniuses suffer and must suffer; they have known intoxication unknown to the rest of men and, if they have wept tears of sadness, they have poured tears of ineffable joy. That is itself a heaven for which one never pays what it is worth.

BERLIOZ on WAGNER:

Wagner is turning the singers, the orchestra, and the chorus of this opera into goats. Nothing can be made of this *Tannhäuser* music.

[84]

Wagner on Gounod:

With Gounod alone did I preserve friendly relations. I was told that everywhere in society he championed my cause with enthusiasm. To repay him for this I gave him a full score of *Tristan,* for his conduct was all the more gratifying to me in that no consideration of friendship had been able to induce me to hear his *Faust.*

Gounod on Wagner:

God give me a failure like that! [*Tannhäuser* in Paris] Let's not be mistaken. You call this a failure. I call it a riot, which is something very different. Let's meet again ten years from now before the same work and the same man. You'll take off your hat to them both. A matter like this cannot be judged in an evening.

Wagner on Donizetti:

La Favorita, as you no doubt know, enjoys a considerable measure of approval. Paris lies midway between Germany and Italy. The German composer who writes for Paris feels obliged to abandon a large measure of his pedantic earnestness, whereas the Italian maestro tends involuntarily to become more serious and sedate, to stop playing the fool and to be on his best behavior. I will desist from drawing conclusions, which would certainly be in Paris's favor, but I will add that *La Favorita* provides immediate proof. Donizetti's music here reveals, beside the recognized merits of the Italian school, those qualities of dignity and good breeding which one misses in all the countless other operas of the indefatigable maestro.

Verdi on Wagner:

Sad, sad, sad. Wagner is dead! When I read the news yesterday, I may truly say that I was completely crushed. Let us not discuss it. It is a great personality that has disappeared. A name which leaves a mighty imprint upon the history of art.

BIZET on VERDI:

Verdi is a man of great talent who lacks the essential quality which makes the great masters: style. But he had bursts of marvelous passion. His passion is brutal, it is true, but it is better to be impassioned in this way than not at all. His music is at times exasperating, but it is never boring. In short, I do not understand the fanatics or the detractors he has excited. In my opinion, he merits neither the one nor the other.

VERDI on BERLIOZ:

Berlioz was a poor, sick man who raged at everyone, was bitter and malicious. He was greatly and subtly gifted. He had a real feeling for instrumentation, anticipated Wagner in many instrumental effects. (The Wagnerites won't admit it, but it's true.) He had no moderation. He lacked the calm and what I may call the balance that produces complete works of art. He always went to extremes, even when he was doing admirable things.

ROSSINI on VERDI:

If the name of the composer had been kept hidden from me, I should have wagered that he could only be an artillery colonel.

BERLIOZ on ROSSINI:

Le Comte Ory. What musical riches! A wealth of felicitous air throughout, and finally, that wonderful trio. Rossini's masterpiece in my opinion.

WAGNER on BERLIOZ:

The audience [at *Benvenuto Cellini*] went to sleep and awoke hissing.

BERLIOZ on GOUNOD:

There is nothing in the score of *La Reine de Saba,* absolutely nothing. How can one support something which has neither bone nor muscle?

GOUNOD on MOZART:

Oh, mama, what music! This is truly music!

VERDI on GOUNOD:

Gounod is a great musician, a great talent, who composes excellent chamber and instrumental music in a manner all his own. But he isn't an artist of dramatic fiber. *Faust* itself, though successful, has become small in his hands. *Roméo et Juliette* and this *Poliuto* will be the same. In a word, he always does the intimate piece well; but his treatment of situations is weak and his characterizations are bad.

TCHAIKOVSKY on VERDI:

I spit upon "effects"! Besides what are effects? For instance, if *Aida* is effective, I can assure you I would not compose an opera on a similar subject for all the wealth of the world; for I want to handle human beings, not puppets. I would gladly compose an opera which was completely lacking in startling effects, but which offered characters resembling my own, whose feelings and experiences I shared and understood. The feelings of an Egyptian Princess, a Pharaoh, or some mad Nubian, I can't enter into, or comprehend. I want no kings, no tumultuous populace, no gods, no pompous marches—in short, none of those things which are the attributes of "grand opera." *Aida* is so remote, her love for Radames touches me so little—since I can't picture it in my mind's eye—that my music would lack the vital warmth which is essential to good work.

Verdi on Bellini:

Bellini is weak instrumentally and harmonically, it's true; but he is rich in feeling and in a certain personal melancholy, which is completely his own. Even in his less well-known operas like *La Straniera* and *Il Pirata*, there are long, long, long spun-out melodies, like nothing that had been written before.

Donizetti on Verdi:

My heyday is over, and another must take my place. The world wants something new. Others have ceded their places to us and we must cede ours to still others. I am more than happy to give mine to people of talent like Verdi. Friends are always worried, but you may rest assured of this young man's success. Talent can win esteem all over. In any case, even though his success may not measure up to the complete hopes of his friends, that will not prevent Verdi from occupying shortly one of the most honorable places in the galaxy of composers.

Verdi on Puccini:

He follows the new tendencies, which is only natural, but he keeps strictly to melody, and that is neither new or old. But it seems that he is predominantly a symphonist; no harm in that. Only here one must be careful. Opera is opera, symphony, symphony; I don't think it is a good idea to insert a symphonic piece into an opera just for the pleasure of letting the orchestra cut loose once in a while.

Puccini on Debussy:

Debussy's *Pelléas et Mélisande* has extraordinary harmonic qualities and the most delicate instrumental effects. It is very interesting, in spite of its coloring, which is sombre and unrelieved like a Franciscan's habit. The subject is interesting.

[88]

Debussy on Wagner:

Wagner's art can never completely die. It will suffer that inevitable decay, the cruel brand of time on all beautiful things; yet noble ruins must remain, in the shadow of which our grandchildren will brood over the past splendor of this man who, had he been a little more human, would have been altogether great.

In *Parsifal,* Wagner tried to drive his music on a looser rein and let it breathe more freely. We have no longer the distraught breathlessness that characterizes Tristan's morbid passion or Isolde's wild screams of frenzy; nor yet the grandiloquent commentary on the inhumanity of Wotan.

Although it must be admitted that Wagner's peculiar conception of human nature is also shown in the attitude of certain characters in this drama. Amfortas, that melancholy Knight of the Grail, whines like a shop girl and whimpers like a baby. Good heavens! As for Kundry, that ancient rose of hell, I confess I have but little affection for such a sentimental draggletail. Klingsor is the finest character in *Parsifal.* His bitter hatred is amazing; he knows the worth of men and scornfully weighs the strength of their vows of chastity in the balance. This crafty magician, this old jailbird, is not merely the only human character but the only moral character in this drama, in which the falsest moral and religious ideas are set forth, ideas of which the youthful Parsifal is the heroic and insipid champion.

Here, in short, is a Christian drama in which nobody is willing to sacrifice himself, though sacrifice is one of the highest of the Christian virtues!

The musical beauty of the opera is supreme. It is incomparable and bewildering, splendid and strong. *Parsifal* is one of the loveliest monuments of sound ever raised to the serene glory of music.

Wagner on Rossini:

In *Guillaume Tell,* maestro, you made music for all times, and that is the best.

Rossini on Beethoven:

I told him of all my admiration for his genius, all my gratitude for his having allowed me an opportunity to express it to him. I felt such a painful impression of my visit to that great man—thinking of that destitution, that privation—that I couldn't hold back my tears.

That very evening I attended a gala dinner given by Prince Metternich. Still completely upset by that visit, I couldn't, I assure you, protect myself from an inner feeling of confusion at seeing, by comparison, myself treated with such regard by that brilliant Viennese assemblage. That lead me to say stoutly and without any discretion at all what I thought about the conduct of the court and the aristocracy toward the greatest genius of the epoch, who needed so little and was abandoned to such distress.

I added that it would be so easy, by means of drawing up a very small subscription, to assure him an income large enough to place him beyond all need for the rest of his life. That proposal didn't win the support of a single person.

Beethoven on Rossini:

Ah, Rossini, you are the composer of *Barbiere*? I congratulate you, it is an excellent *opera buffa*; I read it with pleasure, and it delights me. It will be played as long as Italian opera exists. Never try to do anything other than *opera buffa*; wanting to succeed in another genre would be trying to force your destiny.

Opera seria—that's not the Italians' nature. They don't have enough musical science to deal with real drama; and how could they acquire it in Italy? In *opera buffa* nobody would have the wit to match you, you Italians. Your language and your vivacity of temperament destine you for it.

Then, wishing me a good performance and success for *Zelmira,* he got up, led us to the door, and said to me again, "Above all, make a lot of *Barbers.*"

BIZET on BEETHOVEN:

I place Beethoven above the greatest, the most famous. Neither Mozart with his divine form, nor Weber with his powerful, colossal originality, nor Meyerbeer with his thundering dramatic genius can, in my opinion, dispute the crown of this Titan, this Prometheus of music. He is overwhelming.

TCHAIKOVSKY on BIZET:

Yesterday evening—to take a rest from my own work—I played through Bizet's *Carmen* from cover to cover. I consider it a masterpiece in the fullest sense of the word: one of those rare compositions which seems to reflect most strongly in itself the musical tendencies of a whole generation.

Contemporary music is clever, piquant, and eccentric, but cold and lacking the glow of true emotion. And behold, a Frenchman comes on the scene, in whom these qualities of piquancy and pungency are not the outcome of effort and reflection, but flow from his pen as in a free stream, flattering the ear, but touching us also. It is as though he said to us, "You ask nothing great, superb, or grandiose—you want something pretty, here is a pretty opera."

Truly I know of nothing in music which is more representative of that element which I call *le joli*. I can't play the last scene without tears in my eyes. I am convinced that ten years hence *Carmen* will be the most popular opera in the world. But no one is a prophet in his own land. In Paris *Carmen* has had no real success.

BIZET on WAGNER:

Rienzi is a badly constructed piece. A single role—Rienzi. A racket that can't be described; a jumble of Italian motives; a bizarre and bad style; music of decadence rather than of the future. Wretched numbers! Admirable numbers! All in all, an astounding work, terrifically *alive:* a grandeur, and Olympian breath! Genius, immoderate, disorderly, but genius! Will it be a success? I don't know! Some maintained: "It's bad Verdi!" others: "It's good Wagner!" It is sublime! It's frightful! It's mediocre! It isn't bad! The audience is perplexed! It is very amusing. Few people have the courage to persist in their hatred of Wagner. . . .

Wagner is no friend of mine and I am fairly indifferent to him, yet I can't forget the immeasurable enjoyment which I owe to this original genius. The charm of his music is inexpressible. Here are voluptuousness, tenderness, love.

This man is the nineteenth-century German spirit incarnate. Fortunately for Wagner, he is endowed with such insolent conceits that criticism can't touch his heart—admitting that he has a heart, which I doubt.

Of course, in spite of my admiration, if I thought I were imitating Wagner, I would never write another note.

FAURÉ on BIZET:

That Mérimée's novelette should have seemed scarcely to conform to the traditions of the *Opéra Comique* is understandable. What is not understandable is that Bizet's music, so utterly clear, so sincere, so colorful, sensitive and charming should not have conquered the public from the outset. Dramatic eloquence of such pathos, so vigorous and direct, should immediately have moved the audience.

The youth, joy, passion, and life which it contains remain as overflowing as they are unalterable. And the indifference and hostility of yesteryear have given way to the most brilliant, most universal favor.

BIZET on ROSSINI:

Rossini is the greatest of all because he has, like Mozart, all the qualities: loftiness, style, and, finally, the melodic sense . . .

I am by conviction, heart and soul, German. But sometimes I lose myself in low artistic places. And I must confess to you in a whisper that I get infinite pleasure from it. In a word, I love Italian music as one loves a mistress, but she must be charming. And when we have cited two thirds of *Norma*, four pieces from *Puritani*, three from *Sonnambula*, two acts of *Rigoletto*, an act of *Trovatore* and just about half of *Traviata*—add *Don Pasquale*—we

[92]

can throw the rest away anywhere you please. As for Rossini, he has his *Guillaume Tell*—his sun—*Comte Ory, Barbiere,* and one act of *Otello*—his planets. Because of these we may pardon the terrible *Semiramide* and all his other sins.

PUCCINI on BIZET:

Yesterday I sneaked in for nothing to hear *Carmen.* It really is a beautiful work.

FAURÉ on PUCCINI:

Puccini is the most famous of the musicians who today represent the Italian school; he is one of the most gifted, certainly the best equipped and the most experienced. Though he translates moving situations by means one may find too uniform; though accents, emphatic and often wanting in invention, take too important a place in his works; on the other hand, he excels in scenes of movement. His verve, his taste for harmonic and orchestral quests, his manner of adorning the most slender ideas with charming details, present a feast of pleasure to the listener.

PUCCINI on STRAUSS:

Last night I was able to go the premiere of *Salome,* conducted by Strauss, and sung (?) by Bellincioni, whose dancing is marvelous. It was a success, but there must be many who doubt the verdict. The playing of the orchestra was like a badly mixed Russian salad, but the composer was there, and everybody says that it was perfect.

At the rehearsals when Strauss was trying to work up his orchestra to a rough and tempestuous kind of execution, he said, "Gentlemen, this is not a question of music, but of a menagerie. Make a noise! Blow into your instruments!" What do you think of that?

STRAUSS on PUCCINI:

La Bohème, Tosca, Madama Butterfly, I can't tell them apart.

FAURÉ on STRAUSS:

A great part of the emotion which the presentations of *Salome* have stirred up, wherever they have taken place, is due to the extraordinary strangeness of the work. *Salome* is a symphonic poem with vocal parts added.

Atmosphere and color are portrayed in their finest nuances, all by means of mediocre themes, it is true, but developed, worked, interwoven with such marvelous skill that their intrinsic interest is exceeded by the magic of an orchestral technique of real genius, until these themes—mediocre, as I said—end by acquiring character, power, and almost emotion.

This cleverness, this prodigious facility, has its drawbacks. The instability of the music, the fleeting changes of orchestral effects, always new, always arresting, scarcely absorbed before replaced by others, end by creating a perpetual dazzle which tires not only the spirit but—does this seem absurd?—even the eyes. Is it because of the particularly brutal character of the subject, or is it solely to shock that Strauss has introduced so many cruel dissonances which defy all explanation? His bewitching orchestra, it is true, makes everything permissible.

Nevertheless, as far as I am concerned, these criticisms do not denote weaknesses, but only musical means with which I can't sympathize, in a work vigorously conceived, executed with skill and virtuosity of the first order, and which contains some very very impressive pages: especially the final scene, one of genuine beauty.

STRAUSS on MOZART:

Though it is correct to say that he was one who solved all "problems" before they were even posed, that in him passion is divested of everything earthly and seems to be viewed from a bird's-eye perspective, it is equally true that his work contains —even when transfigured, spiritualized, and liberated from reality—all phases of human experience from the monumental, dark grandeur of the Commendatore's scene in *Don Giovanni*, to the daintiness of the Zerlina arias, the heavenly frivolities of *Figaro*, and the deliberate ironies of *Così*.

Almost immediately on Bach does the miracle of Mozart follow, with his perfection and absolute idealization of the melody of human song. Not to be recognized by the eye, not to be grasped by the understanding, but to be divined by consciousness as most godly, which the ear is permitted to "breathe in."

MAHLER on STRAUSS:

Salome is truly a work of genius, a very strong work, which definitely belongs among the most significant which our age has brought forth. It seethes under a mass of lava, a volcano, a subterranean fire—not merely fireworks. It is the same with Strauss's entire personality. At the same time it is so difficult to separate the wheat from the chaff in him. But I have achieved a tremendous respect for the entire phenomenon and confirmed it anew. I am very happy about it! Here I can go along all the way!

STRAUSS on WAGNER:

Richard Wagner combined all kinds of rich passage work with the most evocative melodies to serve dramatic expression. *Tristan, The Ring, Meistersinger,* and *Parsifal* constitute the peak toward which all species of "form in tonal motion" and "musical expression" strive. In Wagner, music reached its greatest capacity for expression.

WAGNER on WEBER:

The score of *Der Freischütz* is a finished whole, perfectly rounded in every part, as well in thought as in form. Would not the omission of the smallest part be to maim or distort the master's work? In this drama, where the song has so deep a significance and so important a meaning, you will find none of those noisy combination passages, of those deafening finales, to which the grand opera has accustomed you.

Weber breathed a fresh warm lovely life into the music of the stage. He touched the heart of the German people. Its basis was the simple soulful ballade decorated in the noblest style of early romanticism, celebrating the imaginative life of the German nation at its most characteristic.

SCHUMANN on WAGNER:

Wagner, though certainly a brilliant fellow and full of original, audacious ideas, can hardly set down (and think out) a four measure phrase beautifully or even correctly. He is one of those people who have not learned their harmony lessons, nor learned how to write four-part chorales, as this work makes plain [*Tannhäuser*]. The music is not a bit better than *Rienzi;* if anything, more pallid and forced. It is certainly a genial work. Were he as melodious a composer as he is an intellectual one, he would be a man of our times.

WAGNER on VERDI:

Pig.

VERDI on ROSSINI:

I can't help thinking that, for abundance of real musical ideas, for comic verve, and truthful declamation, the *Barbiere di Siviglia* is the finest *opera buffa* in existence.

MUSSORGSKY on VERDI:

But Maestro "Senatore" Verdi is quite another matter! This one pushes ahead on a grand scale, this innovator doesn't feel shy. All his *Aida* outdistancing everything, outdistancing everyone, even himself. He has knocked over *Trovatore,* Mendelssohn, Wagner—and almost Amerigo Vespucci, too. The spectacle is wonderful, but demonstrates a fabulous impotence in personifying (with reminiscences!) the teeth-champing, hot African blood.

[96]

TCHAIKOVSKY on MUSSORGSKY:

He is "used up." His gifts are perhaps the most remarkable of all, but his nature is narrow, and he has no aspirations towards self-perfection. He has been too easily led astray by the absurd theories of his set and the belief in his own genius. Besides which, his nature is not of the finest quality; he likes what is coarse, unpolished, and ugly. He is the exact opposite of the distinguished and elegant Cui. He even seems proud of his lack of skill, writing just as it comes to him, believing blindly in the infallibility of his genius. As a matter of fact, his very original talent flashes forth now and then.

DVOŘÁK on TCHAIKOVSKY:

I confess with pleasure that your opera [Eugene Onegin] made a very deep impression upon me—an impression such as I expect from a true work of art, and I do not hesitate to say that none of your compositions has given me such pleasure.

It is a splendid work, full of warm feeling and poetry, and, at the same time, worked out to the last detail; in short, this music speaks to us and penetrates so deep into our soul that it is unforgettable.

I congratulate you and ourselves on this work and pray God that you may be spared to give the world many more such compositions.

TCHAIKOVSKY on CUI:

Cui is a gifted amateur. His music is not original, but graceful and elegant; it is too coquettish, "made-up"—so to speak. At first it pleases, but soon satiates us. That is because Cui's speciality is not music, but fortifications. He himself once told me he could only compose by picking out his melodies and harmonies as he sat at the piano. When he hit upon some pretty idea, he worked it up in every detail, and this process was very lengthy, so that his opera, Ratcliff, for instance, took him ten years to complete. But, as I have said, we can't deny that he has talent of a kind—and at least taste and instinct.

CUI on DONIZETTI:

Dramatic music must always have an intrinsic worth, as absolute music, independent of the text. Because composers have been mainly preoccupied with pure melody and vocal virtuosity, guarantees of success, the most astounding and naive banalities have been justified and accepted. What would have been discarded with justifiable disdain in a symphonic composition, found its way naturally into opera. In this business, the Italians are masters beyond compare. Content with facile successes, based on florid passages and on high B flats and C sharps, keeping step with and sustaining the public's bad taste, they not only resort to using the most banal themes, but they parade these horrors in all their nakedness, never so much as attempting to mitigate them with even slightly elegant harmonies. The best among these musicians either repeat each other or repeat themselves, in style, themes, and harmonies.

One has merely to glance at the thirty-odd Italian operas of Rossini, at the seventy and more of Donizetti. Both offer two or three typical works, of which the rest of their output is only a more or less feeble and pallid reproduction. And even in their masterpieces, what commonplaces, what insignificant and stale pages!

DONIZETTI on BELLINI:

The only musical event of extraordinary importance has been the production of *Norma.* I am happy beyond measure at the splendid reception accorded the above opera at the Scala after its opening on the 26th of this month, a gay and festive reception which was repeated at subsequent performances.

A lucky outcome, all the more significant considering that *Norma* had a somewhat chilly greeting, even, to tell the truth, a hostile one, from the numerous public the first evening it was presented. After four evenings, however, an immense crowd besieged boxes, galleries, balconies, orchestra, and filled the vast hall to overflowing, applauding every piece in the opera with tremendous enthusiasm.

Everybody is praising the music of my friend, or rather my brother, Bellini to the skies. Everyone is overwhelmed by his sovereign genius and is discovering in his work undreamed-of beauties and treasures of sublime harmony. The whole score pleases me immensely, and I have been going to the theater the last four evenings to hear Bellini's opera, remaining through the last scene.

I shall only say that I am completely won over by this moving composition, by the rich elegance of its orchestration, and by the union of the emotional and dramatic with the greatness of inspiration.

BELLINI on ROSSINI:

The musical oracle of Paris.

ROSSINI on WAGNER:

Wagner has beautiful moments but awful quarter hours.

WAGNER on BELLINI:

I shall never forget the impression that a Bellini opera lately heard made on me, after I had become heartily sick of the eternally allegorizing orchestral bustle, and a simple and noble Song made its appearance again. The German connoisseur of music listens to one of Bellini's operas with the spectacles off his tired-out eyes: delight in lovely Song, the limpid melody, the simple, noble lovely Song of Bellini. It is surely no sin to confess this and to believe in it; perhaps even it would not be a sin if before we went to sleep we were to pray Heaven that some day German composers might achieve such melodies and such an art of handling song. Song, Song, and yet again Song, ye Germans!

CLARA SCHUMANN on WAGNER:

We went to *Tristan und Isolde* this evening. It is the most repulsive thing I ever saw or heard in my life. To have to sit through a whole evening watching, listening to such love-lunacy till every feeling of decency was outraged, and to see not only the audience but the musicians delighted with it was—I may well say—the saddest experience of my whole artistic career. I held out till the end, as I wished to have heard it all. Neither of them does anything but sleep and sing during the second act, and the whole of Act III—quite forty minutes—Tristan occupies in dying—and they call that dramatic!!! Levi says Wagner is a better musician than Gluck.

The subject seems to me so wretched: a love-madness brought about by a potion—how is it possible to take the slightest interest in the lovers? It is not emotion, it is a disease, and they tear their hearts out of their bodies, while the music expresses it all in the most repulsive manner. I could go on lamenting over it for ever, and exclaiming against it.

Are they all fools or am I a fool?

WAGNER on BEETHOVEN:

I inspected the five daily playbills. Heavens! On one of them I read, "*Fidelio,* Opera by Beethoven." I had to go, never mind the state of my finances. They were giving the new revised version of the opera which, under the title of *Leonore,* had already been played in Vienna and accorded the honor of being damned by its discriminating public. I too had never heard the revised version; imagine therefore my delight at the fresh marvels it contained! It was as though the heavens had opened; I prostrated myself before the genius who had led me, like Florestan, out of the darkness of tyranny into the light of freedom.

Wagner dashed off his letter, added his name to the bottom of the list, and sent his copy to L. von Beethoven. By this time, however, Beethoven was quite deaf and couldn't hear the postman's insistent knocking. The letter was thrown away.

Since the chain was now broken, the threat of ill fortune would forever plague opera composers. Now, we ain't afraid of no ghosts, but do you know of any good works written in the last fifty years?

[100]

─────── • *Intermezzo* • ───────
Having an Acts to Grind

Have you ever had one of those days? The new, expensive IBM computer "goes down," setting off the entire sprinkler system on the 33rd floor. Moments before the big presentation to the client, your partner announces she's joining a religious cult and begins chanting, "Down with Capitalist Goons!" You can hardly contain your excitement when the boss informs you that you get the all-expense-paid business trip to Paris—Paris, Missouri! And, at 7:50, your date frantically telephones to remind you that you were to meet at the Met. Have you forgotten? You rush off into the rain, there are no cabs, your dinner consists of a cup of cardboard coffee and a $4.00 box of stale mints at the theater, and the "fun little opera" turns into a Germanic five-act cement dumpling, set in what appears to be outer space, and sung by the fattest cast this side of Barnum and Bailey.

Face it, wouldn't you rather be eating dinner, or having a martini, or folding your laundry? Not every work of musical art requires four hours of your time for its treasures to be enjoyed. Intermissions are a waste of time. Come on, this is the 80's. Can't those stagehands change sets any faster? And if those singers have got to rest their voices, why did they become singers in the first place? We'd rather be given the option of sitting there in one fell swoop and getting the whole damned show over with. Since this is not to be, we offer the following tips in what acts to miss so you can save time, your health, and your sanity when you're also squeezing in the opera.

1. *Fidelio.* Acts I or II.

Admit it, nobody really likes this prudish strudel, this German *Cage aux Folles,* this sanctimonious paean to conjugal love. The so-called comic moments (?) are embarrassing and stale (Ludwig was not a party guy); most singers can't even begin to negotiate the difficult passages—even if they can, they don't look good in Leonore's drag; that arch-fiend Pizarro is not nearly as frightening and mean as the least-animated of Disney villains; and the lumpy plot and creaky devices were out of date and out of shape centuries before Beethoven tried to rejuvenate them. Back to the spa, Florestan.

If you can suffer through the maddening *singspiel* until the quartet and the sublime *Abscheulicher* and the *Prisoners' Chorus,* you can go home after Act I. Or, come fashionably late, watch Florestan go mad, listen to a love duet, hear another *Leonore Overture,* and suspend disbelief as overweight chorusers pretend to be starving political prisoners. As Pizarro says, "Hell and Death." Choose!

2. *La Verismo.* Acts I and III.

Written by the team of Mascagni, Leoncavallo, and Puccini, this triple bill collaboration, known familiarly as the *Cav/Pag/Tab* trilogy, is actually the same opera not-so-cleverly disguised. *Cavalleria* has unhappy peasants, unwed mothers, adultery, mother-love, live donkeys, oenophilia, ear biting, dust, and the Church (whose teachings go unheeded, but it gives a good parade). Is it any wonder that this cobbled together, piecemeal, jerky opera is beloved in Italy? What you may not know, however, is that Turiddu recovers from the knife fight, sees the error of his ways, forgives the whining Santuzza, and the happy duo hop a ferry to Calabria and join a traveling circus. Here, in *Pagliacci,* Turiddu disguises his chewed ear with clown make-up, Santuzza has taken Mama Lucia's advice and become a liberated woman, and Alfio changes his name to Silvio and follows the motley crew since he never loved Lola anyway. There's much made—too much, really—about life as theater and theater as life and theater as theater and . . . Anyway, the police close in, and everybody takes off for the freedom of Paris. Santuzza always wanted a vacation on a barge trip down the Seine. In *Tabarro*, history repeats in the undulating shadows of the Eiffel Tower. Santuzza, changing her name to the chic Georgetta, is awfully tired of gourmet meals on a lurching boat, Turiddu has second thoughts about his wife's constancy, and Alfio, taking out a membership at Jacques La Lanne, has become a stevedore, still following Santuzza. He needs all his extra strength: have you ever seen the size of most Giorgettas? You can tell by the crashing chords in minor keys that this story is going to have an unhappy ending, just like the others. But don't fear, these characters have amazing resiliency and recuperative powers. You never know where they're going to show up; you just know that they can't be killed off. A little less Verismo, maestros, if you please.

3. *Siegfried.* Act II.

On his way to the orchestra to conduct the Bologna premiere of *Siegfried,* Toscanini was stopped backstage by the nervous tenor making his debut. "Maestro, will it go well tonight?" "I don't know, too many beasts," Toscanini shot back. "There's that bird, that bear, a dragon. And then there's you."

Right again, Arturo! We suggest skipping the act with the dragon (and the bird, too) which has never worked well at all, even at the Bayreuth premiere. The neck didn't arrive from the property shop in London; poor Fafner made his first appearance with a good head literally upon his shoulders. Usually there's no dragon at all. Sometimes Fafner dresses up as an octopus or some amorphous blob that looks just as silly as a stuffed dragon; sometimes he's a disembodied voice or a bright pin-spot. Whatever guise he assumes, he's never terrifying, but he's always long-winded, as are Mime, Alberich, and even Wotan in this act. Wagner could write glorious music, but a dramatic librettist he was not. Unrelieved by a woman's voice until the Bird flits in, Act II groans on and on, rehashing what we already know. Act I is redeemed through the built-up tension in the forging scene. Will the sword shatter? Will the anvil fall neatly in two before Siegfried touches it? Will the anvil resist cleaving? We always anxiously await what will happen, then we go out for dinner. Full and happy, we can face Wotan's fade-out and Brünnhilde's awakening.

4. Any act by Massenet.

Pick one, any one, in any order, it doesn't matter. They all sound the same, and somebody's going to die at the end, except in *Cendrillon,* where everybody is pretty much dead when it begins. Thaïs loves Le Cid, who is having an affair with Sapho, the illegitimate daughter of Werther, who is, in disguise, Le Roi de Lahore, whose second cousins Esclarmonde and Herodiade have eloped with Le Jongleur de Notre Dame. Listening to such sweet music for over three hours is hazardous to one's health. Better to sit at home, eat a pound of white chocolate, and drink Taylor champagne. It's sick, cloying, and doesn't go together either.

5. *Forza del Destino.* Act III.

We don't know about you, but by this act we've had just about enough of these characters and their infernal disguises and jealousies and religious conversions and Preziosilla, too! Rataplan, indeed! We wouldn't be tempted to return except there is Leonora's Act IV aria to look forward to.

6. *Don Carlos.* Act I.

There have been almost as many versions of Verdi's "flawed masterpiece" as performances: Paris, pre-Paris, Moderna, Milan, Naples, Paris/Milan, pre-Paris/Moderna, ad infinitum. Every scene has its own dizzying array of variations. In 1882, Verdi did a major overhaul and removed the first act, stripped away the ballet, and cut the "purely musical" while "retaining only what is necessary for the dramatic action." This four-act version appeared at La Scala in 1884. In 1886, Act I popped back, with Verdi's consent—so it was said—for Moderna's 1886 production. Take it out, we say! The evening is long enough, and all our favorite tunes show up later in much more dramatic circumstances, underscoring the seething emotions and passions that make this opera one of Giuseppe's juiciest. Plot-wise, the act is a redundant prologue: Act II tells us, in brief, what has preceded it, and gets us right into the action. Go have a drink for a half an hour. Once Elisabeth and Carlos get out of the forest, the opera takes off. There's no need to witness their stalling tactics.

7. *Parsifal.* Act III.

Once Klingsor's dead, what good is this rubbish? Amfortas recovers, Mr. Clean blesses the waspy knights, Kundry shrieks, Gurnemanz keeps talking, and we get to hear every Dresden *Amen* another twenty times, usually slower than the twenty times we've already heard it in Act I. Can't conductors speed up this Sunday school lesson! God, it's lugubrious. Anything this pious is automatically suspect. Klingsor might not have all his pieces; he may not be all man, but he's the only human among these stuffed icons.

8. *Der Rosenkavalier.* Act III.

Next to *Meistersinger,* this is the longest comic opera in the repertoire. It does have ravishing music, as only Strauss can provide, but even this blessing can't redeem the unendurable lethargy of Act III. Ochs doesn't deserve forty minutes of vaudeville before that sumptuous *Trio* gets under way, and we're not waitin' around for it, either. We'll find another tavern. See you at the bar.

Screaming Mimis
and Other Loudmouths

O ver the centuries there has been a multitude of sobri-
quets to characterize various divas and their unique
traits: La Stupenda, the Queen of Song, the Swedish Nightin-
gale, La Divina, The Phenomenon, The Tuscan Thrush, The
False Renata, etc., but there can be only one word to describe
our favorite—the one and only—La Incredible, Florence Foster
Jenkins!

She beggars description. Words fail, *Roget's Thesaurus* proves
inadequate, Shakespeare's genius falters, poets laureate become mute in her presence, Apollo's lyre is stilled. What
power, what unnatural force did this woman possess to drive
wordsmiths to the brink of despair?

Her career spanned decades. She sold out Carnegie Hall in a matter of hours. Her recordings couldn't be pressed fast enough to meet the clamorous demand. Packed with the musically fashionable and society's elite, her anxiously awaited recitals in New York and Newport were reviewed in every major newspaper. Her fans outnumbered the legions of Caesar and were as vociferous as a blood-lusty mob at a double-header at the Coliseum. Tumultuous ovations were as common to her as air to us mortals. Like any great diva, she inspired rumors and scandals that swirled about her and made her a legend in her own time. Indeed, she lived with her manager and agent, St. Clair Bayfield, for thirty-six years outside the bonds of matrimony. She was "liberated" generations before it became *de rigueur*. The proceeds from her concerts went to struggling artists to lighten their financial burdens. She was a patron of the arts who founded the Verdi Club, of which Caruso was a member.

Yes, she had her detractors, some even laughed and scoffed, snickering that she could sing everything but the notes; but those "hoodlums," as she rightly called them, were lured from their dank recesses time after time to witness Madame's fresh triumphs. She appeared in costumes of her own designing that would make Leona Helmsley salivate: draped in sumptuous blue and cream satin, with a rhinestone stomacher and tiara for her rendition of *Vissi d'arte,* or startlingly becoming in a brocaded Slavic gown surmounted by a jeweled headdress for a selection of Rachmaninoff songs. She was, once, her own librettist, setting a song by her accompanist Cosme McMoon to the apt title, *Like a Bird I Am Singing, Like a Bird,* which she always used as her final encore. Opera's *tour de force* arias held no trepidation for her. She spun out Zerbinetta's *Grossmächtige Prinzessin* or Lakmé's mountain-climbing coloratura *Bell Song* with the same ease and gaiety as her renditions of Lehár and Arne. There was nothing she couldn't, or didn't, sing. It can truly be said that one never heard the Queen of the Night's *Der Hölle Rache* in quite the same way after La Jenkins sunk her choppers into it!

[108]

Her *joie de vivre* and utter conviction and love of singing was more inspiring than Joan before the gates of Orleans. Her technique was not flawless, nor was her voice a radiant instrument comparable to Nilsson's steel, Price's velvet, or Rysanek's gold; but since we do not damn Sutherland for her scoop, or Callas for her strident wobble, or Caballé for her cancellations, neither do we damn La Jenkins for her shortcomings. They made her like no other. She *was* her art. She gave everything she had; who could ask for anything more?

Like other unique individuals who have been ahead of their time and have heard that "different drummer," Flo was discouraged from her musical marching by her parents and her first husband. After her divorce from Mr. Frank Thornton Jenkins in 1902, she high-stepped her way from the sedate confines of Wilkes-Barre, Pennsylvania, to the musically adventurous city of New York, where she began her lessons in earnest. Upon the death of her father, a prominent lawyer and member of the Pennsylvania legislature, she received financial independence. This majorette was going first-class, or not at all.

It did not take long before her conspicuous presence was duly noted. As Chairman of the Euterpe Club—she would have balked at being called a chairperson—she supervised their annual fund raising galas. She personally staged their much-written about *tableaux vivants,* the Club's spectacular living paintings, including the subscribers' favorite, "The Angel of Inspiration." Gasps and audible cries of astonishment greeted this lavish vision, wherein Madame Jenkins, bewinged and tinseled in silver lamé, emerged from a cocoon to the delight of all and regaled the stunned audience with a recital. Such was her mesmerizing quality that, during the war rationing, when wire was in short demand and therefore her winged costume could not be refurbished, the audience was disconsolate that their "angel" would not appear. Clever girl that she was, as she stepped forward to sing, the velvet drapes were dramatically drawn back to reveal a magnificent oil painting of Madame in heavenly garb. Grateful pandemonium ensued. A veritable mistress of publicity, who could have given lessons to Barnum, Madame Jenkins and her appearances assured the Euterpe Club of an endless fount of new patrons and much needed cash.

As the musical chairman of the Electric, Pleiades, Rubinstein, Mozart, and the famed Verdi clubs, as well as performing numerous, time-consuming philanthropic activities on behalf of her beloved Order of the Eastern Star, the Society of New England Women, and the National Society of Patriotic Women, she was much too busy to think about joining the roster of an impersonal opera house. Instead, with divine sagacity, she embarked upon a career as a recital performer. In a bold stroke worthy of Gatti-Casazza, she rented the grand ballroom of the Ritz-Carlton Hotel as the site of her annual musicales. They were the talk of the town and awaited with a breathless anticipation that reminded many of Lindbergh's arrival in Paris.

Amid squeals of joy and appreciation, her faithful hordes jammed the ballroom and greedily perused the silver program for the tasty musical morsels that lay ahead. Constant study led her to add many new numbers every year. One never knew what to expect from the reigning "Dean of Coloraturas." It was always a wide range of selections, from Mozart's *Alleluia* to Brahms's *Vergebliches Ständchen,* labeled the "Serenade in Vain," to David's *La Perle du Brazil,* to Verdi's *Ah! fors' e lui.* Another Brahms song, *Die Mainacht,* carried the quote: "O, singer, if thou canst dream, leave this song unsung." Jenkins could dream with an unbridled passion that could have driven Freud into analysis. Her stage manner was an elegant blend of sangfroid and unstudied simplicity, or in the description of her common-law husband, "she had perfect rhythm and star quality, something about her personality that makes everyone look at her with relish." Indeed, Madame Jenkins had more relish than a Coney Island hot dog.

Between numbers, while Madame was changing, the Pascarella Chamber Music Society Orchestra, or some other small ensemble, would play. Invariably, they would not be heard or even paid scant attention to, because the audience's discussions of La Jenkins's unique talents would sweep through the hall "like the hum of mischievous bees riding a farmer's buckwheat field," until the diva made her next amazing appearance. Perhaps this time she would enter in a gown which combined the patterns of early Ming and late Marie Antoinette, complementing the ensemble with an ostrich fan of indefinite period that she maneuvered with telling effect. Her inimitable singing and her infectious joy were communicated as if by magic. Her hearers, transported, "were stimulated to the point of audible cheeriness, even joyous laughter and ecstasy," as the august *New York World Tribune* reported under the headline "Superb Song Recital."

A favorite encore of Madame Jenkins was *Cavelitos,* wherein the diva attired herself in a fetching Spanish shawl, a jeweled comb and lace mantilla, with a red carnation seductively placed in her hair. She held a flower basket in her arm and emphasized her "perfect rhythm" by tossing the rose petals into the audience. As with all great dramatic artists, La Jenkins got carried away with the moment and tossed her basket into the audience, hitting an old admirer on the head. Finishing the aria, the applause and whistles were so deafening that she felt compelled to encore the encore. Before she could continue, Cosme McMoon was dispatched into the audience to retrieve the basket . . . and the rose petals.

Newspapers rhapsodized: "Madame Jenkins's art is many-faceted. It makes no speciality of any one composition, or, for that matter of any one composer." "Needless to state, Mme. Jenkins gave her interpretative abilities full and untrammeled sway last night. The cataract of audible sounds greeted her at practically every one of her nonchalantly tossed off phrases, and again by the torrent of applause that followed every selection." "She may possess a certain unusual method of projecting some of the most elaborate and difficult compositions, a method which most musicians consider a far cry from the rules of correct vocalism, but she was undaunted by either the composer's intent or the opinions of her auditors." "The enthusiasm of last night's public can only be compared, both in intensity and unanimity of reaction, to that of The Voice, currently drawing the same sort of delighted applause at the Paramount Theater."

The woman was indefatigable. And magnanimous. In 1943, in New York, the taxi cab in which she was riding was involved in a collision. Did La Diva sue the incompetent driver? Not at all. She sent him a box of fine Havana cigars, since she had subsequently discovered to her astonishment that she could now sing "a higher F than ever before." What a remarkable woman!

The *World Tribune* in 1944 said it best: "Of all the singers appearing before the public today only Madame Jenkins has perfected the art of giving added zest to a written phrase by improvising it in quarter tones, either above or below the original notes. Think of the difficulties involved in making this possible. It would be a presumption to speak of the artist's achievements in technical terms, for there can be none where freedom of expression is rampant."

Her recordings are still available today, attesting to her phenomenal prowess and staying power. There is not a Scrooge alive who, after listening to her astounding interpretations, will not break into grateful smiles for the unbelievable artistry he is hearing. We urge those unfamiliar with the sublime Madame Jenkins to rush out to their favorite record store and buy one of her albums. You won't be sorry and you won't believe it!

With the grace of a stevedore, the phrasing of an iron lung, the musical insight of Jack the Ripper, she *was* opera, she *was* singing, and she most certainly *was* a diva. There was no one like her before, there will be no one like her again. Brava, Madame! Brava, La Incredible!!

BOOGIE, BOOGIE, BOOGIE!

Celestine Galli-Marié, the originator of Carmen who was confronted by the specter of Bizet on the very day of his fatal heart attack, is far from the only opera singer to experience the supernatural.

Dame Nellie Melba, nee Nellie Mitchell, grew up in the overbearing atmosphere of her mother's constant illnesses. Shortly before Mrs. Mitchell died, she gathered her family about her and entrusted each with a specific task to carry out after her death. Young Nellie was to look after her four-year-old sister, Vere, whose trundle bed was immediately moved in next to Nellie's. One evening three months after their mother died, Vere became ill. It being too late to call the doctor, she was put to bed and made comfortable, and Nellie, having stoked the fire, lay down on her own bed to keep watch over her little sister. Suddenly, Nellie realized they were not alone. In the flickering light, her mother, wearing the same black dress in which she had been buried, walked to the bed of the sick child, pointed at Vere, made a sweeping motion with her arms, and then disappeared. The sick child slept soundly. The next morning Nellie told her father of the nocturnal visit. She thought that it meant Vere's condition was far worse than it seemed. Mr. Mitchell dismissed his daughter's apprehensions and suggested they wait until he returned from work in the afternoon to see if the doctor should be called. By then it was too late. Vere died in midafternoon.

Tito Schipa, the famed tenor, had a vision during his own childhood illness. As he lay in bed he fantasized shapes from the shadows on the walls until a very real and attractive young Spanish woman emerged, veiled in a beautiful mantilla and carrying a fan. She smiled as she walked to his bedside, and then disappeared as suddenly as she had appeared. Tito's mother assured him no one had been in the house all day. Two days after the vision, the Schipas received word from Parma that an elderly aunt had died. Later at a family reunion in Parma, Tito was leafing through the family's photograph album, when he saw a picture of his visitor. It was the recently departed aunt in a picture taken on her honeymoon in Spain. She had posed in authentic Spanish costume with mantilla and fan.

The young Renata Scotto was asked by some friends if she would be interested in joining them at a séance. Scotto knew nothing of such things, but went out of curiosity, knowing it would be a change from the Canossian Convent in Milan where she was living in those early years. Suddenly, after the group had been sitting silently holding hands, the medium, possessed, spoke in an other-worldly voice. She turned to Scotto, "You must sing what I sing. You must sing my roles." She talked of having died too young and of wanting to sing forever. The medium began making writing motions on the table; someone put a pen in her hand. She scribbled frantically on sheet after sheet. A name finally became legible: Maria Malibran. Years later Scotto was given a letter of Malibran's, and she compared the signature with that on the sheets from the séance which she had saved. The signatures were identical.

Malibran was, of course, Bellini's favorite Amina in *La Sonnambula,* even though the role was written for Giuditta Pasta. It was also a turning point role in Scotto's career. In September 1957 at the Edinburgh Festival, Scotto had to replace Maria Callas in the last performance of *Sonnambula.* Being Callas, this was not just a routine cancellation or a minor indisposition. As usual, Callas turned it into a brouhaha, claiming that she had agreed to only a certain number of performances and that this was a performance added without asking her if she could or would perform. The press loved it. She walked out in a furor, they said, while they included detailed reports of the Elsa Maxwell party she attended the evening of that final performance.

Although Scotto was the understudy, she had never sung it and had had little preparation. In a dream before the performance, Maria Malibran appeared to Scotto. Smiling, she reassured the young singer to trust the music because from Scotto's mouth would come Malibran's voice. Scotto trusted and conquered. Despite the hostile atmosphere into which she was catapulted, the performance was a great success and Scotto's first step to stardom.

Even in her own lifetime Malibran was the subject of at least superstition if not supernatural phenomenon. During her debut season in Venice, gamblers at the Casino played the numbers 17 (the announced date of her debut), 24 (the date her debut actually occurred), and 6 (the number of performances she was contracted to sing). The numbers came up winners. With fanatical, unprecedented demonstrations following her every move, Malibran was a hit before she stepped onto the stage. It sounds as if her clever manager, if not a publicity agent, was running the wheels.

ONE WAY TO BECOME A SINGING TEACHER

In 1853 in Iowa, two men vied for the one teaching position at a school for music. It was decided that a singing contest be set up to determine the most qualified. The *Minnesota Pioneer* reported that one man "made such desperate efforts to astonish the natives" that he dislocated his jaw in attempting to sing "high B." He won the post.

LIFE GOES TO THE OPERA

There are those who claim that, one month and a day after her infamous Carnegie Hall solo concert, Florence Foster Jenkins died from a broken heart. That is much too operatic, even for La Incredible. Who could die broken-hearted after selling out such a theater at the age of 76?

Many singers, though, have expired in the best operatic fashion, especially Leonard Warren, who dropped dead on the stage of the Metropolitan Opera House 4 March 1960 during a performance of *Forza*, right in the middle of his Act III aria *Urna Fatale (Fatal Letters of Destiny)*; and Caruso, of course, who suffered—and sang—through hemorrhages, abscesses, and even a concussion after being hit on the head by the falling pillars of *Samson* before he died in Naples.

Less known, perhaps, is that the bass Armand Castelmary also died on the Met stage 10 February 1897, during a performance of *Martha,* in the arms of Jean de Reszke. Aroldo Lindi died of a heart attack in San Francisco after singing *Vesti la Giubba,* and Joseph Mann dropped dead on the stage of the Berlin State Opera during *Aida* in 1921. The English tenor, Walter Widdop, a real trouper, finished his concert before dying of a heart attack, while another tenor, Giuseppe Borgatti, didn't even get to go on, having been struck blind during a *Tristan* rehearsal at La Scala.

Lillian Nordica was shipwrecked en route to Java on a concert tour in 1913. She didn't meet Circe or Bacchus; she caught pneumonia and died in Batavia. Fritz Wunderlich, at the peak of his career, died from falling down the stairs after a Heidelberg concert—he was 36. Other premature losses to the opera world: Ettore Bastianini died of throat cancer at age 44, Conchita Supervia died in childbirth at 41, and Milka Ternina, the Croatian soprano, had her career terminated because of facial paralysis.

Lucia and La Loca have nothing on Lina Bruna-Rasa, an Italian soprano who suffered from schizophrenia. In 1937 at the age of thirty, she threw herself into the orchestra pit during a performance and was hastily institutionalized. Like Elvira in *Puritani,* she recovered and continued to give concerts. The Canadian mezzo Jeanne Gordon, however, didn't recover after going mad at age 36. The Russian soprano Zinaida Jurjewskaya couldn't decide whether she was Peter Grimes or Suor Angelica. Her suicide consisted of the double whammy of taking poison and drowning herself at the age of 31. The twenty-six-year-old Paris Opera soprano, Cleontine de Meo, simply shot herself.

Jealousy pervades the operatic stage. Many a Fricka would love to emulate the wife of Romanian tenor Trajan Grozavescu. She shot her philandering husband when he was only thirty-three. Gertrude Bindernagel, a German soprano, lived to thirty-eight before being mowed down by her husband as she was leaving the Berlin Staatsoper after singing the *Siegfried* Brünnhilde. Sounds more like *Il Tabarro*. And how about Anna Sutter, shot at age thirty-nine by conductor Alois Obrist, who then committed suicide. Add music and it's *Wozzeck*.

John Garris was murdered while on tour with the Metropolitan in Atlanta: a sex-change *I Pagliacci*. Madeleine Bugg, a French soprano, disappeared in 1927 when she was thirty-one. In 1936, a pathologist dissecting a body donated from a charity hospital recognized it as hers. Genevieve Warner, an American soprano, was luckier than *Lulu*. Though beaten and raped in London, she lived, but she did not resume her career. Amelita Galli-Curci's career ended as a result of a goiter. We can't think of an opera for that one.

HOW NOT TO BECOME A CASTRATO

Now that we have your attention! Of course, it takes more than the obvious not to become a "violation of decency," as the London *Times* described Velluti in 1825, making his London debut in Meyerbeer's *Il Crociato in Egitto*, the last of his kind to appear upon the stage. "Humanity itself should rise against such an outrage upon feeling. But women! Can women too attend the scene? Can British matrons take their daughters to hear the portentous yells of this disenfranchised of nature, and will they explain the cause to the youthful and untutored mind? Our opinion was that the manly British public and the pure British fair would have been spared the disgust of such an appearance upon any theater of this metropolis." Are they talking about a castrato or Boy George and Prince? Anyway, there are a few rules to follow if you don't wish to become a neutered gender.

1. Be born anywhere else than Italy. The practice started here, and it ended here. The last castrato, Alessandro Moreschi, the "Soprano of Sistine Chapel," died in Rome in 1922! Al-

though there were some German castrati, and a famous English male soprano, John Abell, everyone else came from sunny Italy. When in doubt, blame the church. Good old Paul, that most mean-spirited, miserly of all saints, prohibited women from the church service and, ever since, male voices were required to sing the heavenly praises of Catholic Christianity. Slowly, the ancient Byzantine practice of using eunuchs—with their ethereal, unearthly sounds—gained popularity. Boys had sweet, eerie voices, but they were unruly and had short singing careers. Men's voices were too deep and impure to convey holy thoughts. What else was left?

2. Be born to rich parents. The wealthy or noble had no need for such suspect, vague chances of fame and fortune for their male child; only the destitute were dumb and greedy enough to risk the fantastic odds involved in turning "their" offspring into a singing, golden gelding. Usually, once the child grew up, no matter how successful he became, he shunned and detested the very people who did the horrid deed to him.

3. Do not tap your fingers during church service. Do not hum idly while at play. Show not the slightest interest in or aptitude for music. If you do, be warned, you soon might be humming in a much higher octave than you ever thought possible.

4. Think up any excuse so you don't have to accompany your parents to Naples, Bologna, or Norcia. These were notorious centers for the operation, although excommunication and a death penalty were on the books for those involved. Bologna was highly prized for its medical facilities, its university renowned since the medieval period. Surprisingly, the operation was painless, except for the inevitable psychic scars. Drugged with opium or a juice distillate of belladonna, the hapless boy, preferably between the ages of six and eight, was placed in a hot bath for an extended period until he was insensate. Then, like a vasectomy, the ducts to the testicles were severed by a

tiny incision. Inevitably, the "stones" shriveled, losing their procreative function and all subsequent virile qualities that come with manhood.

Once the operation was performed, and the parents had their thirty pieces of silver, your rigorous training began, either with a famous singing teacher like Porpora or Bernacchi (if you were lucky and could pay, or if your musical ability was high enough to act as a deferment of payment until you earned a living), or you enrolled at a Naples conservatory allied with a church. Caffarelli, one of the two most famed of all "evirati" (Farinelli being the other claimant), had thorough studies in composition, counterpoint, musical theory, improvisation, and vocal exercises in front of a mirror to practice gesture and deportment. The conservatories also supplied the theaters with needed singers when necessary, and this gave the gifted pupils invaluable stage experience. Again, through church edicts, women were banned from the stage, and the castrati were there to take the female operatic roles.

In the seventeenth and eighteenth centuries, the chances of becoming a rich and famous opera singer were about as remote as our winning the New York Lottery. Once women were singing the female roles, once *opera buffa* became popular, once "realism" and "romance" sneaked into the repertoire, the highly artificial, yet dazzling, style of the castrati went the way of the Nehru jacket and four-inch ties. By the time of Rossini and Meyerbeer, who both wrote for castrati, this capon was comically passé. Amazingly, Wagner toyed with the idea of transposing the role of Klingsor for Domenico Mustafa, the Papal castrato, since that nefarious, necromantic Knight was self-emasculated in his futile pursuit of the Grail. Now *that* would have made *Parsifal* interesting!

If the poor lad was blessed with a massive lung capacity, the coloratura technique of a Marilyn Horne, and the dramatic intensity of a Callas, it just might've been possible to achieve international superstardom. You'd be hard put to rival Farinelli, though, who by singing for the melancholic Philip V of Spain for ten years attained a political position on a par with a modern Secretary of State and received the Order of Cala-trava, an honor reserved for the nobility. When retired by Charles III, who dismissed him saying, "Capons are for eat-ing," Farinelli had served the Spanish court for twenty-two years after already completing a brilliant twenty-year reign as Europe's king of singers, prompting one hysterical woman to shout his forever immortal epithet, "One God, one Farinelli!" Other than this blasphemy, Farinelli is remembered in opera trivia as being the only singer, other than Maria Malibran, to have been the subject of an opera—four, as a matter of fact!

Caffarelli, the anthithesis of Farinelli, was a real prima donna: vain, arrogant, impertinent as a peacock. He fought duels with cuckolded husbands, he got away with insulting Louis XV, he was imprisoned for "disturbing the other per-formers, acting in a manner bordering on lasciviousness with one of the female singers, conversing with the spectators in the boxes, and refusing to sing in the ensembles with the others," he was constantly propositioned by adoring female and male admirers, and was immortalized in Rossini's *Barber.* Following Rosina's lesson aria in Act II, Bartolo sings, "Certainly, you have a beautiful voice, but that song—what a bore! Now, in my day, music was something else. When, for example, Caffarelli used to sing that wonderful air . . ." Like Farinelli, he, too, had a splendid villa in Italy. Its inscription read, "Amphion built Thebes, I this house." The Neapolitan wits quickly flashed, "He with, You without."

Only a handful garnered such riches—fame, fortune, palaz-zos, their lives immortalized in the works of Casanova, the beloved of kings, the lovers of duchesses and cardinals. The rest lived out their sad lives in the second-rate houses of the provinces, their voices never fulfilling the promise their grasp-ing parents craved. It could never have been worth the price.

HOW TO TALK BACK TO A PRIMA DONNA

Mrs. Webb, "an excellent though very irritable actress," was rehearsing in 1785 for William Shield's new opera at Covent Garden called *The Nunnery*. This lady, "who was one of the tallest and most bulky women," came to the theater one morning, and constantly complained of a pain in the small of her back. One gentleman, having had enough of her carping, aroused her ire by asking her, "Pray, Mrs. Webb, which is the *small* of your back?"

SINGING FOR YOUR SUPPER

As we are all well aware, singers make enough money to eat their supper, in perpetuity, at Lutece. Most of them look as if they've also been snacking during intermission at McDonald's and Fanny Farmer. Musical superstars, like their cousins in the other arts, can command astronomical fees, concurrent with the market value. Fortunately, they are paid per performance, not by the pound. Except in Italy, where opera is a second language, the singing art everywhere else is a rarefied entertainment, patronized by a small segment of the musically cognizant, and the entertainers who can pack a house get paid handsomely.

Ever since people opened their mouths and started screaming at each other in musical terms, the star system had arrived. Italian opera established itself in England in 1708, and the enormous terms demanded by the singers were, even then, derided and denounced as a "system of extortion." "It has increased, is increasing, and ought to be diminished." This was the era of the pampered castrati, who, if lucky and invested wisely, could retire to ducal villas. Later, Mara, Banti, Mrs. Billington, and Catalani would increase their terms every season and demand benefit performances, whose grosses went directly to them. Pasta in 1828 received £4,500 and an insured benefit premium of £1,000. Here in America, Adelina Patti sang for Colonel Mapelson at a contracted $5,000 per performance fee, a guarantee of 50 performances, a $50,000 security, *and* a private railway car with "conservatory, fernery, and Steinway." Not even Pavarotti gets terms like that! When Marilyn Horne opened the 1977–1978 season of Rome's Teatro dell-'Opera in *Tancredi,* Italian press scandals seemed far away, but Act II began with a deluge of pamphlets dropped from above. The new manager, Luca di Schiena, was accused of wasting 50,000,000 lire on Madame Horne's seven-performance schedule. The following day, di Schiena stated, in wake of investigations, that Horne was receiving $7,000 per performance, not $8,000. Anyway, he said, if Rome wants *Tancredi,* Rome must have Horne. In the words of Patti, "The success of the cage will depend upon the birds put in it."

W. T. Parke in his *Musical Memoirs* addressed the problem: "It may however happen that an opera manager is compelled, by the precepts of his subscribers, to buy vocal talent at so high a rate. But he should (like the quack doctor who, to keep his chariot, dined thrice a week on cow-heel) retrench in other respects, taking care at the same time that, by avoiding Scylla he does fall into Charybdis, and thereby render his performances less unique, consequently unacceptable to the public. This foreign system, which it is to be hoped has reached its acme, will probably work its own cure, and then these upstarts will, similarly to the man in the fable, regret that, by ripping up the goose, they have lost the golden eggs for ever."

A Night at the Opera addressed the problem in less fabled fashion:

> GOTTLIEB: Well, Mrs. Claypool, was I right? Isn't Lasspari the greatest tenor that ever lived?
> MRS. CLAYPOOL: He's superb, but what would you have to pay him?
> GOTTLIEB: Why, he would be worth a $1000 a night.
> DRIFTWOOD: How much?
> GOTTLIEB: A $1000 a night.
> DRIFTWOOD: What does he do?
> GOTTLIEB: He sings.

DRIFTWOOD: And you're willing to pay him a $1000 a night just for singing? Why, you can get a phono record of Minnie the Moocher for 75 cents. For a buck and a quarter you can get Minnie.

How to Write an Overture

My dear Sir:

You have the reputation of being clever, obliging, and also of being an epicure. To the epicure then I send a *pâté de foie gras.* I appeal to his goodness, and trust the clever composer will reply to my question, and come to the aid of one of his future rivals. My nephew does not know how to set about writing the overture to an opera he has composed. Would you be good enough, you who have written so many, to let me know your rules for the same. When you had still some pretensions to renown, my demand might have appeared to you rather indiscreet, but since you have renounced all idea of glory, you cannot be now jealous of any one. Believe me, dear Sir,

Yours, truly . . .

My dear Sir:

I am much flattered at the preference that you have been kind enough to give my writings above those of my brother composers.

First I must tell you that I have never written anything except by the direct necessity. I could never understand what pleasure there could be in cudgeling one's brains, tiring one's fingers, and getting into a fever, to amuse a public, whose only pleasure in return is to get tired of those who have amused them. I am not at all a true partisan of industry, and think the finest and most precious of the rights of man is to do nothing. That is, at least, what I have been doing since I have acquired, not by my works, however, but by some lucky speculations, the rights of idleness. If, then, I have a counsel to give your nephew, it is to imitate me in that. If, however, he should persist in his fantastic and incomprehensable idea of working, the following are the principal receipts which I have made use of during the miserable epoch of my existence when I was obliged to do something. Let him choose whichever appears to him the most convenient.

First Rule, general and invariable. Always wait for the night before the first performance of an opera to write the overture. There is nothing so inspiring as necessity, and the delightful propinquity of a copyist, who awaits your composition shred by shred; also the sinister appearance of a despairing manager, who is tearing his hair out by the roots. The real chefs d'oeuvre of overtures have never been composed otherwise. In Italy, in my time, all the managers were bald at thirty.

Second Rule. I composed the overture to *Otello* in a small room at Barbaja's Palace, where this most bald and ferocious of managers had locked me up, in company with some macaroni simply boiled in water, and a threat that I should never leave the room alive until I had composed the last note of the said overture.

You could make use of this rule very successfully with respect to your nephew; but mind, no *pâté de foie gras,* they are only good for idlers like myself, and I thank you for the one you have honored me by sending.

Third Rule. I composed the overture to *La Gazza Ladra,* not the night before, but on the same day of the performance of the opera, on the roof of the Teatro alla La Scala, where the manager —a counterpart of the ferocious Barbaja—had placed me under the guard of four machinists. The mission of these executioners was to throw my work, page by page, to the copyists who were waiting below, who having copied it, sent it phrase by phrase to the conductor, who rehearsed it as it came. If I did not write, these barbarians had orders to throw me, instead of my music, to the copyists.

If you should possess a loft in your house, Sir, you might make use of it in a similar way with your nephew.

Fourth Rule. I did much better for my overture to the *Barber of Seville.* I didn't compose any at all; that is to say, that instead of the one I had written for this very comic opera, one was taken which I had written for *Elizabeth,* a very serious one. The public was enchanted with the substitution.

Your nephew, who has yet done nothing, might try this means, and borrow from himself another overture.

Fifth Rule. I composed the overture to *Count Ory,* one day, fishing at Petit-bourg, with my feet in the water, and in company with M. Aguada, who never ceased all the time talking to me of Spanish finances, which teased me to death.

I doubt, Sir, that in a parallel case, your conversation might be of a nature to produce the same invigorating effect on your nephew's nerves.

Sixth Rule. I composed the overture to *William Tell* in the middle of an apartment which I occupied on the Boulevard Montmartre, which was the resort, night and day, of all that Paris contained of the most absurd and noisy people, who came daily to smoke, drink, yell, stamp about, and humbug me, while I worked with fury, so as to hear them as little as possible.

Perhaps, notwithstanding the progress of wit in France, you might find fools enough to procure this stimulant for your nephew. You might yourself powerfully aid in this result, and merit the largest share of your nephew's gratitude.

Seventh Rule. I never composed the shadow of an overture for *Mosè in Egitto,* which is by far the easiest plan. I doubt not that your good nephew may use with success the last-named rule. It is the same that my excellent friend Meyerbeer has employed for *Robert le Diable* and the *Huguenots,* and he appears to have perfectly succeeded. I am told that he has used it also for *Le Prophète.*

Accept, Sir, my best wishes for your nephew's renown, and many thanks for your excellent pie.

Yours very obediently,
Rossini, Ex-composer

Sweet Diva,
Did You See That?

Contrary to medieval scholars and their doctoral exegeses on Dante's *Divine Comedy*, there is a tenth circle of hell. Here, below the icy regions of Lake Cocytus, opera directors are damned to eternally watch other directors' abysmal productions. Watching their own horrid attempts wouldn't be any punishment for them—they think they're heavenly. What do the damned know anyway?

Let us start with the works of Richard Wagner, for here certainly the stage director has been having his way for some time now, even when Birgit Nilsson was the star around whom the production was built. She disliked the darkness of Wagnerian productions so much, especially those directed by Herbert von Karajan, that she threatened to appear on stage wearing a coal miner's hat, but Karajan did not raise the light levels. When his *Ring* was produced at the Metropolitan, Karajan had a falling out with Rudolf Bing who insisted on having Nilsson as Brünnhilde instead of Helge Dernesch, who had sung the part in Karajan's Salzburg production. Karajan withdrew, and Nilsson consequently got her lighting wish, for as the years wore on, the production did seem to get a little brighter without Karajan around to supervise—the hours required for his lighting rehearsals are legendary and it has been said by many that they could have gotten it that dark in minutes.

Needless to say, the most infamous Wagnerian production in recent history was the centennial *Ring* at Bayreuth, conducted by Pierre Boulez and directed by Patrice Chéreau. The problems began early in rehearsals when Boulez informed the orchestra that he had not recently conducted the *Ring* and wanted to relearn it with them. The orchestra disliked a novice leader, disliked his batonless technique and new ideas, and refused to appear with Boulez for curtain calls.

On the production side, things were no better. The designer was used to the slipshod methods of Italian opera houses, had not prepared sketches and designs, and construction got behind schedule despite the efficient Germans who were anxious to work. Some of the scenery was built in Rome and arrived so late that singers were going on stage in surroundings they had never before seen. Technical effects were not completely rehearsed, and comic disasters ensued. Spring arrived fifteen minutes too early in the first act of *Walküre*. In *Götterdämmerung* Valhalla disappeared after an immolation in which the lighting, smoke, and fire did not coincide, only to reappear again from the Rhine, like the age-old story of the Tosca who bounced back up into audience view after leaping to her death from the ramparts of the Castel Sant'Angelo.

It was, however, the concept and production as a whole that capped the "centennial scandal," as the German critics called it. Rhinemaidens cavorted in three spillways of a concrete dam, Nibelheim resembled a budget basement, Hunding's hut was a bombed-out concrete chancellery, and Brünnhilde's rock was a lower ledge in the ruins of a Roman amphitheater. The gods were dressed as Victorian bourgeoisie, the Rhinemaidens as Carmen's trashy sisters, Siegfried in a tuxedo, while Sieglinde and the Valkyries were in flowing dresses of operatic any-period design. The Valkyries rode in on live horses with blood-ied heroes across their saddles, which brought open laughter from the audience, despite the fact that this is what Wagner specified. The production was littered with violence: Wotan pierced Alberich's hand with his spear, Hunding and Hagen repeatedly stabbed Siegmund and Siegfried, all to depict the brutality of capitalism.

The audience repeatedly interrupted the performances, not with applause, but with boos, cries, and whistles. Although one patron's umpire's whistle was confiscated before a per-formance, enough were distributed throughout the theater to make an effect. "Bayreuth is not Disneyland" was the pro-tester's placard which summed up the general consensus.

The outrageous is certainly not new in Wagner's sacred house. In 1961 a production of *Tannhäuser* was set in a gigantic yellow Kleenex box, which made Wolfram's ode to the eve-ning star redundant, if not silly. Ten years later a new *Tann-häuser* was more experimental and more scandalous. The prel-ude started with a pantomime of Tannhäuser's fantasy of Venusberg in which he played a gigantic harp until its strings ensnared him. In the second scene the pilgrims carried a huge cross as if lost from Oberammergau, and the hunters were transported in sedan chairs. Elizabeth was neurotic, and the knights gave the Nazi salute to the Landgraf. When Elizabeth dragged herself off across the floor after her prayer in Act III, one matron commented that a Landgraf's niece wouldn't crawl, no matter what.

Not to be outdone, the Australian Opera put on a pseudo-Bayreuth *Tannhäuser* during the 1973–1974 season at a time when obscure symbolism was beginning to fade. Instead of an orgy in Venusberg, they presented an anatomical slide show of various views of the "Mound of Venus." The Pope's sproutless staff was made of glass, the pilgrims were prisoners liberated during Act II, and the Wartburg and song contest were eliminated. We have no idea what it was supposed to mean anymore than we understand a recent *Tannhäuser* in East Berlin. There, Venus and her lover, suspended over the stage in an upholstered sofa and engulfed in curtains, looked like victims of the plant Audrey in *Little Shop of Horrors.* Below, actors mimed their fantasies amid dancers who could not exude eroticism despite their see-through unitards.

No opera of Wagner's is sacred to stage directors. A Dresden *Tristan* had subtitles for each of the opera's acts—"In the Hothouse," "Dreams," and "Pain." The pain was mostly in the eye of the beholder. Isolde sailed in a pink flower-bedecked tent with her lesbian handmaiden Brangäne. Act II took place in the palm court of a ruined Victorian house with a tilting Plexiglas fan downstage on which the lovers reclined. Tristan, who couldn't decide whom he loved more, Isolde or King Mark, dressed as the mad Ludwig II of Bavaria, died in Act III in the midst of an endless meadow of tufted grass.

The *Ring* operas are still the most subject to idiotic tampering. A 1975 *Siegfried* in Leipzig put vines overhead and stretched colored tape back and forth over the floor for the forest scene. Erde rose up, sleeping, into a marble mausoleum, and Mime's forge was an entire steel mill which swung into action for Siegfried's work. Mime looked like the night watchman in his granny glasses, and the Wanderer was costumed as a fully equipped Swiss mountain climber. The same year in London, the forest was an impenetrable jungle of green fettucine hanging over a giant tilted rectangle. Mime's house was tucked under the forest floor downstage right with a pile driver replacing the forge. The rectangle tilted and revolved in many different directions before revealing Brünnhilde asleep in Act III. As for costumes, Mime and Alberich were in painted clown face, and Wotan was painted in double face. Get it? Erde was wrapped in layers of spaghetti, carrying out the scenic theme. We got it, we got it!

A few years earlier, the Brussels Opera indulged André Ernotte, a young actor-director, and Jean Marie Fievez, his twenty-two-year-old set and costume designer, with a production of *Die Walküre,* in which they attempted "to realize the vision or dream aroused in them on first hearing the Valkyrie music." More nightmare than dream. The stage was flanked with huge black mirrors while a platform in the center represented Valhalla, on which roamed white-clad gods resembling the Coneheads. Only Siegmund and Sieglinde were allowed hair. The singers stood motionless at the sides while more Coneheads, in cowl-collared white caftans, mimed their action. Similarly-clad extras crawled on and off, and pornographic scenes, interspersed with head shots of famous film and pop stars, were projected on a giant screen. Props continually dropped from the flies, including a large Valentine heart in Act I. A foam-rubber bed was provided for the doubles during the love duet, while on high floated a large pregnant doll. It might as well have been "Saturday Night Live."

How about this *Walküre* in Mannheim. Hunding was a Siberian cossack, in fur coat and hat, living in an Arabian tent furnished with nineteenth-century oak furniture. For *Winterstürme* the tent flew to reveal an apple tree in full bloom. Act II found Valhalla on hard times, with broken and battered plastic statues lining the walls and an overgrown sagebrush hedge at the rear. Wotan got lost in it once, missing an entrance. Brünnhilde was accompanied by a white plaster horse on wheels, and Siegmund and Hunding battled in a glass cage, while Wotan and his daughter stood on the roof. The Valkyries, sisters of Conan the Barbarian, stripped their dead warriors almost naked, discarded their weapons and armor, gave them new masks, kissed them back to life, and sent them packing into Valhalla. To top it off, Wotan lay Brünnhilde on the ramparts of his castle to sleep, retreated inside and set his house on fire, engulfing himself in flames but not his daughter. Say, whose opera is this anyway?

A year after the Bayreuth centennial scandal, the Paris Opéra got its own *Ring* with the West Berlin production team who had been the original choices for Bayreuth. Oiy! In *Rhein-*

gold they indicated the nineteenth-century pollution of the Rhine with a bathtub-like dirty ring. The Rhinemaidens sat around in tacky evening dresses taunting Alberich, while doubles flew above their heads. Alberich clambered up a ladder to reach the gold, which was nothing more than an amber light. Wotan and Fricka were found in full evening dress sleeping under a pile of leaves, and their rivals, the Giants, were ordinary humans in painters overalls, protected by a single symbolic giant who shed bloody tears. Nibelheim was equipped with magic monsters and a pneumatic toad, but Erde's subterranean entrance must have taken place offstage since she strolled in from the wings as if awakening from a nap. Wotan paid for Valhalla with flea-market gold flatware, while an Erector set's bridge descended for the gods' entrance. In *Walküre,* Hunding's back wall was made of hundreds of men's black suits on hangers, with one white horse's ass shining amongst them; Siegmund had arrows sticking out from the back of his coat; and the mountain peaks of Acts II and III were piles of sandbags. Stuffed deer stood on the peaks, and stuffed rams' heads were attached to Fricka's skirt to simulate her cart, but the Valkyries' horses were the real thing. The French critics claimed this production was Germany's revenge for the Boulez-Chéreau Bayreuth *Ring.* They never figured out who was the horse's ass.

The *Ring* production for the space age was designed by Thomas Richter-Forgach and directed by Ulrich Melchinger in Kassel. Begun in 1970 and completed in 1974, it set the story in a futuristic world of robots, nuclear reactors, and high technology. Rhinemaidens rode underwater rockets in skindiving gear. Wotan, the quintessential capitalist pig, viewed his new Valhalla, a futuristic oil refinery, out his office window, seated behind a corporate desk in an enormous swivel chair. The remaining gods were straight out of Flash Gordon: Fricka in gold leather helmet and enormous "fun" fur coat, Froh in a metallic blue space suit, Donner in a radar helmet, and Freia as a topless nymphet in green lamé pants with a yellow plastic halter top and long fringe at the waist. The giants were robots who traveled around on little computer wagons. Wotan directed the *Walküre* action on a miniature set, a reproduction of the original 1876 Bayreuth production. Brünnhilde followed her sisters' actions on a TV monitor and their famous Ride was on rocket ships, not horses. Mime, living in a masonry cave with Victorian furniture, was a beaded hippie, and the Wanderer's disguise was the Kentucky Colonel in Stetson hat. Erde arrived from her subterranean slumber to have tea with Wotan. The Norns resided in the cockpit of a huge space shuttle, with their computer "going down" just when it should have revealed the gods' ultimate destruction. Naturally the Gibichungs were neo-Nazis, living in a hall that would warm the cockles of Albert Speer's heart, but Siegfried's murder took place in an old-fashioned picture book setting. After the fall of Valhalla, an apotheosis was added to show Wotan and Alberich, blind and crippled, tapping their way through the world their lust for power had destroyed.

In the words of the inimitable Anna Russell, we're not making this up, you know!

The *Ring* is not the only outrageous Wagnerian production to be seen in Kassel. Their *Flying Dutchman,* again a production by Melchinger and Richter-Forgach, made the protagonist a seafaring Don Juan who offered riches to Scandinavian fathers for their daughters' hands and then abandoned them, claiming to be the phantom Dutchman, when really he was an impostor. The action took place on a giant recumbent cross jammed between a rocky coastal inlet. The Dutchman arrived during the Steersman's erotic dream, flying in amidst numerous skeletons to celebrate a black mass. A disemboweled voodoo doll's gore was emptied into a chalice and then poured over a virgin, who lay spread-eagled over the hatch cover waiting to be deflowered with a samurai sword. The evening ended with Erik accidentally stabbing Senta, who had thrown herself between him and the Dutchman to save his life and, she thought, his soul. Nobody could have saved this production.

Unfortunately, we operatic masochists in the United States have little opportunity to indulge in such theatrical mayhem, but there is an occasional production by Jean-Pierre Ponnelle, however, to give us a glimpse of what we're missing. His production of *Der Fliegende Holländer* was seen both in San Francisco and New York in the late 70's, and here the entire opera was played as the Steersman's dream. The Dutchman, looking like Count Dracula, made his entrance from an outhouse-looking captain's passage at the stern of the ship and strolled down the deck through a nautical nightmare of hanging red sails, ropes, nets, and skeletons. The Dutchman's treasures lined his cape like a nineteenth-century Banana Man, and Daland multiplied into half-a-dozen mad hatters as gold rained down upon him. Senta spent most of the evening on a downstage platform in a Middle European wedding dress, while Mary and the spinning women were bound together by ropes. Naturally, there was no suicide or redemption at the end. The Dutchman just returned to his outhouse, followed by Senta, and then the Steersman woke up.

Mr. Ponnelle is well known for his audacious reinterpretations of the libretto, and his Cologne *Salome* was no exception. He moved Herod's court to a lascivious Indian locale, set in a temple with wall friezes depicting copulating couples. Salomé was dressed as an Indian goddess, and Jokanaan was a naked, hirsute hippie. *Salome* crouched between his legs as she fondled and explored his body, then did a striptease right down to bare breasts and g-string to earn his head. In the same theater, Ponnelle translated *Die Frau ohne Schatten* into Kabuki theater. The only scenery was a rough-surfaced movable bridge over a dark, shiny floor on which no one cast a shadow. Each human was followed by a faceless, black-clad double. These Kabuki stage hands also waved blue silk to represent the fountain waters, threw fish into the frying pan for Barak's dinner, and carried a paper cutout falcon. Back on these shores, San Francisco was blessed with Mr. Ponnelle's cinematic, flashback version of *Rigoletto.* Another of his depraved, erotic nightmares with a plethora of undulating half-naked courtiers.

Verdi's operas have not suffered at the director's hand to the same extent as Wagner's, but they have had more than their share of abuse. How does *Aida* sound with an anti-war message set in the year 2001, an octagonal revolving glass pyramid as the main scenic device with the base of a spaceship in the background? This was seen in East Berlin under the direction of Gotz Friedrich. Or try *Aida* in a high-tech set of five-story towers, connected by a bridge suspended over 25 tons of sand, in front of a giant golden disc and a 25-foot neon-lighted pyramid. This was planned recently for Tulsa, though time pressure and the weight of the set required it to be simplified. Simplified, not scrapped.

Verdi's *Un Ballo in Maschera* had its libretto tampered with by censors from the very start, and directors are still at it. With Ernst Schroder as director and Michael Rafaelli as designer, a new West Berlin production was set in neither Sweden nor Massachusetts, but "anywhere about 1850." Plantation owners in white suits with pastel ties and vests, and soldiers in both Confederate and Union uniforms were waited upon by black servants in livery. Ulrica's hut became a pier furnished with a blue satin loveseat and an electrified crystal ball on a wooden crate. Amelia came in through a door, but the others came and went through the "walls" of the steel-arched unit set. The second act took place in an abandoned train station instead of a secluded spot near the gallows. When Riccardo heard the conspirators approach, he fled in their direction, while Amelia, without disguise or veil, stood only an arm's length from her husband and yet remained unrecognized. Back at Renato's house, a life-size statue of Riccardo in Puritan mufti sat in a wicker rocking chair on the dilapidated front porch. The final ballroom was peopled with mantilla-clad ladies left over from a production of *Carmen.* God knows what all this was supposed to mean. Bring back the censors!

Another West Berlin production in 1970, Verdi's *La Forza del Destino,* proved that poorly thought out productions could be just as ludicrous as those that are intentionally outlandish. The opera opened with the Calatrava home set in a grotto with steps and a stone madonna carved into the wall. The Marquis, dozing in a chair, woke up to sing his first line—*"Bouna notte."*

[135]

The pilgrims of the next scene appeared to walk on the roof of the inn, and Padre Guardino consecrated Leonora in a chapel crowded with enormous melted candles and then showed her to her hermit's cave with a gesture that seemed like directions to the ladies' room. In Italy, the team of Luca Ronconi and Pier Luigi Pizzi have been creating Verdi productions that don't really distort the libretto but set the action of the opera on one stage level with an ongoing pageant on another level. Florence saw their *Nabucco,* which placed the principals on a central platform with the chorus downstage in nineteenth-century formal dress as if they were the audience. The *Va, pensiero* chorus had a Biblical tableau of reapers and gleaners on the central platform. Milan saw their *Don Carlo* opening night in 1977 that had a parade of canopies, carts, processions, crucifixes, and other symbols of power crossing at the rear of the stage for the entire evening. The tomb of Charles V sat downstage center all evening, being used by Eboli for a bench from which to sing her veil song. Other coffins, skulls, and skeletons symbolized life as a carnival of death.

The Carmen story has been presented in many guises, but that doesn't justify what was done to Bizet's *Carmen* in Bologna in 1967. Alberto Arbasino created a production that was pop art, with most of the cast dressed in plastic. Micaëla carried a silver overnight bag, the factory girls slunk around in miniskirts, a captain resembled a South American dictator, and Dancairo and Remendado wore space suits. The Act II inn became a discotheque, and the bandit's camp was set at the bottom of a waterless concrete dam. In 1974, back in Kassel, that hot bed of the avant-garde, *Carmen* was set in a Roman ruin, complete with crumbling mosaics, statuary, and a niche with the Virgin. The Virgin? In a Roman ruin? The unit set had an area downstage left that changed with each act, from a guardhouse to a Casbah-style opium den. Carmen stripped to her bikini underwear to dance for Don Jose at the insistence of Escamillo, who looked like a precursor from "Miami Vice" in his white tropical suit, kid shoes, open-necked shirt, and blond wig. Where's the stubble? This time the gypsy camp was set on a beach with a single palm tree and breakers below a range of mountains.

Don Juan, that other operatic sex symbol, has been the object of directorial tampering. In his Prague and Duisberg productions, Bohumil Herlischka turned Don Giovanni into a syphilitic, senile lecher, living in a decaying castle of provincial pretensions. His perverse world included group sex between Zerlina, Masetto, and their peasant friends; Leporello's fetish for wearing the undergarments of the Don's conquests; and the Don himself and Donna Elvira's trashy maid making it in the churchyard. When the Commendatore rose from the coffin-like dinner table, Giovanni hanged himself from the ceiling. Recently in East Berlin, the cheap sex continued with Leporello and Donna Elvira having a quickie on the floor, while Masetto turned somersaults in slow motion during *Batti, batti* and then leapt upon Zerlina when she finished. The set encased the Commendatore in a glass shrine with a skyscraper in the background. Don Giovanni threw tennis balls at Elvira to get her attention, but he sang his serenade to no one—and without mandolin.

Mozart's *Così Fan Tutte* was updated to the present, a favorite device of directors, for a production in Minneapolis in the early 70's. It was reset in a small New England town. The sisters came from a well-to-do family, and their lovers were soldiers in the reserves who had just been activated. The names were Americanized and an English translation was used, but not updated, so that the libretto did not match the stage action. A few years earlier, once again in Kassel, a *Fidelio* was brought up to the present with Andy Warhol-like paintings of multiple photographed faces used for scenery. A new libretto replaced the dialogue with poetry on political imprisonment and murder. Florestan was suspended in mid-air, like a gymnast's iron cross on the rings, Don Pizarro was a highway patrolman, and Leonore wore a white Mao costume. One more modern-day version was a *Salome* in East Berlin in 1979, set in a Latin American prison, complete with machine-gun toting guards. Herodias impersonated Carmen Miranda, and Salome wore an evening dress and bandanna. After she squeezed the bloody rags containing Jokanaan's severed head between her legs, she was blown away, Rambo-style.

On those occasions when updating the action is not deemed sufficient, a complete rewrite of the story is attempted. Poor *Oberon* suffered this fate in the fall of 1985 by the Scottish Opera. The new libretto by Anthony Burgess added Titania as Yin and Yang, representing universal opposites which can only be resolved by a pair of human lovers who, like Tamino, remain faithful through all dangers. Hugh and Rezia became the two lovers: she being an American secretary held hostage by, who else, an Ayatollah, and he being an American test pilot bent on rescue with the aid of a magic horn whose high notes caused paralysis. Hugh succeeded in his rescue mission, Rezia was recaptured, and had to do it all over again. The Ayatollah was deposed by his westernized brother, a new oil deal was struck, and the heroes were gratefully received at a White House garden party. Ah, yes, a great improvement on the original.

Although the "classics" have been somewhat restored to their original plot lines in the Soviet Union, rewriting the libretto was common after the Revolution. The revival of *Faust* in Moscow in 1925 had a new libretto by order of the Commissar of Public Art. Faust was an American millionaire named Harry living in Berlin. He told "Mr. Mephistopheles" that life was not worth living without Margaret, a poor but pretty Hungarian actress, who lived with her lover Siebel and brother Valentine in communal, communistic bliss. Harry tempted Margaret with an enormous package of thousand-dollar bills laid on her window sill, to which she sang the Money Waltz. She succumbed, then was abandoned, and condemned to death for the murder of her baby. Harry remorsefully came to the prison to rescue her, but she killed him and was saved from execution by the timely arrival of the revolutionary guards. An English National Opera *Faust* in 1985 was hardly more outrageous. In it, Marguerite's prison was a clinically white asylum, run by the Sisters of Mercy complete with wimples and whips, and her end was not redemption but a brutal death at the hands of Mephistopheles, who cracked her neck like a rag doll and flung her body away.

Modern operas are not immune either. Marilyn Horne made her La Scala debut as Jocasta in Stravinsky's *Oedipus Rex* dressed as a plastic purple egg. The motif of the entire production was ovate, with a huge egg center stage for Jocasta's home base which she had to tag all the time. Oedipus wore a golden blindfold with huge red beads dangling from the eyes, and since the singers could hardly move in their egg shells they scrambled around the stage on conveyer belts and elevators.

Many modern operas do not need to be revised, updated, or rewritten to be outrageous. That seems to be their purpose from the very start. Take, for example, the world premiere in 1966 of Kurt Schwitters' *Class Struggle Opera*. The work's only score or libretto consisted of two words, "up" and "down." Up was intoned by three "artists" perched on high ladders, while down was intoned by two more "artists" seated below. The action took place on a small wooden platform floating in a reflection pond in New York's Central Park. One of the performers was a certain Charlotte Moorman, a cellist with Leopold Stokowski's American Symphony, whose small claim to fame came from her participation in such "happenings." She once jumped into Venice's Grand Canal while playing Saint-Saëns's *Le Cygne,* and on another occasion was carried in a parade in New York while playing topless. The question of the day was whether Pablo Casals would have been a greater artist had he played bottomless.

About the same time, Minneapolis gave us *Horspfal,* composed by Eric Stokes to a libretto by Alvin Greenberg. The set consisted of a bed, 16 by 22 feet, jutting out into the audience, on which slept the title character, an American Indian. Bit by bit he lost his bed to Mom, Dad, Junior Tourist, Betsy Ross, D.A.R. Ladies, highway surveyors, real-estate brokers, and other would-be helpers, whom he berated for dirtying his clean white sheets. By the opera's end, they had completely taken over his bed, burned it down, and replaced it with the trash of modern society. The creators claimed no conclusions were to be drawn from their work. O.K.

In 1969 seven Dutch artists collaborated on an opera entitled *Reconstruction*. It dealt with American power politics in South America and the collaborators' admiration for Che Guevara. They personified his antithesis in the character of Don Juan and made this point musically by dissecting two phrases from the *Don Giovanni* overture and recomposing them by computer. Everything was done collectively, including conducting the performance, with four leaders at four different desks. The libretto contained Erasmus, Tarzan, Martin Bormann, and Quetzalcoatl, in twenty-six scenes of non sequiturs. By the end a gigantic plastic statue of Guevara had been built center stage. Aren't collaborators shot?

Robert Wilson's *The Life and Times of Joseph Stalin* had everybody and everything but the kitchen sink. Presented at the Brooklyn Academy of Music in New York in 1974, the 12-hour marathon began at 7 P.M. and lasted through the night. It contained Stalin, Freud, Queen Victoria, real sheep, a live dog and a snake, fake lions, oxen, flying horses, giant turtles, camels, and nineteen life-sized dancing ostriches. A frogman pounded his fist on the dining table, demanding a drink, and Stalin read a lecture on dialectical materialism in a glass isolation booth. There were whirling dervishes, a burning parasol, an Egyptian temple, and an endless panorama from sunset to sunrise.

In 1979 West Berlin witnessed a "happening" with *The Sinking of the Titanic*, written and composed by Wilhelm Dieter Siebert. Only 250 people could attend each performance, which began with speeches christening the unsinkable ship on the steps of the opera house. Before the ceremonies were over, the third-class passengers arrived from the adjacent subway stop to board the ship. As the audience entered the lobby, they witnessed first-class passengers at leisure and heard their commentary on society. Of course, the ship's orchestra played, and the sailor on lookout sang his aria from the highest level of the lobby. Then as an ominous scrape was heard, the participants moved on into the ship's bar where a frantic formal party was going on. Soon, the crew began handing out life jackets to performers and audience members alike, though only one person out of every five received one. Gradually everyone was ushered down stairwells, past bleeding steerage passengers to the smoky lower decks, represented by the stage, and hurriedly led through the auditorium to the rear courtyard. Only the first-class ladies were permitted to board the one lifeboat. While emergency flares lit up the night sky, the lights of the makeup room galleries were gradually extinguished as the liner sank. A lone voice sang "Nearer my God to Thee."

Hell is very crowded these days.

A Toscanini Tetrad

Early in his career Arturo Toscanini was engaged to conduct
the Italian premiere of Verdi's *Four Sacred Pieces*. It was during
the composer's lifetime, and Boito had arranged for Toscanini
to go through the score with the composer. Don't be nervous,
Toscanini was told, "You will find Verdi all right." Despite the
advice the young conductor was very nervous. A passage in the
Te Deum had puzzled him. He felt that the tempo should be
definitely broader at a certain place, although there was no
such indication in the score.

Toscanini wrestled with the problem for many days and
sleepless nights in anticipation of his meeting with the maestro. When the day arrived, Toscanini sat down at the piano
and commenced playing. At the spot in question, Toscanini
went considerably slower despite his desire to maintain the
tempo. Verdi, with the first sign of approval he had given,
slapped him on the back, saying "Bravo!"

Greatly relieved, Toscanini said: "But, Maestro, you don't
know what anguish that place has caused me. You gave no
indication of a retard."

Verdi replied: "And can you imagine what some asses of
conductors would make of it if I *had* marked a retard?"

Many years after Toscanini and Geraldine Farrar had ended
their notorious affair, Farrar invited the maestro to a dinner
party. Caviar was served, to the pleasure of all except Toscanini, who furiously remarked: "I slept with that woman for

seven years. Wouldn't you think she'd remember that I hate fish?"

On another occasion a leading singer was being sought for one of the operas Toscanini conducted with the NBC Symphony. After scrutinizing the available talent, the reluctant suggestion was made to engage a certain singer with a very good voice but whose intelligence, it was sadly conceded, was not on the same level. The conductor considered the suggestion carefully and finally said: "Let X do the singing. I will do the thinking."

Toscanini was rehearsing an opera at La Scala with a well-endowed soprano who couldn't sing a particular phrase the way the maestro wanted. "No, caro, no! Parole! Don't eat the words," Toscanini kept yelling. The hapless creature began the phrase again and was cut short by Toscanini banging on the scoreless podium. *"Canta come è scritto!* Is written this way; sing it the way is written! One phrase, one breath!" She was losing it under his merciless black stare. She tried again and mangled the music. This time, with uncharacteristic and therefore frightening slowness, Toscanini pointed his baton at her bosom. "If only those were brains."

Son of Beckmesser

Fidelio (Ludwig von Beethoven)
20 November 1805. Vienna. World Premiere.

Suppose you wrote an opera, and nobody came. That's the problem good ol' Ludwig von faced when he stepped to the podium of the Theater an der Wien. Turning around, he looked out upon a half-empty house; the other half filled with dour-faced soldiers. Surly, glum, French, enemy soldiers. Napoleon's soldiers. A few scurvy prostitutes plied their wares; and, somewhere amidst the dust motes, a tired businessman was scribbling in his diary.

Might the Great Titan, at this moment, have regretted tearing up the dedication to Bonaparte that he had prefixed to his *Eroica* Symphony? Of course, for that matter, he might just as well have been contemplating yet another *Leonore* Overture.

Having waged an intermittent war with France for the last thirteen years, the Austro-Hungarian empire, in 1805, faced its most serious threat, for Napoleon's Grand Army was marching swiftly toward Vienna. Riots and food shortages plagued the capital. Then, on 20 October 1805, the Austrians were defeated at Ulm, and Vienna, defenseless, waited for the inevitable occupation by the barbarians. Emperor Franz, being the perfect and wise ruler, fled south to Baden to stick his head in the hot waters of the spa, leaving his city to fend for itself.

Everyone who had the means and the opportunity deserted the city, including Beethoven's wealthy friends and patrons. Under royal edict, the theaters remained open; although who was to attend the performances, only Franz knew. On the day of the premiere, the editor of the city's most prestigious newspaper, the *Wiener Zeitung,* was dismissed from his post and replaced by a Viennese quisling. There would be no review of any German opera for that edition.

Since the Viennese trollops did not write their memoirs of that important evening (oh, if only they had!) we have a nineteenth-century Pepys to thank for our knowledge of *Fidelio*'s premiere. Joseph Carl Rosenbaum, a successful Viennese businessman, married to the opera singer Theresa Gassmann, chronicled the events leading up to opening night.

4 November 1805.

> Every moment one sees baggage and carriages passing. In the afternoon I went with Theresa to the Danube. The court is sending everything away, even bedwarmers and shoe trees. It looks as if they have no intention of ever coming back to Vienna.

6 November 1805.

> Devastating news that the Russians have retreated. Vienna is in great danger of being swept over by marauding Chasseurs.

8 November 1805.

Theresa along with the rest of the company is summoned by Braun [manager of the court theaters] to the Redoutensaal for half-past nine. His situation is extremely awkward. By the command of His Majesty he has to remain, but it is possible that he as court banker and landowner would be taken in custody as hostage by the enemy, who are expected to arrive in a few days. He is prepared to share fortune and misfortune with all his people. Performances are to continue. Only in case of a bombardment would he have passes for all.

10 November 1805.

His Majesty has determined not to permit a single shot to be fired on the city and has sent a deputation to the enemy to begin negotiations about the fate of Vienna.

13 November 1805.

At half-past eleven a mass of people pressed through the portals of the Burg. Everyone was screaming, "The French are coming!" The cavalry was in the vanguard. The infantry looked very sloppy, not uniformed alike. The troops look quite wild. Nothing is known of our army. They have retreated far from Spitz. The French are masters of the whole region.

14 November 1805.

The French behave most considerately, even gallantly. All the streets are still full of people. Here they are received amicably. If only they would amicably go away again from Vienna!

15 November 1805.

Nothing is to be found in the market. Yesterday a pound of butter cost two, even three florins. Nobody dares to bring anything here because they take everything; even the horses are unharnessed. Women are hardly to be seen in the theaters, except the whores.

20 November 1805.

At the Wien today for the first time, Beethoven's grand opera *Fidelio, or, Conjugal Love,* in three acts, freely adapted from the French by Josef Sonnleithner. The opera contained beautiful, artful, heavy music; a boring, uninteresting book. It had no success. And it was empty.

Recently, little new of significance has been given. A new Beethoven opera *Fidelio* has not pleased. It was performed only a few times and after the first performance remained completely empty.

Also the music was really way below the expectations of amateur and professional alike. The melody as well as the general character, much of which is affected, lack the happy, clear, magical impression of emotion which grips us so irresistibly in the works of Mozart and Cherubini. The music has some beautiful passages, but it is very far from being a perfect, yes, even successful work.

The text, translated by Sonnleithner, concerns a story of rescue which has been in fashion ever since Cherubini's *Deux Journées.*

Freymuthige. 26 December 1805.

Up to now, Beethoven has sacrificed beauty so many times for the new and strange that this characteristic newness and originality was expected from this first theatrical production of his. It is exactly these qualities that are least in evidence.

The whole is distinguishable neither by invention nor execution. As a rule there are no new ideas in the vocal pieces; they are mostly too long; the text repeats itself endlessly; and the characterization fails remarkably. The choruses are ineffectual and one, which indicates the joy of prisoners over the sensation of fresh air, miscarries completely.

Allgemeine Musikalische Zeitung. 8 January 1806.

It was probably for the best that the French militia couldn't understand the German text. We don't think they would have appreciated Beethoven's lofty paean to political freedom, nor his condemnation of tyranny and its oppressions on the human soul.

But what in the world could they have thought of Leonora's drag? Were they even paying attention? It's time to unearth those harlots' diaries.

Il Trovatore (Giuseppe Verdi)
2 May 1855. New York. U.S. Premiere.

We hate to record our impressions of the new opera, and would fain ascribe them to the imperfect conditions of a first hearing. But in all candor we have little hope that any number of repetitions of *Il Trovatore* could increase our liking of Verdi's style of music. Once, when we first heard *Ernani* after the monotony and languor of a long continuance of Bellini's sentimental sweetness, we found a certain vigor therein quite refreshing. But now we have the mannerism of *Ernani* all over again, without its freshness; *Ernani* arias, *Ernani* unisons, *Ernani* chromatic climaxes—all the *Ernani* characteristics, only much diluted and run into a mere habit.

But we were surely in the minority. The people liked it. It was really a marvel to us, and discouraging in view of any progress of sound public taste, to witness the almost insane outbursts of applause which uniformly followed every aria, scene, and effect last evening (May 2), from that large and fashionable audience at the Academy. We could not account for it, except that everybody had been prepared to think that they *must* like what has been having such a run in Italy, and that the intensities and horrors of the plot, the *red hot* character of so much of the music, the frequency of dance rhythms too in the most serious portions, and the elaborately contrived scenic effects fastened upon the idle imagination, after the manner of the intense yellow-covered novels, and the like.

The plot is about as far-fetched and full of vicious appetite for horrors as the plot of *Rigoletto.* Nothing but ginger and red pepper seems to suit the modern Italian appetite. To see and hear all that scenically and musically illustrated, must it not be almost as good as "going to a hanging," if one has a taste for that!

But we find nothing that is new in kind, nothing that shows progress; above all, no signs of a more true and wholesome tendency, but only a hardened habit in the old false way—the way of substituting strong, glaring, and intense *effects,* at whatever cost of theme and treatment, for the real inspirations of sincere human life and feeling. Whatever power, whatever beauty, whatever brilliancy it may possess, this never strikes

[149]

you as *sincere* music. These are not the natural tones and melodies of human loves and griefs, and joys and longings, clothed in nature's sympathetic harmony.

When in Art it comes to this, are we not very near the expiring stages? If this be the logical and necessary result of the unfolding genius of Italian Opera, then what more can there be to hope from the Italian Opera except the end? Such fiery, lurid, overstrained intensity in music indicates a half burned out state.

Dwight's Journal of Music. 12 May 1855.

10 May 1855. London Premiere.

In the accumulation of horrors the *Trovatore* gives the sack even to *Rigoletto*. But the terrible earnestness of the last scene of *Rigoletto* would redeem a multitude of sins. The final scene of *Il Trovatore* is horrible without relief, and ineffective in the bargain.

It is apparently written with more care than the majority of his works; the unisons are fewer; and the desire to give a true dramatic interest to the scene is more manifest. On the other hand—which surprised us—the tunes are not so frequent as in his former operas. Much of the music of *Il Trovatore*, however, has *character*, is often pleasing, oftener well adapted to the situations, and occasionally in point of freedom and breadth worthy of unqualified praise. The audience, though favorably disposed towards the work and its composer, were not roused to enthusiasm. There were only two encores.

If not precisely the best, *Il Trovatore* is one of the longest operas of Signor Verdi, and in some respects the one in which he has attempted most. Signor Verdi, had he known more, there is no doubt, would have done better. As it is, he may rest satisfied with the applause of the mob, and effect to despise the educated few. Applause is to him as the breath of his nostrils. To gain applause he must conciliate mobs, and ignore "ears polite." He writes exclusively for mobs, and is accepted and worshipped as their idol. His aim is to be less a musician than a popular composer.

Meanwhile the grumblers are in the minority; *Il Trovatore* is

[150]

applauded; and the directors of the Royal Italian Opera put money in their pockets every night it is performed.
London Musical World. Reported in *Dwight's Journal of Music.* 16 June 1855.

Don Giovanni (Wolfgang Amadeus Mozart)
29 October 1787. Prague. World Premiere.

Monday, the 29th, the Italian Opera Company presented Maestro Mozart's eagerly awaited opera *Don Giovanni, or, the Stony Banquet.* Connoisseurs and musicians say that nothing like it has ever been performed in Prague. Herr Mozart conducted himself, and when he entered the pit, he received a triple ovation, repeated when he left. Incidentally, the opera's very difficult, and everyone admires the good performance, despite the limited time of study. Stage and orchestra did everything to reward Mozart with a good execution. Much expenditure was required by choruses and scenery, all provided splendidly by Herr Guardasoni. An unusually large crowd guaranteed the applause, which was shared by all.
Prager Oberamtszeitung. 3 November 1787.

Aladdin (Henry Rowley Bishop)
26 April 1826. London. World Premiere.

We may all be grateful that Sir Henry Rowley Bishop's operas have mercifully disappeared. Of his 100-odd dramatic works or arrangements (odd, indeed) only two songs have survived: *"Lo! here the gentle lark"*—although you'll never hear it in an elevator—and the eternal inspiration for countless samplers, *"Home, Sweet Home,"* from his comic opera *Clari, The Maid of Milan* (1823). The sheet music to this classic, in its first year, sold over 100,000 copies. Today, Bishop would have gone platinum!

When Covent Garden was rebuilt after its disastrous fire of 1808, Mr. Bishop was named its musical director, a post he held until 1824. As was the execrable habit of the times, he rearranged the music of whatever happened to be scheduled at his theater, be it *Fidelio, Barbiere, Don Giovanni,* or *Figaro,* and added his own music where he thought necessary. Perhaps for his steadfast adherence to this practice or for writing *"Home, Sweet Home,"* we really don't know, he was knighted in 1842, the first composer of the realm to be so honored.

Bishop would be completely out of the picture, and this book, except that the opening night of his *Aladdin* had a most refreshing happenstance. By 1826, Bishop was at Drury Lane, making a mess of the masters and writing a few more of his own messes. Carl Maria von Weber, though, was across town working on his last opera *Oberon* for a world premiere scheduled for 12 April 1826 at Covent Garden.

With his nationalism rising like pigeons in Hyde Park, Bishop countered Weber's fairy-tale opera with his own oriental bauble *Aladdin* (26 April 1826). He should have known better. It was a dismal attempt and had to be withdrawn. The ultimate humiliation was that he had composed a *"Hunting Chorus,"* which clearly reminded the audience of Weber's by-now-familiar and beloved *"Hunter's Chorus"* from the third act of *Freischütz.* With Weber himself in attendance at Bishop's premiere, the audience showed their contempt and stopped the show by whistling Weber's tune to the disgruntled knight-apparent.

Sometimes the English behave just like Italians. And we're glad they do.

Tannhäuser (Richard Wagner)
13 March 1861. Paris Premiere.

> The appearance of *Tannhäuser* on our first lyric scene, has not, I suppose, answered the expectation of Monsieur Wagner and his partisans, nor even those of his adversaries.
>
> We would have desired a different reception for *Tannhäuser* and its author. But the artist must be honored, who, even in the eyes of his most determined adversaries, is a man of intelligence, conviction, and will; and whose talent, regarding him simply as a composer, is vigorous, full of color, if not original, and wanting neither in elevation nor depth. We should have

desired, therefore, for Monsieur Wagner a reception at once sympathetic and respectful.

Journal des Débats. March 1861.

A second trial has come off, far from being more successful than the first. On the contrary, the public disapprobation was manifested with increased energy, and we do not recollect such another evening in the arena, ordinarily so calm and serene, of our Grand Opera. True that we can manage to dispense with hissing, but to avoid laughing is another affair; and, on the very first night, we involuntarily yielded more than once to the feeling which had irresistibly laid hold of the entire audience.

On the second night, precautions had been taken to guard against such inconvenient manifestations. The oboe solo after the *"Herdsman's Song,"* the redoubtable *trait de violins,* the pack of hounds at the end of Act I, and the reappearance of Venus in the third were one and all suppressed. Curtailments, too, had been effected in various places, and the rose gauze curtain sent back to the property room. But, alas! nothing could save *Tannhäuser.* This time there was less laughter, perhaps, but a great deal more hissing.

We have been assured, nevertheless, that Richard Wagner continues obstinate, attributes the check he has received in Paris to a cabal organized against him by his enemies. In his double capacity of poet and composer, the author of *Tannhäuser* is, doubtless, furnished with a double dose of pride, and should, therefore, perhaps be accorded a double amount of indulgence. This last we willingly extend—nay, we can even pity him, for we know of nothing more sad and hopeless than the fatuity, too common now-a-days, which induces authors to contemplate and admire themselves in their works, and to pronounce in a tone of sovereign authority, without the slightest deference to public opinion, that those works are good.

The second performance of *Tannhäuser* merely served to bring out in still bolder relief the talent and courage of the singers, who had to answer in person for the sins of the composer.

Revue et Gazette Musicale de Paris. 24 March 1861.

On Sunday the *Tannhäuser* was played for the third and last time. The theater was crowded, the receipts reaching 10,000 francs. The performance was the stormiest of all. Never was there such an uproar in the Opera House. The spectators were provided with whistles, and the whistling was heard in cadences and roulades. Wagner is certainly the first composer ever hissed by the aristocratic public of the Grand Opera. The proscenium box, situated above the Emperor's, was filled with hissers in straw-colored kids. The storm raged not only in the theater, but the foyer was also excited; the hubbub resembled the roar of the sea.

Philadelphia Bulletin. Byline-Paris. 25 March 1861.

The last ennui, but a colossal one, was *Tannhäuser*. Some say that Wagner has been sent to us in order to force us to admire Berlioz. As a matter of fact it is prodigious. It seems to me that I could write tomorrow something like it by taking inspiration from my cat walking over the keyboard of my piano. The Princess of Metternich took terrible pains to make people think that she understood it, and to start applause which would not come. Everybody was yawning; but at the same time everyone wished to appear to understand this riddle without an answer. The fiasco is enormous. Auber calls it Berlioz without melody.

Prosper Mérimée. *Lettres À Une Inconnue.*

My sufferings *before* the performance, which I unfortunately could no longer cancel, were far greater than *after* it. The truth is that I am glad to have been prevented by the Jockey Club from getting my work actually heard. I, myself, could not have listened to it any more!

Richard Wagner.

Elektra (Richard Strauss)
19 February 1910. London Premiere.

One thing is quite clear about *Elektra,* it will divide the opera-going public into two great classes, and the more deliberate remnant who recognize in it great merits and great defects will probably get their heads broken by both parties in the dispute.

It seems that we are allowed to think the music a little noisy, but we must admit that the tendency of the drama is a real

[154]

advance. For the music we must express a bewilderment that is ready to pass into enthusiasm.

The air is indeed so full of slaughter that by the time Aegisthus is seen flying about the Palace at the back of the scene, even the blood-thirsty spectator must feel that he cannot care very much what happens—for tragedy has apparently found it necessary to cast off the buskin for the galosh.
The Times. 20 February 1910.

Aida (Giuseppe Verdi)
24 December 1871. Cairo. World Premiere.

When Ismail Pasha succeeded his uncle to the title of the Khedive of Egypt in 1863, he embarked—with a Pharaoh's expense account and a typically Pharaonic megalomania—to beautify and modernize medieval Cairo. With an army of French counselors and an unlimited supply of manpower, he planned to out-Paris Paris. With new factories, bridges, schools, boulevards, railroad lines, telegraph and postal systems, a redrafted legal code, brackish swamps shoaled, public housing begun, he almost attained his dream. However, even Pharaoh had a budget director. With his lavish spending for the forthcoming celebrations in honor of his crowning achievement, the opening of the Suez Canal on 17 November 1869, his treasury was nearing depletion, and his subjects all the poorer for the capital's vast improvements.

But before the money ran out, the Khedive built the Italian Theatre to coincide with the Canal's gala premiere. Basically a wooden structure, it was shot throughout with chryselephantine decorations, colonnades, a grand foyer of floor-to-ceiling mirrors, and Ismail Pasha's initials wrought into the grillwork of the entranceway. Now, all it needed was an opera for opening night. The Khedive weighed Wagner, Gounod, and Verdi as suitable contenders for such an honor. He choose Verdi, and emissaries were sent to Italy. Verdi refused. It was too late to contact the runners-up, so the house opened on 1 November 1869 with *Rigoletto.*

The Khedive still wanted a world premiere for his theater.

He was not used to being said no to. In spring of 1870, while Verdi was in Paris, he was approached again. He refused. On the third try, a four-page story outline by Egypt's Inspector General of Monuments, Auguste Mariette, was sent along to the composer. Verdi was hooked. He agreed to write an opera for Cairo with the following stipulations: he would choose his own librettist, conductor, and singers; he would not go to Cairo (he feared sea voyages); he would retain all rights to the work except in Egypt; and his fee would be 150,000 francs. The Khedive readily accepted all of the maestro's terms.

The premiere was set for July 1871; the opera was completed after four months, but no one foresaw the outbreak in July 1870 of the Franco-Prussian war. Sets, costumes, and properties, all designed and constructed in Paris, were warehoused behind the barricades. Even the librettist Ghislanzoni was unable to get out. The premiere was postponed. By May 1871, the war was over, Napoleon III deposed, France ceded Alsace and portions of the Lorraine to the German victors, and *Aida* was rescheduled for 24 December 1871.

During one of the rehearsals, the Egyptologists supervising the accuracy of the production noticed Radames's bit of business at the end of Act III's *Nile Scene*. Aida and her father flee the approaching priests, while Radames gives himself up. He hands over his sword as the curtain falls. The scholars said this would never do. A pharaoh's general would only submit to Pharaoh himself, never to a priest. In Italy, Ghislanzoni received a telegram from Cairo, "Should the high priest be handed the sword of Radames?" In Cairo, they received his reply, "If it is a wooden sword, yes. If gold, do not trust him."

The premiere would not have been more of a smash had the Khedive written the opera himself. Members of his seraglio, bejeweled, veiled, and mysterious, occupied three boxes of the first tier. The sumptuous production was greeted by so many outbursts of applause that during the *Triumphal Scene,* Giovanni Bottesini, the conductor, had to shout at the first-nighters, "Quiet, quiet, it's not over."

By 1879, *Aida* was making its speedy conquest of Europe

and the Americas; the Suez Canal was happily turning a profit for England, who had bought the controlling interest to save the financial empire of the Khedive; and the profligate prince of Egypt who had commissioned the world's most famous opera was tossed out on his padded posterior—with his harem —by the Sultan of Turkey.

A very remarkable and interesting work, certain to be appreciated in France as well as Italy. Certainly the old Verdi still survives; we find him, in *Aida,* with his exaggerations, his sharp oppositions, his negligencies of style, and his wildness. But another Verdi, touched with Germanism, also manifests himself, with a clever manner, with a science and tact of which we did not think him capable; with all the artifices of fugue and counterpoint, coupling tunes with rare ingenuity, breaking the old forms of melody, even those of his own preference, giving to the accompaniment more interest, often more importance than the melody itself. Those who know the abrupt nature and the undisciplined character of the Italian master will see something more and something better than vague promises for the future in the aspirations and tendencies which AIDA reveals. *Journal des Debats.* Dispatch from Cairo. 24 December 1871.

Signor Verdi,

On the second of this month, attracted by the sensation which your opera, *Aida,* was making, I went to Parma. I admired the scenery, listened with great pleasure to the excellent singers and took pains to let nothing escape me. After the performance was over, I asked myself whether I was satisfied. The answer was in the negative. On the way back in the train carriage, I listened to the verdicts of my fellow travelers. Nearly all of them agreed that *Aida* was a work of the highest rank.

Thereupon I decided to hear it again, so on the fourth I returned to Parma. I came to the following conclusion: the opera contains nothing thrilling or electrifying, and if it were not for the magnificent scenery, the audience would not sit through it to the end. It will fill the theater a few more times and then gather dust in the archives.

[157]

Now, my dear Signor Verdi, you can imagine my regret at having spent 32 lire for these two performances. Add to this the aggravating circumstances that I am dependent on my family, and you will understand that this money preys on my mind like a terrible specter. Therefore I address myself frankly and openly to you, so that you may send me this sum. Here is the account:

> Railroad: one way. . . . . .2.60 lire
> Railroad: return trip. . . . 3.30 lire
> Theater. . . . . 8.00 lire
> Disgustingly bad dinner
>   at the station. . . . . . 2.00 lire
>   15.90 × 2 = 31.80 lire

In the hope that you will extricate me from this dilemma, I am yours sincerely,

Bertani

On condition that this young man never again attend any of his new operas and so wouldn't expose himself to the danger of being persued by ghosts, Verdi paid the bill, but deducted 4 lire for the two suppers. Said the maestro, "He could perfectly well have eaten at home."

26 November 1873. New York Premiere.

Clearly the offspring of an almost Wagnerian system. Loud applause was elicited last night by many portions of *Aida.* To excite continuous admiration, however, the subject needs a closer acquaintance than one sitting can beget. Artistically nothing finer could be wished than the reproductions on canvas of the gorgeous temples of Egypt. An augmented orchestra, a complete brass band, a small corps de ballet—including a rather undisciplined force of Ethiopian juveniles—and brand-new dresses of every one of the two hundred beings who, in the Second Act, are gathered at once upon the stage, were beheld during last's night's entertainment.
New York Times. 27 November 1873.

Much of the success of the performance was due to the scenery, and we think this ought to be a lesson to managers. *New York Herald.* 27 November 1873.

22 June 1876. London Premiere.

"At The Opera"

HABITUÉ (much distressed): It really *is* a pity that Patti has made herself such a red brick-dust fright.

FACETIOUS PARTY NO. 1: Yes! Look here! (Points to book). See what Amneris is saying about her. (Reads.) "Yon deadly pallor —her bosom panting." She's panting hard enough, but I'll be hanged if she could show any deadly pallor, unless someone would kindly empty a flour bag over her. However, her singing is admirable.

(ENTER Signor Graziani as Amonasro, King of Ethiopia, and looking blacker than Otello.)

FACETIOUS PERSON NO. 2: I say, he's supposed to be Aida's father. He's as black as my hat, and she's as red as a brick wall. I say, this won't do, you know. (Appeals to his Friend, who can't account for it himself, but suggests writing to Darwin on the subject.)

Punch. 1 July 1876.

The Beggar's Opera (John Pepusch and John Gay)
29 January 1728. London. World Premiere.

On Monday was represented for the first time at the Theatre Royal in Lincoln's Inn Fields Mr. Gay's new English opera, written in a manner wholly new and very entertaining, there being introduced instead of Italian airs about sixty of the most celebrated Old English and Scottish tunes. There was present there, as well as last night, a prodigious concourse of Nobility and Gentry, and no theatrical performance for these many years has been met with so much applause.

London Journal. 31 January 1728.

The piece was received with greater applause than was ever known. Besides being acted in London sixty-three days without interruption, and renewed next season with equal applause, it spread to all the great towns of England . . . The ladies carried about with them the favorite songs of it in fans, and houses were furnished with it in screens. The fame of it was not confined to the author only. The person who acted Polly [Lavinia Fenton], till then obscure, became all at once the favorite of the town; her pictures were engraved and sold in great numbers, her life written, books of letters and verses to her published, and pamphlets made even of her sayings and jests. Furthermore, it drove out of England, for that reason, the Italian opera, which had carried all before it for ten years.

The Dunciad. Alexander Pope. 1728.

The play, like many others, was plainly written only to divert, without any moral purpose, and is therefore not likely to do good; nor can it be conceived, without more speculation than life requires or admits, to be productive of much evil. Highwaymen and housebreakers seldom frequent the playhouse or mingle in any elegant diversion; nor is it possible for anyone to imagine that he may rob with safety because he sees Macheath reprieved upon the stage.

Dr. Johnson.

POLLY PEACHUM

Of all the toasts that Britain boasts,
The gin, the gent, the jolly,
The brown, the fair, the debonair,
There's none cried up like Polly.

She's fired upon the town, has quite cut down
The Opera of Rolli:
Go where you will, the subject still
Is pretty, pretty Polly.

There's Madame Faustina Catso!
And the Madame Catsoni,
Likewise Signor Senesino,
Are tutti abbandonni!

Ha, ha, ha, ha, Do, re, me, fa
Are now but farce and folly.
We're ravished all with Toll, loll, loll,
And pretty, pretty Polly!

Ballad by Henry Carey.

Neues vom Tage (Paul Hindemith)
8 June 1929. Berlin. World premiere.

Hindemith's caustic one-act burlesque on Germany's yellow journalism was not greeted with smiles by the Nazis. As we know, these cretins never possessed a sense of humor. The opera's scene in the Savoy Hotel with Laura singing in the bathtub among cotton soapsuds caused a scandal. That the heroine also praised electric heating over gas ("constant hot water, no horrid smell or danger of explosion") was enough for the Breslau Gas Works to order—and receive—an injunction against the work when it was to be performed in that city. Nobody in Germany was smiling. With his Jewish wife, his Jewish friends, and his continued associations with Jewish musicians, his "utilitarian" music was condemned as degenerate "cultural bolshevism." He wisely fled his homeland and settled in America, becoming a citizen in 1946.

When a man like Hindemith commits the foulest perversions of German music we have the right to reject him. The accomplishments of such an artist and the laurels received by him in that now-overthrown Republic, are by right of no value to our movement.
Die Music. January 1935.

Technical mastery is not an excuse but an obligation. To misuse it for meaningless musical trifles is to besmirch true genius. Opportunity creates not only thieves but also atonal musicians who in order to create a sensation will exhibit on the stage naked women in the bathtub in the most disgusting and

[161]

obscene situations and will further befoul these scenes with the
most atrocious dissonance of musical impotence.
Dr. Joseph Goebbels.

La Traviata (Giuseppe Verdi)
6 March 1853. Venice, Italy. World Premiere.

Operatic legends and myths are more difficult to dispatch
than New York City cockroaches. Hiding from truth's light,
they scurry about from one source book to another, dragging
their accumulated falsehoods with them, becoming more outrageous with each retelling. Accreditation comes to those particular stories that have stayed longest in circulation. Tell
something for a lengthy enough period of time, and everyone
will believe it must be so. Survival of the falsest.

La Traviata is one such case. Contrary to numerous books on
the opera—and to Verdi's own letters—this intimate work,
"simple and filled with love," was neither a disaster on opening
night at Venice's Teatro La Fenice, nor was it performed in
contemporary settings and costumes (i.e., circa 1850). If our
book serves no other purpose than to deal the *coup de grace* to
these unsubstantiated fables, we will glow with satisfaction.

Granted, *La Traviata* did not soar into musical history until
its run at the Teatro San Benedetto, also in Venice, over a year
later on 6 May 1854, but it received a very respectable and
honorable schedule of ten performances at La Fenice, with
Verdi called out repeatedly for curtain calls during the first
three performances.

If anything happened on that first night to warrant censure,
it was the singing of the two male principals. The tenor,
Lodovico Graziani, suffered from a hoarse voice; while the
baritone, Felice Varesi, didn't think his part was important
enough and just wasn't in the mood to do justice to Germont.
During rehearsals Verdi fretted that the singers didn't understand the music and were indifferent and lazy to his instructions.

Prior to his coming to Venice to supervise the production,

he had written to the general manager to have Signora Salvini-Donatelli replaced by a "real prima donna," but nothing was done, and Verdi resigned himself to the soprano since it was now too late to engage anyone else. Nothing in the coeval reports say anything about her unsuitability for playing Violetta. She was not a cow, and her singing is singled out as exemplary. No one laughed or hooted when consumption did her in.

We are so used to seeing *La Traviata* set in the period of Napoleon III and Eugénie that it seems quite perverse to think of a production in the style of Louis XIV, but, bizarre or not, that's how these early productions were staged. (Jean-Pierre Ponnelle, eat your heart out.) The blatant inaccuracy of Arthur Pougin (1834–1921), a renowned biographer of Verdi who was the first to state that the disaster of opening night had been caused by "modern costumes, so cold, so sad, so monotonous," stubbornly resists any attempt at correction.

Early on, Verdi did have misgivings about setting Dumas's timely tale in such a remote period; but, once he arrived in Venice, he didn't demand new sets and costumes because he knew damned well that opening night was just around the corner. He had worked in the theater long enough to know just what he could demand and what he could hope to receive. Perhaps, when he saw the lavish production in rehearsal, he liked the sumptuousness of it.

Newspapers, posters, playbills, and the original libretto of 1853 refer to the production as set in the time of "the Great Louis," i.e., the early 1700's. The ultimate corroboration are the extant original sketches of the scenic designer Bertoja in his collection at Pordenone, Italy, which clearly show long wigs, knee-length breeches, buckled shoes, etc. At certain Italian opera houses, this eighteenth-century treatment of *La Traviata* persisted until 1918!

We will never know for certain why Verdi wrote to no less than three colleagues saying that *La Traviata* was "a solid fiasco!" except that he was *not* pleased with the singers at his disposal. For such a consummate artist, anything second-rate would veer perilously toward the abyss. On the other hand, he could have been taking sweet revenge against apathetic divas and listless divos. "I won't say anything about the music; and allow me to say nothing about the singers." "I don't know whose fault it was; and it is better not to talk about it." "Is it my fault or the fault of the singers? Time will tell." For not wanting to talk about the performance, he says a great deal.

After the two Venice productions, *La Traviata* waltzed into Rome in 1854, and galoped through London, Paris, Buenos Aires, Rio de Janeiro, Mexico City, and New York City by 1856. She might have worn old clothes, but she was not a cow, and the music delighted all who heard it. Now, where are those roach motels?

The music was magnificently played by the orchestra, so much so that the delicious prelude of the third act got and deserved a unanimous round of shouted cheers. The public was ravished by the most beautiful and lively melodies that have been heard in a long time.

Anyone who does not see the beauty of *Un dì, quando le veneri;* anyone who does not feel moved by those *Piangi,* neither played nor sung but spoken by the orchestra; anyone who does not feel his heart tremble with that musical sigh of *Pietà, gran Dio di mé;* anyone who is not moved by those moments has no right to talk about music.

Three things are needed for the art of music: voice, voice, and voice. And truthfully, Verdi has created something beautiful, even though he does not have an artist who understands and can perform what he creates. Last night, Verdi had the bad luck to lack those three things mentioned above, and all the pieces not sung by Mme. Salvini-Donatelli went by the line, so to speak. She ravished the public, which deluged her with applause.

La Gazzetta Uffiziale di Venezia. 7 March 1853.

Venice—Gran Teatro della Fenice. The first performance of *Traviata* by Maestro Verdi. Theater was packed, great anticipa-

[164]

tion: the result was wretched! What shall we blame? The music? The singing? The libretto, which is a horror? Misericordia! On top of everything else to disturb the show, a table was carried in with two candelabra, which fell and the candles rolled across the stage to the proscenium.
Pirata. 10 March 1853.

24 May 1856. London Premiere.

On Saturday night one of those important experiments was made that are generally preceded by a vast amount of conjecture and—we may almost say—trepidation among the patrons of lyrical drama. We do not, of course, allude to the production of a new opera by Verdi, since it is one of the virtues of that prolific composer that he does not disturb the equanimity of the public, either by raising expectations or by weighing on the memory.

The book is of far more consequence than the music, which, except so far as it affords a vehicle for the utterance of the dialogue, is of no value whatever.
The Times. 26 May 1856.

10 June 1857. Boston Premiere.

The recent compositions of Mr. Verdi afford a remarkable example of what might be called the "Art of Sinking in Music." Each of the last four or five operas he has given to the world has been considered inferior to that immediately preceding it, and it now becomes a matter for anxious consideration what we are to expect in his next lyrical production, should he continue in this manner. It can hardly be anything better than a series of brilliant and somewhat noisy quadrilles, polkas, and waltzes, for ponderous orchestra, with weak vocal accompaniments. Indeed, while listening to the *Traviata* one's first thought is—what a beautiful writer of quadrilles was lost to the world when Mr. Verdi devoted himself to the manufacture of operas. That the *Traviata* is more deficient in science and imagination than anything he has previously written cannot be denied.
The Courier. June 1857.

The reign of Verdi, according to the European journals, is about over. No composer ever went up so much like a rocket, scintillated and flashed into a thousand stars, and afterwards came down into Cimmerian darkness, so much like a stick. The world fifty years hence will scarcely believe that we, the originators of ocean steamers, sub-marine telegraph, builders of big Opera houses, and otherwise "posted" on matters and things in general, should have ever endured his excruciating music.

New York Atlas. September 1858.

Le Prophète (Giacomo Meyerbeer)
25 November 1853. New York Premiere.

The first performance of *The Prophet* took place at Niblo's Theatre last night, and attracted, as might be expected, a very large and discriminating audience. The opera was an indisputable triumph.

The costumes are new and generally appropriate and in some instances elegant. The scenery, too, is mostly new. Above all, the announcements in the advertisements were simple and truthful, not made up of lying appeals to public gullibility by statements of fabulous sums expended for costumes, scenery, etc.

We cannot compliment Mr. Salvi upon the manner in which his head and face were made up. If it was after that "picture of K. David in the Cathedral at Munster"—as described by Mr. Marini—it was painted by a shocking bad artist.

New York Tribune. 26 November 1853.

Der Fliegende Holländer (Richard Wagner)
23 July 1870. London. First Wagner performance in England.

If we are to welcome such music and ultimately to adopt the Wagnerian doctrine of the "Art-work of the Future," it is well to begin from the beginning—with an opera composed when the Prophet was more like other men. We have always thought that Herr Wagner's very best, least extravagant, dramatic work was the *Holländer,* which, amid much that is incoherent and formless, contains some genuine music, and the promise of more to come. Every step since taken in advance of it seems to us a step in the wrong direction. Perhaps a more remarkable instance could scarcely be cited than the *Holländer* of the power of making something—a great deal, indeed—out of little or nothing.

The Times. 25 July 1870.

> The music of the future, eh?
> Well, some may think it pleasant!
> But when such trash again they play,
> I'll for the future hope I may
> Not be among the present!

Punch. 6 August 1870.

Salome (Richard Strauss)
22 January 1907. New York Premiere.

In the Year of Our Lord 1907, tunafish was put in its first can; the Hoover vacuum cleaner swept the nation; Korea became a protectorate of Japan; the "all-electric" washing machine began its spin cycle; l'Oréal perfume scented the ears of Paris; Flo Ziegfeld dazzled Broadway with his premiere *Follies;* the Brothers Ringling somersaulted into the center ring with Barnum and Bailey; Canada Dry Ginger Ale effervesced and tickled the palette; the long-distance swimmer Annette Kellerman was arrested at a Boston beach for wearing a skirtless, one-piece bathing suit; the Plaza Hotel unrolled its red carpet; the United Press wire service sent out its first dispatch; Neiman-Marcus peddled its first millinery to the miladies of Dallas; the Chicago Cubs mauled the Detroit Tigers to win the World Series; bubonic plague decimated India; the *Lusitania* was launched; women were granted suffrage in Norway and Austria; Oklahoma added its 46th star to the American flag; metered taxis cruised the streets of New York City; Gulf Oil Co. spewed forth its "black Texas tea"; yogurt was apotheosized as prolonging life; and Gifford Pinchot coined the word "conservation."

[167]

As if all this weren't enough, the year really began when that lubricious, concupiscent, Fescennine teen-ager stripped off her veils on the stage of the august Metropolitan Opera House.

Heinrich Conried, the Met's general manager, had witnessed the original Dresden production and was as goggle-eyed over Strauss's bad girl as had been the audiences in Germany and Italy. Toscanini never forgave Strauss for reneging on his promise to give the maestro the first Italian performance of the work. After conducting *Salome* at La Scala during the 1906 season, he never performed another Strauss opera. Whoever said Italians don't hold a grudge?

Negotiating with Herr Strauss for what he considered an exorbitant per performance fee of $250, Conried announced *Salome* as his "annual benefit" with tickets at double price. Apprehensive, he wisely paired the naughty girl with a standard gala evening to mollify the response. It was quite a gala.

The first half of the program, a concert potpourri, included: Farrar and Scotti in the *Là ci darem la mano* duet from *Don Giovanni,* Caruso singing the hymn of praise *O paradiso* from *L'Africaine,* Louise Homer in the *Barcarolle* from *Contes d'Hoffmann,* two songs from Marcella Sembrich, and the *Trio* from *Faust.* Intermission. And then, at 10 P.M., the curtain rose on *Salome* with Olive Fremstad, making her American debut. Hell didn't actually break loose; but it quietly slipped its bonds.

Unlike their European counterparts, the New York audiences have always been polite—to the point of serenity. They rarely boo or hiss. When they are truly outraged, it's a solo, almost wistful sotto voce display, never an organized, gallery-filled demonstration. They only walk out when the curtain comes down, for they dread being watched during their escape as they inelegantly lumber over their neighbors, especially in the almost aisle-less caverns of the New York theaters. New Yorkers would rather sit there, as still as stones, watching the abuse, and then leave at the earliest convenient moment. The sound of rustling coats is usually more devastating than a khamsin of insults.

[168]

The Metropolitan audience, packed to the rafters, behaved itself on that Tuesday evening in January like little angels. A few moans, quite a few demurely turned heads, many walk-outs, but no cacophonous outrage. Bianca Froehlich's hootchy-kootchy belly dance à la "Little Egypt" caused but slight discomfort; and even Fremstad's caressing of Jokanaan's severed head (which some wag described as a poorly put together pudding) played out at the blazing footlights counter to Strauss's explicit stage directions for beclouded obscurity, did not elicit the wrath of the audience—that was saved for the reviews. There was a smattering of brief applause from those brave few who remained, and Strauss's notorious third opus was over.

If anyone could be said to have lost his head over *Salome*, it was Heinrich Conried, who was plagued with a manic-depressive management throughout his directorship. Credits and debits aligned equally. He had to contend with Oscar Hammerstein's increasingly successful, rival Manhattan Opera Company; he caused Cosima Wagner a *petit mal* seizure when he flouted the "bitch of Bayreuth" and staged *Parsifal* against her explicit injunction; he added the illustrious Geraldine Farrar and Lina Cavalieri to the roster, but allowed Charles Gilibert, Maurice Renaud, and Luisa Tetrazzini (three of the most remarkable artists in an age of remarkable artists) to slip through his fingers and land in Hammerstein's enemy lap; and he had brought over Humperdinck and Puccini to supervise their own operas. While the Met was on tour in San Francisco, the earthquake and fire of 18 April 1906 destroyed a major portion of the sets and costumes, and the remainder of the profitable tour had to be canceled and subscribers repaid. On top of everything else, the season suffered a financial loss, the first since Henry Abbey in the 1890's. The board and stockholders were not happy. Even when in New York, Conried was on shaky ground. The mess of *Salome* helped bump him out the door.

Little Conried tilted valiantly for the "daughter of Sodom," but he was no match for the snorting Clydesdale in Box 35,

J. P. Morgan, whose Victorian sensibilities were as overpowering as his bank statement. "Pip" and his daughter detested what they saw on the boards, and so the directors of the Metropolitan Opera and Real Estate Co. (of which they were the most formidable members) threatened that if Conried didn't remove the detestable creature from moral Christian eyes, the Met would lose its lease. Conried could face any opposition but that. The house was dark for her second and third scheduled appearances, while the fourth was hastily programmed with something completely different—*Hänsel und Gretel!* *Salome* was given the boot. Conried followed after the next season.

Wily Hammerstein, knowing the untold riches to be garnered from such free publicity and scandal, produced *Salome,* in French, with Mary Garden, two years later (when much of the heat had dissipated) and had a smash hit and no notoriety.

When *Salome* was allowed back into the Metropolitan, she was twenty-seven years older; now, more than eighty, she shows nary a wrinkle. Wherever she goes, she's still the youngest girl in town.

A reviewer ought to be equipped with a dual nature, both intellectual and moral, in order to pronounce fully and fairly upon the qualities of the drama by Oscar Wilde and Richard Strauss. He should be an embodied conscience stung into righteous fury by the moral stench with which *Salome* fills the nostrils of humanity, but, though it makes him retch, he should be sufficiently judicial in his temperament calmly to look at the drama and determine whether or not as a whole it is an instructive note on the life and culture of the times and whether or not this exudation from the diseased and polluted will and imagination of the authors marks a real advance in artistic expression, irrespective of its contents or their fitness for dramatic representation.

There is a great deal of ugly music in *Salome*—music that offends the ear and rasps the nerves like fiddlestrings played on by a coarse file. What shall be said when music adorns itself with its loveliest attributes and leads them to the apotheosis of that which is indescribably, yes, inconceivably, gross and abominable? Music cannot lie. Not even the genius of Richard Strauss can make it discriminate in its soaring ecstasy between a vile object and a good.

There is not a whiff of fresh and healthy air flowing through *Salome* except that which exhales from the cistern, the prison house of Jokanaan. *Salome* is the unspeakable; Herodias is a human hyena; Herod, a neurasthenic voluptuary.

Mme. Fremstad accomplished a miracle. A sleek tigress, with seduction speaking in every pose, gesture, look and utterance, she grew steadily into the monster which she was when she sank under the shields of the soldiers while the orchestra shrieked its final horror and left the listeners staring at each other with starting eyeballs and wrecked nerves.

22 January 1907. *New York Times.*

Carmen (Georges Bizet)
3 March 1875. Paris. World Premiere.

Depressed over the dismal reception given to his new opera *Carmen,* exhausted from four months of strenuous rehearsals, and ailing from recurrent bouts of rheumatism, heart trouble, and chronic throat infections, Georges Bizet had fled the "poisonous air of Paris" to the sweeter serenity of neighboring Bougival, France. There, exactly three months after the gypsy girl's premiere, he died, aged 37, from complications suffered from a double heart attack and stroke. On the stage of the Opéra-Comique in Paris that same evening, his specter suddenly materialized to Célestine Galli-Marié during Carmen's portentous fortunetelling in Act III.

"The blow to my side felt as if it had been struck by a hammer. For a few seconds I saw his face before me. How pale he was." Momentarily dazed, she finished the scene, rushed backstage, and collapsed.

News of Bizet's death reached the company a few days later. Only then did Galli-Marié realize the ghastly timing of the

[171]

phantom's appearance and the accompanying pain. After that night, it was said that her portrayal of Carmen during the divination scene was positively uncanny.

Ironically, with Bizet dead, business at the Comique picked up, but it still wasn't enough the fill the theater, and Camille du Locle had to resort to papering the house for the final stretch. Even though *Carmen*'s run of 48 performances would indicate a very successful season, business was mediocre. The prehistoric regime refused to revive the opera until 1883, long after *Carmen* had redeemed herself and was playing to full houses everywhere but in Paris: Vienna, Brussels, Antwerp, Budapest, London, Dublin, St. Petersburg, New York, and Christiana, Norway.

Ernest Guirard's recitatives, orchestrated and added for the Vienna production in October 1875 (sung in German) were never the reason for Carmen's ultimate worldwide success and popularity. Saint-Saëns called these recensions "nonsense." Simply, the French critics stayed put in France; thereby allowing Bizet's "lively, unaffected, simple" work (in Nietzsche's phrase) to seduce the listener on its own terms, without the parochial moralizing that so encrusted the Parisian reviews of the Second Empire.

Though they sanitized and freely adapted Mérimée's much more brazen tale, Bizet and his librettists Halévy and Meilhac whipped up quite a spicy *paella* using such diverse ingredients as gypsies, smugglers, dragoons, cigarette smoke, mother-love, fortunetelling, passion, fate, revenge, and the blazing white heat of mid-day Seville. It is an opera fashioned "near perfect" by its sensuous spin of continuous melody, with its leading roles tailored to demolish every available piece of scenery, and with its tunes that the world now whistles in its sleep. (Although Bizet pilfered Sebastiàn Yradier's song *"El Arreglito"* for the *Habanera.*)

The critics had their come-uppance, for although Bizet died without ever having known a popular operatic success, his *Carmen* is forever beloved and immortal. The ripe flavor of

Spain was never again so fortunate as to be so tastily prepared by a Frenchman.

The music of the future has been a standing joke for some years, and it is high time that we heard the last of it. The leader of the school, since it must be so called, Richard Wagner, has been banished from our theaters and concert rooms. Had it not been for the war, we might even now be at the mercy of his braying German trumpets, to the destruction of all real music. But Monsieur Wagner has sowed such baneful seed which should be stopped from reaching maturity.

These remarks apply particularly to Monsieur Bizet. This work is by no means without merit. The hand of a musician who knows his business thoroughly is plainly seen in it. But it is all head and no heart.

The gypsy girl is an odious creature at best; and Mme. Galli-Marié accentuates the least attractive side of her character. The actress's gestures are a very incarnation of vice, and there is something licentious even in the tones of her voice. She was fascinating by reason of her animal beauty ard in the exposure of her animal instincts. There was the swaying of restless hips, the curving of amorous arms, the languishing eye that encouraged, promised, pursued.

L'Art Musicale. March 1875.

The *Carmen* of the Opéra-Comique is a very much sweetened, very purified edition of the novel which everyone has read, except perhaps young girls. The composer could hardly dispense with looking for the Spanish atmosphere. His memories have helped him there, for it would be absolutely out of place so to point to a composer with as much talent and imagination as M. Bizet.

The song of the first act, with its very original chromatic phrase, comes straight from South America; they sing it a great deal in Havana; they sing it a great deal in Paris.

Journal des Débats. March 1875.

Otello (Giuseppe Verdi)
5 July 1889. London Premiere.

Without going to the length of admitting its superiority to the many other works Verdi has produced, the skill and genius of the composer in *Otello* may certainly be conceded. It is without question a most remarkable production, even if it does not possess those qualities which secure popularity.
Morning Post. 6 July 1889.

Otello is the effect of Verdi conVerdid to Wagnerism.
Punch. July 1889.

X (Anthony Davis)
9 October 1985. Philadelphia. World Premiere.

X is an untidy corpse, and it would take a sharp-eyed operatic pathologist to discern the exact cause of death, the possibilities being so many. First, the title role is invested with none of the expressive or musical charisma that might set him apart from the rest of the cast. Surely the real-life Malcolm was not so languid. This Malcolm discloses little inner existence or conflicting emotions: hence, his conversion experience in prison—a sure-fire operatic scene—played hollowly. Second, the work discloses no awareness that the attention span of an audience must be confronted, manipulated, teased. This lack led every scene to sprawl beyond its dramatic point and congeal into a *tableau vivant.* Third, the libretto tells its "story" with a hailstorm of clichés ("The chickens will come home to roost".) Finally, the music of *X* is wearyingly homogeneous, except for some Harlem jazz interludes: mainly hand-me-down Stravinsky of the *Les Noces* sort and angular, heavily declaimed, truncated phrases doled out to every character in equal measure.

Clearly, *X* is a heartfelt memorial to the martyred black leader (it is dedicated to him). But little heart feeling and much dramatically inert piety reached the Walnut Street Theater stage. The bloody climax at the Audubon Ballroom in Harlem (also bumbled in conception) came as a relief.
Opera News. 4 January 1986.

La Forza del Destino (Giuseppe Verdi)
10 November 1862. St. Petersburg. World Premiere.

The first performance of the opera composed expressly for our Italian Opera House by Verdi took place last night. The work has been adapted for the Italian stage by Piave, who has had to shorten and alter it considerably. Even as it is, and although reduced to four acts, it is still too long, and the habits of our public will certainly render cutting necessary.

The subject of *La Forza del Destino* was, doubtless, a seductive one for the maestro, whose talent is particularly partial to violent situations. We do not pretend, after having heard it only once, to pronounce a decided judgment on an opera of such a length. But there is one thing that struck us at once: in the whole course of the work, there is not a trio, a quartet, or a concerted piece. The entire opera is a succession of cavatinas, duets, and choruses. In the fourth act, the second scene contains nothing but an air for Leonora.

Revue et Gazette Musicale. 11 November 1862.

Les Pêcheurs de Perles (Georges Bizet)
22 April 1887. London Premiere.

To lovers of poetry the pearl fisher is known as one who "held his breath, and went all naked to the hungry shark." To the patrons of the Opera he is now familiar as an expensively got-up Oriental, with an elaborate ritual conducted in temples not unlike Parisian newspaper kiosks, the precincts whereof are laid out in the manner of a Brussels tea garden. The chief ceremony is a ballet; and though here, if anywhere, we might expect to find our pearl fisher in the condition mentioned by Keats, such is by no means the case. He—or rather she—is clothed and, within operatic limits, in her right mind. As to holding his breath, he turns that accomplishment to account for the better execution of roulades and fiorituras. He keeps the hungry shark in order by the prayers of a virgin priestess, who remains veiled and secluded from all intercourse on a rocky promontory during the oyster season.

Out of these simple and plausible conditions we get a pretty poem. Leila is the priestess. Nadir and Zurga fall in love with her. Nadir sacrilegiously serenades her on the promontory. She responds; and the two, amid a hideous tempest, are seized and condemned to the stake. Zurga effects a diversion, and enables them to escape by setting Ceylon on fire: an extreme measure. The natives then burn him; and really, under the circumstances, it is hard to blame them. That is all.

George Bernard Shaw. *Music in London.* 20 May 1889.

The Emperor Jones (Louis Gruenberg)
7 January 1933. New York. World Premiere.

Eugene O'Neill, Lawrence Tibbett, and Jo Mielziner were the making of the hour and a quarter of terror which on Saturday afternoon engrossed one of the largest audiences that the Metropolitan Opera House has ever held. Louis Gruenberg's share in the orgy of rasped nerves was more problematic. *The Emperor Jones* has been familiar to followers of the drama for a dozen years, both as a stage production and as a play for reading. In turning it into an opera Mr. Gruenberg bravely faced a hazard. Should he or should he not be able with his music to heighten the effect of the original? Unless through the music the play acquired a mightier emotional punch, that music must be more or less in the way.

The orchestral commentary, for the most part, sounded less like the issue of an inspired imagination than like a remembered convention. And when the people took to singing, the words lost clearness and the pace turned leaden. Nor did it seem to me that Mr. Gruenberg made a particularly pungent use of syncopated rhythms or of an inserted spiritual. In time the scales may fall from my ears and I may hear *The Emperor Jones* as an authentic masterpiece.

At the end of the brief world premiere there was an ovation, principally, it appeared, for Mr. Tibbett, though others bowing acknowledgments included Messrs. Gruenberg, Mielziner, Serafin, Setti, and Sanine.

New York World Telegram. January 1933.

Die Meistersinger von Nürnberg (Richard Wagner)
30 May 1882. London Premiere.

As for the *Meistersinger,* the shock of hearing it for the first time is too much to make criticism possible till the listener has pulled himself together. *There are tunes in it! There is a waltz!!* Hooray for Wagner waltzing! Shall hear the *Meistersinger* again, as will many others. It is charming throughout. A simple and sufficiently interesting story illustrated by thoughtful, mirthful and delightful melody, which is never wearisome from first to last—and it is a long opera. No one fond of melodious opera, and no unbeliever in Wagner, should miss seeing the *Meistersinger.*
Punch. 10 June 1882.

Giulio Cesare (George Frederick Handel)
20 February 1724. London. World Premiere.

Some say, compared to Bononcini,
That Myn Heer Handel's but a ninny;
Others aver that he to Handel
Is scarcely fit to hold a Candle.
Strange all this difference should be
'Twixt Tweedle-dum and Tweedle-dee.
John Byrum. February 1724.

Our Souls so tuned, that Discord grieves to find
A whole fantastick Audience of a Mind.
In Place of promis'd Heaps of glitt'ring Gold,
The good Academy got naught—but Cold.
Where cou'd they fly for Succour, but to You?
Whose Musick's ever good, and ever New.
The Post Boy. 7 March 1723.

Transpose a few words in the Soviet editorial below, and, amazingly, it would read like a French diatribe against Wagner, or an English sermon on Verdi's worthlessness, or a German exegesis on the perfumed decadency of Saint-Saëns, or . . .

Lady Macbeth of the Mtsensk District (Dmitri Shostakovich)
22 January 1934. Leningrad. World Premiere.

With the general cultural development of our country there grew also the necessity for good music. At no time and in no other place has the composer had a more appreciative audience. The people expect good songs, but also good instrumental works, and good operas.

Certain theaters are presenting to the new culturally mature Soviet public Shostakovich's opera *Lady Macbeth* as an innovation and an achievement. Musical criticism, always ready to serve, had praised the opera to the skies and given it resounding glory. The young composer, instead of hearing serious criticism, hears only enthusiastic compliments.

From the first minute, the listener is shocked by deliberate dissonance, by a confused stream of sounds. Snatches of melody, the beginning of a musical phrase, are drowned, emerge again, and disappear, in a grinding and squealing roar. To follow this "music" is most difficult; to remember it, impossible.

Here is music turned deliberately inside out in order that nothing will be reminiscent of classical opera, or have anything in common with symphonic music or with simple and popular musical language accessible to all. This music is built on the basis of rejecting opera—the same basis on which "Leftist" art rejects in the theater simplicity, realism, clarity of image, and the unaffected spoken word. Here we have "Leftist" confusion instead of natural human music. The power of good music to infect the masses has been sacrificed to a petty-bourgeois "formalist" attempt to create originality through cheap clowning. It is a game of clever ingenuity that may end very badly.

Lady Macbeth is having great success with bourgeois audiences abroad. Is it not because the opera is non-political and confusing that they praise it? Is it not explained by the fact that it tickles the perverted taste of the bourgeoisie with its fidgety, neurotic noise?

The talented acting deserves gratitude, the wasted efforts—regrets.

Pravda Editorial. 29 January 1936.

Voice of Ariadne. (Thea Musgrave)
30 September 1977. New York. American Premiere.

One left the theater feeling this was not an opera about to join the permanent repertory.
Opera News. 3 December 1977.

Peter Grimes (Benjamin Britten)
12 February 1948. New York Premiere.

A musical composition skillfully put together, with effective instrumentation and an interesting rhythmical and contrapuntal scheme, would seem to be the main reason for the considerable degree of acclaim that has met this work. Its story is a grim one, and in itself potential of powerful drama. But the libretto is foggy, and both undramatic and untheatrical.

The story is told in rhythmed, and high-falutin' verse—verse of a symbolic, pseudo-philosophic, and undramatic sort, in which there is little emotional reality.

For all that, it is artificial and exterior. The melodic outburst of unmistakable feeling and genuineness, revealing character and emotion in a flash, is not there. So the opera, for us, is only the facade of an opera. The orchestration is one of the strongest features of a virtuoso score.

But in essence this is instrumental, not lyrical music. Music thought throughout as if for instruments. The worst feature of the performance was the very poor and indistinct English. Why it is that with much clamor for opera in English, with an opera that particularly requires distinct enunciation and diction of the best, with American singers singing in their own tongue, the English language suffers as no other language does on the Metropolitan stage?
New York Times. 13 February 1948.

Die Tote Stadt (Erich Wolfgang Korngold)
19 November 1921. American Premiere.

Whether the new opera has the elements making for a long popularity was not entirely made clear yesterday; there are, it may be feared, pages that may be found oppressive. *New York Times.* 29 November 1921.

Der Ring des Nibelungen (Richard Wagner)
13, 14, 16, 17 August 1876. Bayreuth. World Premiere.

During the whole first series of the Wagner tetrology, food was everyone's primary interest, with artistic concerns considerably behind. There was much more talk about steaks, chops, and fried potatoes than about Wagner's music.

From the point of view of a materialistic benefit to mankind, the Bayreuth festival has, of course, no meaning; but from the point of view of artistical ideals, it is destined one way or another to have an enormous historic significance. But in any case what happened in Bayreuth will be well remembered by our grandchildren and our great-grandchildren.

His music has been deeply thought through; it is always interesting music, sometimes splendid and captivating, sometimes a little dry and difficult to understand, a music incredibly rich from the technical point of view and provided with an exceptionally beautiful orchestration.

Wagner shows an astonishing wealth of harmonic and polyphonic technique. The wealth is too great. Constantly forcing our attention, Wagner finally tries it so that at the end of the opera, your fatigue becomes such that the music ceases to be a harmonious combination of sounds and gets to be some kind of tiring noise. What must have been the fatigue of the unprofessional listener?

For the present, speaking quite frankly, the *Ring* impressed me not so much by its musical beauties, of which there may be too generous an amount, as by its lengthiness, its gigantic size. I have a feeling of great fatigue, but along with it I have a desire for further study of this most complicated of all music ever written.

Moscow Gazette. P. I. Tchaikovsky. August 1876.

We conclude our critical sampling with an excerpt from the master who had more than his share of scathing reviews. As a man of the musical theater, he was unparalleled in his dramatic instincts, his melodic inventions, his uncanny rightness in phrasing music to reveal the sublime in the human voice; as a man, he was utterly devoted to music and gave of himself the best that he possibly could to the art that has not seen his better. He was also as Italian as a pizza—Giuseppe Verdi. To you, beloved maestro, we give the final word:

Besides, this is the question: the opera is either bad or good. If it's bad, and the journalists spoke badly of it, they were right; if good, and they preferred not to appreciate it because of their own or other people's whims or for any other reason, it was better to let them have their say and not mind them.

And as to the public, when your conscience tells you that you have written something good, never mind if it is abused (sometimes it's a good sign). The day of justice will come, and it is a great pleasure for the artist, a supreme pleasure, to be able to say: "Imbeciles, you were wrong!"

Ein Heldenlieben

Oh, my life, don't forget, don't betray me ever, faithfully cling to me, remain my Minna, and if you ever felt love, so give it all to me and never let me share it with anyone else. Never forget that my whole heart is yours.
Wagner to Minna Planer. 6 May 1835.

Ah, my Minna, I could never be unfaithful to you!
Wagner to his wife Minna. September 1837.

She was wholly nothing but love. To the God of Love we dedicated ourselves, and despised all the idols of this miserable world so deeply that we did not even think them worthy of mention.
Wagner writing about Jessie Laussot. April 1850.

No one is worth a toss unless he can really be loved by a woman. If only there were more of them.
Wagner to his niece Franziska. October 1852.

In the morning I was reasonable again, and from the depth of my heart could pray to my angel, and this prayer is love! Love! My soul rejoices deeply in its love, the source of my redemption. Be good to me. Take my whole soul as a morning greeting. . . . To save you for me means to save myself for my art. . . . You know that I am yours, and that only you dispose of my actions, deeds, thoughts and resolutions. Now I know that it still is granted to me to die in your arms.
Wagner to Mathilde Wesendonck. 1858.

Overcome, and firmly believe in the perfect sincerity with which I now aspire to nothing—nothing on this earth—but to make up for what has been inflicted on you, to support and guard you, preserve you in loyalty and love.

Wagner to his wife Minna. 14 November 1858.

Adieu, Adieu! Love me, and keep loving me!

Wagner to Cosima von Bülow. 21 September 1862.

Ach, God! How delighted I am to be able to rest again with you there. (I hope the rose-colored pants are ready?) You must be very pretty and charming. I deserve to have a thoroughly good time once more. I leave it wholly to you as to whether you will meet me at the station. Perhaps it would be nicer if you met me first in the house, in the warm rooms. Many kisses to my sweetheart. Au revoir!

Wagner to his maid Marie. 1863.

My dearest love, go on loving me.

Wagner to Mathilde Maier. 3 December 1863.

Ah! Kiss the children and love, love, love me! I breathe you in and feel great strength in you, with you! I want to work wonders and I can do so, but only for you!

Wagner to his wife Cosima. 24 April 1872.

Your love is the most exquisite intoxication, the highest pride of my life, the last gift of the gods, whose will it was that I should not break down under the misery of the delusive glory of the *Nibelungen* performances. Why in heaven's name did I not find you in Paris, after the failure of *Tannhäuser*?

Wagner to Judith Gautier. 1877.

Oh, if I were only vain.

Wagner to Wagner.

Geraldine Farrar
Goes to Hollywood

Cecil B. DeMille. The very sound conjures up shades from Hollywood's mythic past: orange groves, megaphones and puttees, hand-cranked cameras, onyx bathrooms, leashed leopards, Locomobiles, the ramparts of Acre, the hosts of Pharaoh, Gloria Swanson, Yes men, Cooper and Arthur riding across the Great Plains, Claudette Colbert in a bath of asses' milk, Technicolor, Rembrandt lighting, Hedy Lamarr bedecked in a gown of peacock feathers, a masked ball aboard an exploding Zeppelin, Wallace Reid, Leatrice Joy, a malevolent giant squid, a circus train wreck, Charlton Heston stretching forth his staff to part the Red Sea, Cleopatra's barge, the

[185]

burning of Rome, Lux Radio Theater, William Boyd, and Geraldine Farrar.

When Farrar decided to breach another bastion in her glamorous conquest of the world and set her sights upon the movies, she was fortunate indeed to have signed with Jesse Lasky and his Feature Play Company, whose "Director-General" was none other than C. B. DeMille. Although at this time, 1914, Hollywood was yet to be christened the "film capital of the world," overshadowed by the New York and New Jersey studios' prodigious output, and DeMille was not quite yet "Mr. Movies"; the Lasky product, distributed by Paramount Pictures, bespoke quality and prestige, and, perhaps more importantly, was turning a handsome profit for all concerned. Farrar might also have been swayed by a recent DeMille/Lasky success, the screen adaptation of *The Girl of the Golden West.* Farrar, Lasky, and DeMille would all eventually benefit from this alliance.

Approached by the theatrical agent Morris Gest, Lasky was asked what he'd do if Miss Farrar could be convinced of working for him. "What wouldn't I do," was his reply. Choosing her recent Met triumph *Carmen* as her first film, Farrar and entourage set out for California. As the reigning American diva, she was treated to an unprecedented star treatment: a private railroad car outfitted with a Bechstein grand piano and her current honey, Jimmy Sullivan, to provide music and evening amenities; a lavish two-story bungalow equipped with maids, butlers, and cooks; a Hispano-Suiza limousine with chauffeur; a private bungalow at the studio with piano—and Sullivan, apparently; an augmented orchestra on the set to provide mood music for her scenes; living expenses for her companions; billing as "Miss" Farrar; a working day of six hours, to be divided with a midday rest of two hours; and a contract stipulation for Lasky's "best director."

In those faraway days when Hollywood was inventing itself, anyone who had been around since 1908 was already passé. Every day seemed to bring forth a new technique, some new scientific gadget, a better grade of muslin for the sun shades, a new face to be photographed, a different way of photographing that new face. Constant improvisation on and off the set was responsible for turning these pre-war years into an adventure for those lucky enough to have been there. Pushed into Cahuenga Valley, a dusty orange and lemon grove against the Pacific, American ingenuity and western expansion piled on top of each other. The abundant, hot light was perfect for the slow film emulsion; Mexico was close enough to escape into during the constant Patent Wars waged on cameras, projectors, and moviemakers; the landscape had one of everything, unlike Florida, where the New York-based companies shot in the winter; and interference from the east coast offices was checked by the amount of time needed to reach the producers at the far end of the country (when their edict finally reached the moviemakers, the men in the west had already done their dirty work).

It was a new world and a new time. America couldn't get enough of this new amusement, and when Hollywood started supplying it, the world changed a little. This one-horse town in California was the last place where opportunities seemed limitless. Where else could a glove salesman named Sam Goldfish change his name, change his career, and become a movie mogul called Samuel Goldwyn? Not overnight, but certainly within a few years. Hollywood, however, did appear to blossom overnight into the creator and promoter of the twentieth-century's art form.

DeMille arrived in 1913, rather late for a pioneer, intending to go only as far as Arizona with his troupe of Broadway actors to film *The Squaw Man.* The Flagstaff location proved unsuitable because (1) it didn't resemble these city slickers' romantic vision of the West, or (2) it was raining, or (3) the troupe arrived in the midst of a rangeland war between cattlemen and ranchers. Apropos of Hollywood, which gave the world its modern myths and fables, its own history thrives on, and is concealed under, layers of legend and conflicting stories. Since some film companies were already based in Los Angeles—Sennett, Nestor, Biograph—DeMille and entourage piled back into the train and came the rest of the way west. Behind him was an unsuccessful career as actor and playwright. For the next half century, he *was* Hollywood, and his films are paragons of what made the movies the movies.

Except for science fiction, there isn't a genre that DeMille, at one time or another, didn't grace with a film. Although his name is synonymous with gargantuan historic and/or Biblical spectaculars, his neglected early-silent period and his scandalous comedy-of-manners films of the late-teens and twenties are brash, vigorously physical, and always visual, symbolizing and epitomizing America's style, or, even more subtly, America's myth of its own style. His work was highly respected and compared equally to the Grand Master himself, D. W. Griffith, but mercifully free of the latter's cloying Victorian sentimentality, which would eventually be responsible for the slow, agonizing descent of cinema's first great artist. Griffith couldn't change with the times, and his gentlemanly and sometimes perverse view of life, and of women especially, did not suit the Jazz Age; it barely suited the pre-war years. DeMille was blessed: he knew what the audience wanted and he gave it to them with style, energy, and the fresh innocence of a born storyteller. He believed as much in his fantasy visions as did his audience. It's not surprising that his most glorious creation was Cecil B. DeMille—the world's idea of a movie director.

These early films, gloriously photographed in painterly swathes of chiaroscuro, played in solid substantial sets in costumes that look as if they had been lived in by the characters, not freshly sewn by the wardrobe department, and propelled with a dramatic surety that DeMille had honed from his New York days with Belasco, even then had a realism and an elegance of production that was DeMille's own watermark. No one else's movies "looked" like DeMille's, no one else's movies "moved" like DeMille's.

By the time Miss Farrar made her triumphant entry into Los Angeles, DeMille had directed only 15 films. Compared to

D. W. Griffith's 450, this amount might seem to indicate a journeyman's knowledge of cinematic technique, but DeMille was born to the new medium. Innovative, experimental, and sumptuously visual, he was able to retain his own uncompromised vision. He was incredibly shrewd, and lucky, this way. There have been but a handful of cinema artists whose films have been enormously successful and good at the same time. C. B. DeMille is right up there in that pantheon, probably front row center.

In a clever masterstroke, DeMille announced to a startled Jesse Lasky that *Carmen* should not be their first film with Miss Farrar. He was well aware that film acting was something quite different than theater dramatics. Underplayed and subtle, it demanded a naturalism that was the antithesis of "playing to the gallery." Here, the camera was the gallery; the flicker of an eyebrow could say a paragraph of dialogue. Anything emoted would play false. Since opera is, perhaps, the most artificial of the arts, his doubts were well founded. He wanted Miss Farrar to "cut her motion picture teeth" on *Maria Rosa,* a Spanish love story not unlike *Carmen. Carmen* could then be released first, since it had already been announced as her debut, but after she had become accustomed to how the movies worked. Both Lasky and Farrar, to everyone's relief, heartily agreed. DeMille's worries proved unfounded. "I learned more than our star did," he confessed.

DeMille was pleased with Farrar's professionalism. "I have no compliment in my vocabulary higher than to call anyone a good workman." That she was indeed a good workman is evident in her performances, but she could be every bit as temperamental a diva as she was at the Metropolitan. Dissatisfied with her lavish studio bungalow, she ordered it redecorated by DeMille's master set designer Wilfred Buckland; she fought with Jeanie Macpherson, DeMille's scriptwriter, receiving endless revisions; she detested the garish klieg lights which made her eyes swell up and water constantly; and she complained about the heavy grease paint makeup with its lurid blue or green eyeshadow. To both Farrar and DeMille's consternation, the blinding klieg lights washed out her pale grey eyes and most of her teeth. When photographed, Farrar looked like a toothless Little Orphan Annie. DeMille and his magnificent cinematographer Alvin Wyckoff expertly solved the problem the next day by draping black velvet behind the camera and using more side light. Farrar regained her beauty, but the grease paint remained. In those primitive days of intensely hot, harsh studio lighting, there was no other way for skin tones to record on film and appear natural without the impasto of mask-like makeup. Only when a photographic emulsion was perfected which had a higher sensitivity to light were the arcs able to be toned down, and then Max Factor and The House of Westmore could rise to prominence. Of course, when Technicolor was introduced, the very same problems of incredibly bright, hot light and thick makeup returned with a vengeance.

Maria Rosa is a second-hand *Carmen* with a similar love triangle set in Spain, but with Micaëla substituted as the lead. Andreas and Ramon vie for the affections of this earthy peasant lass. Having killed a fisherman who made passes at Maria Rosa, Ramon, jealous of his friend Andreas, plants Andreas's knife at the scene of the crime. This heroine remains pure and steadfast while her lover languishes in prison, framed for a murder he didn't commit. Rebuffed in his wooing, and told by her that she will not wed "while Andreas lives," the jilted suitor cracks through her resistance by having a letter forged saying that Andreas has died in prison. Falling for the scam, Maria Rosa agrees to marry Ramon. On the prison work gang, Andreas saves the life of the Minister of State's child, who has wandered into the construction area that is being dynamited, and is granted a pardon. Returning to the village after the marriage ceremony, he surprises Maria Rosa as she prepares for her wedding night. Overjoyed, to say the least, she still intends to fulfill her vow of revenge upon her false husband. Playfully seducing Ramon to confess both to the killing and to sending his friend to prison, Maria Rosa stabs him with a butcher knife.

Unsullied and true to her word, she and Andreas greet the dawn with renewed hope.

Seeing this film almost seventy years after its premiere, there can be no doubt that Miss Farrar knew what she was doing. Under DeMille's sure guidance, her performance is remarkable. She could give lessons to Meryl Streep. We tend to encapsulate silent picture acting as an unending reel of florid gestures and Bernhardt posings, eyeball poppings and grand flourishes. Some of that, to be sure, existed; it still exists today on the screen. But the freshness, the naturalness, the believability, the insightfulness that these "old-timers" brought to film acting is wonderful to behold. Jane Fonda, Robert Redford, Dustin Hoffman, and many others in current cinema stardom look like ciphers next to Mae Marsh, Leatrice Joy, Robert Harron, and Mabel Normand. The modern breed tries too hard to act; their efforts are mistakenly applauded, not their results. Farrar is luminous in a way that Garbo and Dietrich would later be—you can't take your eyes off her. She seems to do everything right, nothing is overwrought or false. She is, at once, charming in the first scenes as a peasant girl hitching her wagon to take her vegetables to market, playfully alluring as she's wooed simultaneously, and graceful in her pantomime rebuff of the fisherman as she indicates that she doesn't want him or his fish. She conveys her character's inner strength as she reads the bogus letter and stands like an oak; and, later, crossing herself upon seeing Andreas's specter in the mirror, she reveals herself as a real pro when she realizes with a mixture of abundant joy and equal horror that her lover has returned upon her wedding night. If *Maria Rosa* shows just what a first-rate job Farrar could do in her first attempt in the movies, *Carmen* proves her a star.

Farrar's stage Carmen was much lauded in the press and, thanks to the film version, her interpretation has been preserved. Now we know what prompted all that clamor and praise. She must have been a knockout at the Met, because she's dazzling in the movie. A seductive tigress, an amoral spitfire, a stunning beauty wrapped in her shawl with a carnation in her teeth. The story has been compressed into a zippy one-and-a-half hours. Mercifully, Micaëla has been dropped, and Carmen is in league with the smugglers right from the start and is already Escamillo's lover when she volunteers to lure Don José from his post so the contraband can be smuggled into the city. "Every man can be bought . . . with something." Standing in the breech of the ramparts, she brazenly flirts with him, shoving her carnation into his face. With her beauty, fiery charm, and a heavy dose of modern sex appeal, no Don José could resist her. At Pastia's tavern, while embracing Escamillo, she gives the once-over to the handsome officer who has followed her. After a tabletop dance with castanets, she falls into Don José's arms in close-up. She's hooked him. Hearing the bugle call for the soldiers' return, Don José carries her to the doorway. She closes the heavy door on him but peeks out through the window slot, taunting him, "My kisses are not so easily won." She then turns and woos Escamillo with a cigarette in her mouth.

Farrar's a dangerous, sexy, tremendously physical lady of Spain—kicking away admirers, fighting alongside Don José in his tavern brawl wherein they make their escape, or slugging it out in a rowdy catfight with one of the factory girls. She's not ruled so much by fate as by a desire to have fun on her own terms. When Escamillo tempts her with visions of wealth and respectability as his mistress in Seville, she tosses Don José's ring into the fire and rides off with the matador. Arriving at the bullring with the successful Escamillo in a sumptuous carriage and wearing a white lace gown, she has indeed achieved the outward trappings of propriety. When Don José, disgraced, in brigand's attire of bandanna, rolled-up sleeves, and open shirt, confronts her with: "I wait for your lover," she yawns in his face. "My love is mine to give or deny." Enraged, Don José prevents her escape in the narrow corridor to the bullfighter's entrance. Blazingly backlit so the flies and dust motes swirl about them, he viciously pulls her down by the hair from her attempted climb over the gate and stabs her and then himself. It's a claustrophobic and terrifying death scene, punctuated and contrasted, as in the opera, by Escamillo's brilliant flourishes in the arena.

Farrar's temptress is matched by Wallace Reid's virile yet woebegone Don José and Pedro de Cordoba's macho Escamillo. Reid, launched into stardom by DeMille in *Maria Rosa*, would be Farrar's leading man in three subsequent films and, by 1923, be among the pantheon of Hollywood's great male stars when he tragically died from morphine addiction. His death, along with Fatty Arbuckle's rape trial, and the still "unsolved" murder of the Paramount director William Desmond Taylor—the three great scandals of early-twenties Hollywood—ushered in the censoring Hays Code and firmly implanted in the minds of staid Americans the eternal image of Hollywood as modern Sodom, Babylon, and every other imaginable den of iniquity. That Reid's addiction was caused by treatment for an injury sustained on a movie set, and his habit nonchalantly encouraged by the studio, and that he died in agony in a sanatorium trying to go cold turkey; or that Arbuckle was acquitted after three trials with a fulsome apology from the jury—although he and Hollywood were tried and found guilty by Hearst's yellow rags, his films blacklisted, and his career virtually destroyed; or that Taylor was killed by Mary Miles Minter's harpy of a stage mother, Charlotte Shelby, although gossip and innuendos implicated Minter and Mabel Normand—whose floundering careers were also destroyed by implication—was not nearly as juicy as the fantasyland the press created.

Immediately upon completion of *Carmen*, DeMille and Farrar made *Temptation*, also to be withheld until the release of *Carmen*. The title refers to a physical choice Miss Farrar must make in order to secure funds for her ailing boyfriend. That the offer comes from a lecherous opera impresario and that Farrar plays an aspiring singer must have seemed like a fun way to prick the Met. In heavy mustache and opera cape, Theodore Roberts even looks like Gatti-Casazza. Naturally, with the sacrifice close at hand, the impresario is neatly dispatched by a jealous mistress, and all ends happily. Just like in opera. The screenplay was written by Hector Turnbill, the dramatic critic for the

New York Herald Tribune, who was lured into DeMille's writers stable by C. B.'s brother, William, an unrepentant Broadway playwright. Although bits of backstage theatrics were supplied by him, the film is not a prime feather in anyone's cap, although Farrar, as usual, is radiant, whether singing at the piano in the composer's meager apartment or veiled and crowned for performance. Turnbill's great success would be his screenplay for DeMille's *The Cheat* (1915), a scandalous success of a melodrama with its famed and lurid scene where Sessue Hayakawa brutally brands Fannie Ward on the shoulder when she tries to repay her debt with cash instead of the implied flesh.

Farrar's specified contract period was concluded with these three films and she returned for her next season at the Met to cause a stir when she bit Caruso's Don José and actually kicked and fought with one of the cigarette girls. The audiences loved it, Caruso decried what the movies had done to her and to his hand, while Gerry's beloved stagehands described the show as "a pip!" At the end of the season, she was also responsible in large part for Toscanini leaving the Met. She had apparently given him an ultimatum: your wife or me. Toscanini vacillated, but with his Italian sense of duty and honor rising like the plume of Vesuvius, he chose his wife. He couldn't bear to be in the same theater with the powerful force of Farrar lurking among the sets, forever reminding him of their affair. That Gatti-Casazza and Kahn were also giving him trouble helped persuade him to leave. Fortunately his indecision cancelled his first booking on the ship to Europe—the ill-fated *Lusitania.* However, if Farrar was disconsolate with Toscanini's rebuff, she had these new operatic successes and the rave responses to her new career to console her. If not Toscanini, Farrar had conquered the movies . . . and the reviewers:

> Geraldine Farrar has put her heart and soul and body into this picture, and without the aid of the magic of her voice, has proved herself one of the greatest actresses of all times. Her picture *Carmen* will live long after her operatic characterization

has died in the limbo of forgotten singers. Her acting in this production is one of the marvels of the stage and screen, so natural, so realistic that it is hard to believe that it is acting. *New York Dramatic Mirror.* 6 November 1915.

One cannot do justice to *Carmen.* It is a picture of finesse, encompassing the sincere efforts of a great player—even to the point of a very rough treatment accorded the expensive person of a prima donna—of a great director and of a loyal studio support. It is all done with a swift deftness that makes the point without the wearisome tediousness of other directors less artistic than Cecil B. DeMille.
Chicago Tribune. 6 October 1915.

It is a curious commentary on the crazy economy of the theater that a supreme dramatic soprano should give any of her precious time to a form of entertainment, to an art if you will, wherein the chief characteristic is a complete and abysmal silence. But, though the call of the movies is audible enough, there is small reason to fear that, after Miss Farrar's success, there will be a great rush of prima donnas to California, for precious few of them could so meet the exactions of the camera.
New York Times. 1 November 1915.

Having seen Geraldine Farrar in all her great roles, both on the singing and on the silent stage, I have no hesitation whatever in saying that in the part of Maria Rosa she has reached her greatest histrionic triumph.
The Moving Picture World. 13 May 1916.

The manner of the telling makes this old story [*Maria Rosa*] of the triangle seem new. Its mountings, settings, and acting are sufficient to make it distinctly a "worthwhile" picture, and its star, Geraldine Farrar, is a guarantee of box-office quality.
Motion Picture News. 13 May 1916.

The wonderful personality, the magnetism, and above all the inimitable histrionic power of Geraldine Farrar are brought out in this picture [*Temptation*] even more strongly than in *Carmen.*

[195]

The photography is of the highest standard, and the master hand of director DeMille is discernible throughout.
New York Dramatic Mirror. 8 January 1916.

When La Farrar returned to California in the spring of 1916, DeMille's inspired choice for her fourth motion picture was the story of John of Arc, *Joan The Woman.* This is certainly Farrar's best film and one of DeMille's finest productions. In drama there's no role more difficult to play than a good woman. What actress wants to be burdened, unappreciated, with a thankless character like the suffering Krystal when she could vamp it up, oh so wickedly, as the bitch Alexis? Joan Collins is no fool. When you must play a good woman *and* a saint, the problems increase exponentially. Fortunately, the Maid of Orleans has a historically built-in escape hatch: she was a great soldier. Rampaging through battle scenes, she managed to tarnish the halo with all that spilled English blood. She may have heard voices and been as pious as an icon, but she marched in front of her men, swinging her broadsword, and whacked off limbs like a deranged charcutière.

Joan The Woman was DeMille's first spectacle picture and it's a stunning eyeful. The key to his later, great successes in this genre lay here. He never sacrificed the personal story for screen-filling excess for its own sake; the former was always given precedence and played out against the historical background. Mere pageant never interested him. After a brief one-shot prologue where she stands up from her spinning wheel and assumes the martyr's crucifixion pose against a blinding fleur-de-lis pattern throw on the wall (so DeMillian!), Joan is established as a gusty peasant lass who is ashamed to witness her village's craven desertion before the English. When she hides an English soldier, whom she has taken a fancy to, in the hay loft to recuperate from wounds, she playfully brings him a bouquet of flowers. Trent, played by Wallace Reid, awakens feelings of love in her, but when she absently tries on his gauntlet her face is suffused with light and we know she has found her fate. The appearance of an armored androgynous angel commanding her "to save France" is quite unnecessary when we've just seen the command visually burned into her face. (Audiences needed help in 1916.)

Farrar, in DeMille's words, had "lost a little something of the great spark of genius that animated her last year and, also, has gotten pretty plump. Although she is tremendously enthused over the story and says it is the greatest work of her life, at the same time, that little spark is missing. She may get it as we go on in the work." Get it she did, for Farrar is ideal as Joan. Her plumpness works in her favor, she looks as if she could command a legion and swing a sword and carry a banner at the same time, which she does. It's a remarkable performance, with only one-too-many gazes skyward to suggest her saintliness. In the early scenes, she drives sheep with a mastery she would later use with her flock of geese in *Königskinder* at the Met. Later, she plows across the moat during the fortress siege of La Tourelle treading on dead soldiers and horses, scales the wall holding her banner aloft, is shot with an arrow, defiantly pulls it out herself, and leads her men onward in the final winning surge. During the trial scene and threatened with torture in the dungeon, she conveys a real sense of helplessness and despair over her torments, while fearful visions of hooded inquisitors dissolve around her. The shooting of the moat scene required Farrar to spend five days up to her waist in water. DeMille was worried that her voice would suffer, but Gerry carried on like a trooper. It was DeMille who came down with laryngitis.

Apart from Farrar's portrayal, it is DeMille's unfailing visual sense which keeps this story from turning into a sanctimonious morality play. When Joan takes leave of her sleeping family to seek help from the Governor, she kisses her sister and simply, slowly, backs out of the frame, leaving a void. As she pleads to Charles for soldiers to command, the court is trampled by victorious knights on chargers—in double exposure—symbolizing France's great need. The siege's final victory is shown by an English soldier on the parapet, shot by an arrow, desperately clutching at the flag to stop his fall, and tearing it from the flagpole as he topples to his death with the standard billowing behind him. When Joan renounces her love for Trent, saying "there is room in my heart for one love—France," she stands alone in the vastness of Reims Cathedral, strewn with the trampled remains of thousands of flowers that had been previously thrown at her feet in praise. Successful in his ransom of Joan from the English, the Bishop of Cauchon reaches into the frame and latches onto Joan's shoulder. The burning at the stake is chillingly evoked: first the cartman hauls in his load of sticks and piles them offhandedly around the stake; then the curious townsfolk assemble for a bit of entertainment; Trent offers Joan a twig crucifix; against the blackness of the roiling smoke, the hand-tinted orange flames radiate a horrifying heat.

If anything in the way of evidence were needed to convince the photoplay-going public that Cecil B. DeMille belongs in the front rank of the day, his direction of *Joan The Woman* should supply it in full measure.
Moving Picture World. 13 January 1917.

Joan The Woman is a triumph for Geraldine Farrar, but equally as much is it a triumph for Cecil DeMille, its producer. Through his long picture he has interpolated the personal and the spectacular veins of interest with the fine result of dramatic contrast.
Motion Picture News. 6 January 1917.

It is impossible to describe in detail what producer DeMille accomplished with such a wealth of material. Suffice it to say that no one else could have done more and few, if any, could have done as much.
Weekly Variety. 29 December 1916.

Don't let anyone convince you otherwise. Surrealism did not begin in France with André Breton's *Manifeste* of 1924; it started in Hollywood, and Farrar and DeMille's *The Woman God Forgot* (1917) is a prime example. This bizarre film, barely over an hour, recounts the tale of the Spanish conquest of the Aztec empire, based upon R. Haggard's *Montezuma's Daughter*. It happened, so the film makers tell us, because Tezca (a feeble use of anagram), the daughter of Montezuma, opens the gates of Tenochtitlán under promise by Cortez not to harm her people so that he can save her lover, Cortez's Captain, from human sacrifice. Of course, once Cortez enters the city, all hell breaks loose. After a magnificently stirring battle around, about, and atop a steep-sided teocalli, all Aztecs are destroyed and only Tezca, cursed by her own gods, is spared since she is the last of the line. Living quietly in a valley that looks suspiciously like Yellowstone National Park, the Captain finds her and declares his love. Very happy fade-out.

There are more quetzal feathers, jaguar skins, and leopard pelts than a Blackgama showroom. Farrar, slimmed down from the rigors of *Joan,* is arrayed in a startling wardrobe that mixes Art Deco-Mexico with jeweled brassieres and chic Poiret-inspired gowns that would look most becoming at a Noel Coward dinner party. As we expect from DeMille, his visuals propel the action and say more than a reel of subtitles. Bowers of magnolias and magnificent blooms encircle the menagerie of tropical birds and animals wandering through Montezuma's gardens, while Farrar munches on figs and is surrounded by scantily clad Indian maidens; Montezuma's writing desk is supported on the backs of slaves; Alvarado makes his entrance into the court of the Aztec emperor on horseback, scattering the startled attendants; pierced by arrows, Alvarado makes his escape but leaves blood stains on the wall that will be traced to his hiding place in Tezca's bedroom. The whole thing is a fantasy parade that marches by without the slightest thought to historical accuracy except in the sets and costumes other than the star's. Theodore Kosloff, a refugee from the Ballet Russe, hams it up in the highest camp possible, flexing his massive thighs to register emotion, while Wallace Reid epitomizes a picturebook's idea of the dashing conquistador. The film is such a harmless, mindless bauble that, in contrast, the battle on the pyramid is truly shocking. Horses stumble up the steep staircase, men plummet off its heights or slide sickeningly down its slick polished sides. In long-shot, the teocalli teems with ant-sized armies. In the days before the ASPCA and SAG, how many horses were sent to the glue factory and how many extras were hurt filming such spectacular scenes we can only guess at—but it's exciting cinema, to say the least.

Variously described by the critics as "piffling," "calculating," or "a production of excellent artistry and photography," *The Devil Stone* (1917) was described by Farrar as "almost like a holiday on the beaches." She might have thought it so, but DeMille and Lasky were growing frustrated with their temperamental diva, and their last film together is a half-hearted affair stitched together out of a story by DeMille's mother and Jeanie Macpherson. Here, Farrar gets a chance to be a Breton fisherwoman, a society grande dame, and the incarnation of a cruel Norse queen, who looks like Brünnhilde with a headache. It's a patchwork that includes a cursed emerald, a debauched tycoon, superstition and witchcraft, and, guess who, Wallace Reid as the hero. At this time, Farrar was pushing Lasky to rehire her husband Lou Tellegen as a director. Tellegen, Bernhardt's former co-star, had acted in minor roles and had worked for Lasky, but his directing debut was a flop and both Lasky and DeMille wanted no more work from him. While Tellegen lay on a couch in full view of DeMille, Farrar, blocking the doorway, was his spokesman. "Geraldine met me with the air of a lioness defending her young," DeMille recalled. "She was magnificent, but I was firm. Both Geraldine and I have some small gift of forceful speech when aroused. All through the conversation, the subject of it lay blandly on his couch, letting Geraldine defend him." Six years later, Farrar would divorce him, and upon his death would say, "May those tormented ashes rest in peace."

Both parties knew that a renewal of Farrar's contract would not be forthcoming, and an amicable parting was achieved.

Farrar signed with Goldwyn, who had broken inimically from Lasky. She made four undistinguished films in his studios at Fort Lee, New Jersey, in 1918, and three final ones with Tellegen as her leading man at Goldwyn's new studios in Culver City. Whatever else Goldwyn might have been as a motion picture producer and a veritable source of malapropisms, he was no DeMille. Even Farrar noticed this, and describes her final fade-outs in the movies as "tepid narratives," "lunatic fancies," and "irritations." For Goldwyn, she might have worn bird of paradise hats and sable coats from Bendel's, but DeMille had always valued story over wardrobe. At the very least, he had given her star vehicles—and two recognized classics, *Carmen* and *Joan The Woman*. The Goldwyn films lost money, the studio was compromised, yet Farrar still had a two-year contract with a guarantee of two hundred and fifty thousand dollars. Knowing this venture was a lost cause, she magnanimously tore up the contract, to Sam's amazed consternation but eternal gratitude. A pathetic Pathé effort followed in 1920 called *The Riddle-Woman,* which Farrar said was "spoiled by poor writing, poor camera-work, and impossible direction." And she was out of the movies, soon to leave the opera stage as well.

Upon Farrar's first arrival in Hollywood, she was greeted with *Photoplay*'s boorish assessment of her decision to appear in films: "The Mona Lisa without her smile; a Stradivarius without its strings." As if she needed her voice! She and DeMille went on to prove the magazine wildly mistaken. Writing about this amazing part of her varied career, Farrar said, "I had greatly enjoyed them, and only regret my own era was too early for the combination of the present acting and talking features. . . . Didn't we have fun, though!"

You're not alone in your regrets, Miss Farrar, but your silent voice, your DeMille voice, still sings out to us loud and clear. And the fun couldn't be more evident, or infectious.

Backstage at Bayreuth

The whole place is uninteresting—a mere peasant's town, with close, narrow, dingy streets; it is very ancient but far from honorable, and our first impressions were anything but agreeable. The inhabitants are homely, simple and primitive, and their heads are completely turned by the Festival. They think their golden harvest has come, and regard Richard Wagner as their Messiah. Everything and everybody are in the direst confusion and excitement—a continual stream of people coming and going; but the worst rush was for the first series of performances.

It is useless for me to name all their jaw-breaking titles: princes, dukes and grand dukes, etc., the Emperor William, with suite of thirty-eight persons, attended by his daughter, the Grand Duchess of Baden, and her husband, and the Emperor of Brazil and suite. The young king, Ludwig of Bavaria, arrived here the 6th and immediately retired to a small summer castle called the Hermitage, from whence he did not emerge except to attend the opera, which was to be performed for him *alone;* not a soul was allowed to see it save His Majesty, in order that he might enjoy it undisturbed and unmolested.

He was shy and peculiar as ever, coming and going like a thief in the night, and avoiding every possible contact with the people. He attended only the general rehearsals and then left, but he is now expected for the last representations, with the queen mother.

Saint-Saëns, Sullivan, Tchaikovsky and other musical celebrities are here, and it is rumored that Von Bülow is in an insane asylum because he cannot be present, on account of his embarrassing family relations with Wagner. Though he adores his music, it would never do.

I have seen Von Bülow's four daughters, Senta, Isolde, Eva, and Elisabeth, and they are perfect likenesses of their father. They are called Wagner and are very pretty, charming girls. The oldest is about eighteen and assists her mother to entertain the guests. But the favorite of all is little Siegfried, seven years old and Wagner's only child, a perfect little hero and a chip off the old block.

Mme. Wagner is exceedingly gracious and affable. She is a magnificent-looking woman, a perfect queen (some call her a despot), and dresses elegantly, always with a great deal of expensive white lace, and is never seen in the same dress twice. She is at home mornings from eleven to twelve and gives a reception to the Patrons once a week. They are very grand affairs, and all the great people attend them.

Liszt does not look at all formidable, but very much like a good old grandpa; he shows his seventy-two years and walks rather feebly. Whenever he appears, all salute him.

Here I have been gossiping all this time about everything else but the one important subject, Music. I shall not attempt to give you any learned dissection of the opera, although I am quite familiar with it now, having heard it four times. It is so very absorbing that when one is not in the theater itself one is studying—before and after the performances and the three days between the representations—either the exquisitely beautiful text, with its deep poetical meaning, or the grand music itself with its wonderful variety, richness, and difficult instrumentation. Your whole life here is *Der Ring des Nibelungen,* and the very atmosphere you breathe is Wagner.

I think I enjoyed the rehearsals even better than the performances; they had such an element of sociability and freedom about them. It is a question with me which is stronger, Wagner or his music. It was overpowering and miraculous to me as I watched the stage during the rehearsals and saw the little man with the big head, seated on a chair in a corner, directing his own creation.

He was indefatigable. At one moment on the stage, the next he was beside you; but, of course, we pretended not to see him

[203]

and seemed all absorbed in the drama. He is exceedingly nervous, sits quiet for an instant, then, "Potzausend Donnerwetter," he rushed off and appears on the stage, knocks off very unceremoniously Gunther's crown, giving him to understand it should not be on his head at that particular passage; then he stamps up and down in front of "the mystic circle" and scolds Hans Richter. The great conductor holds his own and does not give in one iota to W., as he knows the score even better than the composer. It was very entertaining to listen to the quarrel, for it seemed like an imaginary one, as we did not see Richter but only heard his calm voice coming up from the depths below. The illusion of the concealed orchestra is perfect, but many think it is sunk too low and that the "chaise-top" muffles the sound too much.

I was somewhat crestfallen when I arrived at the theater, at my first rehearsal, with my four large books of the music that I had dragged with me all the way from America, to find the auditorium so pitchy dark that one could barely stumble into a seat. It is one of Wagner's theories that the audience shall sit completely in the dark; people are expected to know the text and music thoroughly before they come here. Not once are the lights turned on during the acts.

Suddenly from some part of the house, Wagner frantically shouts, "Darker! darker! It's much too light!" And then again we are shrouded in night. The stage itself is rarely very bright —a rather subdued light that seems to have a sort of gloom cast over it.

On the whole there is not much enthusiastic demonstration, as Wagner has rather quelled it by forbidding the actors to appear before the curtain and putting up posters all over the house saying that the company were very grateful for the applause of the public but had decided to remain "in the frame" of the composition they had figured in. Wagner is very willing to show himself, and appears after each series. He is most always "overcome with emotion" and frequently "speechifies."

One word about Mme. Materna. It is utterly impossible to conceive of her voice. I write without any partiality, for I did not believe such a voice existed as hers. It is the grandest, the most powerful, the most magnificent voice I have ever heard. She is also a dramatic actress, a queen of tragedy; but all, *all* is forgotten while listening to her voice. Her conception of Brünn-hilde is complete; she is a perfect goddess with a woman's heart. The way she rolls out the high C's and flings away the A flats is petrifying; your very blood stops circulating.

Oh, believe me! Engrave the name of Materna in your mind, so that you may be prepared to enjoy the feast should she ever visit America, which she talks of doing very soon. I would make a pilgrimage on my knees to her shrine, any time.

The Boston Gazette. Grace M. Tilton. August 1876.

Skeletons to Be Exhumed

hat's a nice romantic guy like Carl Maria von Weber doing without a date? Here he sits—the inspirer of Wagner; the "child" who single-handedly transformed the musty, shopworn operatic conventions of the nineteenth-century into a true, dramatic musical theater; the precursor of Toscanini who ruled the podium with his "iron scepter" and expected "implicit obedience," tempered with justice, "but pitilessly severe with all who need severity—myself included"; the first great piano virtuoso who toured Europe; perhaps the first composer to be thrown into jail; a writer and critic; a lithographer; *and* the musical Father of German Romanticism —lonely, like a wallflower at the ball, his ravishing works languishing for want of performance other than those token revivals that reek of embalmed roses and yellow dance cards.

Why are *Der Freischütz* (1821), *Euryanthe* (1823), and *Oberon* (1826) not in the standard repertoire? Are managers deaf? Dumb? Unless you're fortunate enough to be in Germany for the opera season, you'll have nary a chance anywhere else in Europe to see these; here, in the U.S., the only performances of the three you're likely to hear are the ones you play on your stereo. And as for seeing Weber's adorable, *buffa singspiel Abu Hassan* (1811), you might as well be living in Tanzania. It's a sad, sad, sorry state of operatic affairs when the magnificent von Weber goes unheard and unseen.

Ever since its precedent-shattering premiere, *Der Freischütz* has been appreciated for the swift kick it had given to the rotund posterior of Italian opera, which had been sitting around, eating chocolates, becoming useless. Romanticism swept in with Weber's spontaneous freshness, his atmospheric tone painting, his folksy, danceable tunes, and his other-worldliness. Audiences had neither seen nor heard such things in the opera house. The revolution began!

Weber was fortunate to be born into an age undergoing spectacular transition. The Enlightenment, culminating in the French and the Industrial revolutions, had nowhere else to go. Reason had hit a brick wall; the illusive Romanticism went straight through the chinks. When man's emotions were allowed predominance, classicism was doomed, and art flourished for its own sake. The novel ideas of personal expression, "beauty without bounds," a renewal in things Eastern, fantasy, an awareness of nature's wonders, and individual freedom sprouted and grew rampant throughout the West. Everything seemed to offer rich, nurturing soil: politics, literature, architecture, fashion, painting, and especially music. Weber made it just in time. That grand old titan Beethoven, with the help of Schubert, straddled the old and the new worlds, but it was Weber who had both feet on the other side, although he would be dead one year before Ludwig and two before Franz.

Weber's evocative musical imagination and his utter dramatic power is hard to beat. His music for the theater is fresh and absolutely right. *Freischütz's* justly famous Act II *Wolf Glen* scene is chilling, and you can understand why women and men felt faint and lightheaded, and physicians of the day coined the term "Freischützfieber" for what ailed them. *Euryanthe,* commissioned by that ubiquitous impresario Barbaja, has been damned ever since its premiere in Vienna because of Ms. Chézy's overheated story, but there's no more silliness here than in *Lohengrin,* which it remarkably resembles, except for its happy ending and a large snake that appears in Act III. It has the same medieval pomp, a "good" couple and a "bad" couple, who even sing a vengeance duet and make a pact with the powers of evil, the same seriousness of purpose, a chorus used as a protagonist, and an uninterrupted and continuous musical flow—Weber's first work without spoken dialogue. However, there is that problem with the snake. Within the book's chivalrous subtext of "trials by combat," this ophidian apparition is fairly acceptable, it's just impossible to stage. Even brilliant music can't disguise papier-mâché. Try as he might, even Wagner couldn't make his Fafner serious.

After the lukewarm success of *Euryanthe,* Weber didn't write anything for a year and a half, but sudden anxieties over leaving his family without sufficient funds convinced him to accept Charles Kemble's commission to write a work for Covent Garden. Weber knew he was dying, but he tore into the work with an unconcerned vigor, learning English in the process. There seemed to be nothing this nineteenth-century Renaissance man couldn't do. In spite of dire consequences foretold by his doctor, he traveled to London to fulfill his contract. Proceeding via Paris to visit his mentor Cherubini, he met his *bête noire,* Rossini, who also urged him to return, but Weber was determined to provide for his family.

Oberon, light-years away from the work of a dying man, is Weber's masterpiece. The Romanticism here is delightfully storybook, awash with a fairy tale's primary colors. Oberon, Titania, and Puck mix it up with a manly knight, a caliph's daughter, the Emir of Turkey, the Emperor Charlemagne, magic horns and spells, Persian princes, pirates, and mermaids. It is a captivating hodgepodge, ravishingly scored to sublime, enchanting melodies. The great set-piece, Rezia's second-act aria *Ocean, thou mighty monster,* a concert favorite of many dramatic sopranos, requires the lyric declamations of Leonora's *Abscheulicher* belted with the lungs of Kate Smith. Once more, the text was blasted as being a major hindrance and fairly stupid, but if you love *Zauberflöte,* you'll have no problem with this. Weber wasn't entirely satisfied with the spoken dialogue either and planned a revision for the German premiere, which he did not live to see, dying in London three months after he had arrived, just as his doctor predicted. *Oberon* has seen more recutting and revisions than *Heaven's Gate.* One can choose versions with dialogue, a little dialogue, or no dialogue. Whichever one should be chosen, the production will not suffer since it is set to such intoxicating music.

While Carl Maria von Weber was, surely, a man of his time, he was just as surely a man ahead of his time. The sumptuousness of his melody, his dramatic power, his descriptive evocation of character, nature, and emotion are truly some of the musical wonders of the world. Certainly, it should be possible to mount these operatic jewels in appropriate settings where they could sparkle and be appreciated for their uncommon, multi-faceted beauties. Fortunately, they are priceless, so keeping these gems locked in a drawer won't devalue them. But when they are displayed, what is currently admired will seem like paste.

Poor Pietro Mascagni reached the heights of his creative talent at the age of twenty-seven and lived another fifty-five years trying to rescale them, dying at the age of eighty-one on 2 August 1945. He assessed his career perfectly: "It was a pity that I wrote *Cavalleria* first. I was crowned before I was king."

Pietro's parents wanted him to study law, so he had to sneak off and surreptitiously study his beloved music. For a while in his youth he lived with an uncle who was willing to care for the family outcast. As early as 1879, at the age of fifteen, his

Symphony in C minor and a Kyrie were performed at the Instituto Luigi Cherubini, where he studied. Later he attended the Milan Conservatory, but academic life did not agree with him and he joined a touring opera company as conductor, spending a number of years in virtual starvation. After marrying, he settled in Cerignola near Foggia, eking out a meager living teaching piano and managing the municipal school of music.

Dire poverty caused young Mascagni to enter a contest for one-act operas sponsored by the Milan publishing house of Eduardo Sonzogno. He won handsomely with *Cavalleria Rusticana.* The opera's premiere at the Teatro Costanzi in Rome on 17 May 1890 marked not only the end of poverty for Mascagni but also the birth of "verismo." Like wildfire, *Cavalleria* spread throughout Italy and within two years had been heard in Berlin, New York, London, and Paris. Pietro Mascagni was famous overnight, and his fame endures to this day, resting upon that one crude and common melodrama.

Mascagni composed more than a dozen operas thereafter, to decreasing success with each work. First was *L'amico Fritz* (1891) followed by *I Rantzau* (1892). *Guglielmo Ratcliff,* a rewritten work from his student days, and *Silvano* were given at La Scala in 1895, both decisive failures. In 1896 *Zanetto,* scored for only strings and harp, saw the brief light of day, and *Iris,* a tear-jerker set to a Japanese story, had its debut in Rome in 1898. The year 1901 saw *Le Maschere* audaciously premiered in seven cities simultaneously, including Milan, where the audience greeted it with cries of "viva, Puccini" and Genoa, where the audience didn't even allow the performance to be finished. *Amica* was a flop in 1905, as was the 1911 *Isabeau,* based on the Lady Godiva legend. Mascagni's remaining bombs were *Parisana* (1913), a sentimental melodrama *Lodoletta* (1917), his attempt at operetta, *Si* (1919), *Il piccolo Marat* (1921), *Pinotta* (1932), and finally *Nerone* (1935). In the early part of this century *L'amico Fritz, Iris,* and *Lodoletta* were given at the Metropolitan with the greatest singers of the day, yet the total number of performances for all three operas at the Met was twenty-six, whereas *Cavalleria* has been given there hundreds of times.

[211]

Out of all these turkeys there is one which deserves to be heard more, *L'amico Fritz*. It is performed with some frequency in Italy, but even there it's been met with derision, reputedly laughed off the stage in Parma in 1892 and again in 1908. The opera is set in Alsace at the home of a wealthy young bachelor, Fritz, who has sworn never to marry, making a bet with his friend, the rabbi David, that if he should take a wife, David will get his vineyard. David, the matchmaker, through machinations connives to marry him off to Suzel, the daughter of Fritz's steward. In the end Fritz asks for Suzel's hand, and David gives her the vineyard for her wedding present. In 1938, adopting the Nazi's racial laws, David became a doctor, not a rabbi, a practice that occasionally occurs to this day in Italy.

As you can tell, the plot is as delicate as a bouquet of spring violets and just as refreshing and evanescent. Gustav Mahler, a lifelong champion of Mascagni, said that it showed a decisive advance over *Cavalleria,* particularly in its harmonic and instrumental refinement. True enough, but the opera's also of a piece, a unified love poem that gracefully flows with unprepossessing lyricism. If you sneeze, you'll blow its tender petals all over the house.

Coming so soon from the pen of the blood-and-thunder creator of *Cavalleria,* it's an eye-opener. The simple cut and paste job that's so evident in *Cavalleria* (you can hear the glue), the lurid sensationalism of *Iris,* the barbaric splendor of *Nerone* has given way to a bucolic, never-never land filled with melodic tenderness and a ravishing human warmth. George Bernard Shaw called the *Cherry Duet* such a perfect picture of youthful infatuation that it should hang in the Tate Gallery. And anyway, if we must have a singing rabbi, better Mascagni's life-confirming David, than Halévy's baleful, whiny Elíazar.

Operatic first-borns, like their human counterparts, are much beloved, sometimes spoiled, and usually forgiven their shortcomings because the parents recognize how much their child's rearing was due to experimentation and guesswork.

That the first children of Wagner, Puccini, and Strauss, not without their glaring faults, should be treated like medieval bastards is "cruel and unusual" punishment, not fitting to their rightful place in opera history.

Die Feen (1834) was Wagner's first completed opera, having abandoned *Die Hochzeit* in 1832 upon the urging of his sister, Rosalie, who objected to the tale's gory sensationalism. In deference to sibling intuition, and sorely needing sibling financial support, he stopped scoring and tore up the libretto. Only the Introduction, Chorus, and Septet to Act I are extant. The book included a blushing bride, a love-crazed youth who climbs into her bridal chamber and attempts a rape, the defenestration of her attacker, and her subsequent Freudian "death by guilt" upon seeing his body on the funeral bier. Other than the window, it sounds like Wagner to us.

In a way, it's unfortunate that Rosalie didn't convince her brother to complete *Hochzeit* and tear up *Die Feen* instead. This "Romantic opera," based on the Gozzi tale *The Snake Woman,* has a libretto that even von Weber might have balked at. This attempt at a stage work "in the German style," only seemed to confuse poor Richard. He threw everything he could think of into it, except the inherent simplicity of the source. It's a terribly confusing, complicated libretto. The fragile fairy tale is crushed under cumbersome analytic psychology and a granite solemnity. Here, we have battle scenes, an underwater Magic Garden, enough scenic effects to make Steven Spielberg swoon, curses that turn characters to stone, resurrected children, a tenor driven mad, magic shields, men of bronze, more fairies, elves, and sprites than a Halloween parade, no less than three couples, popping in and out of charmed disguises to test their love, and a final blazing apotheosis in the realm of the Fairy King! Wagner's strong suit was never subtlety.

From this incredible fairy farrago, you'd think this opera would be in "I Bombieri," but the wizard of Bayreuth managed an amazing feat of musical prestidigitation. He set this berserk, out-of-control story to a youthful, radiant score that presages the greatness yet to come, and, as the Opera Gods know,

Wagner would later hobble himself with books just as wayward. Snatches of *Lohengrin, Tannhäuser, Tristan,* and even *Parsifal* are to be savored, and the fairy music has an unconscious nod toward Mendelssohn. The structure follows the conventions of the day with arias, duets, ensembles, and chorus proceeding in a set pattern, but the music is fresh and lively, belying the pompous story. For Wagner fans, this long (of course!) first attempt is a must; for impresarios, it requires imagination, charm, and bags of cash to do it justice on the stage. We don't know about their imagination and charm, but their cash wouldn't be wasted.

Wagner never saw his first child performed on the stage. It was announced for production at Leipzig, but the directors waffled, delaying it indefinitely, and in the meantime Wagner ran off to Magdeburg in pursuit of Minna and the conductorship of the Magdeburg Opera, or whichever came first. Five years after his death, *Die Feen* saw the footlights of Munich in 1888, in a version that Wagner had previously edited, and eighty years later this romantic opera arrived in England for four performances by the Midland Music Makers Grand Opera Society. Just who was spinning faster in the grave, Richard or Rosalie, is unreported.

Giacomo Antonio Domenico Michele Secondo Maria Puccini's first operatic child, *Le Villi,* or as it was then entitled *Le Willis,* was completed in December 1883 and just beat the entry deadline for the first Sonzogno Competition. He didn't even have time to get a proper copy of his scribbled score transcribed and had to submit his ink-blotched manuscript. Having graduated that June from the Milan Conservatorium, Puccini decided that his future lay in the musical theater. Not wanting to return home to Lucca where two positions had already been granted him—organist/choirmaster at the Cathedral of San Martino or teacher at the Pacini Institute—Puccini decided to take his chances with the one-act opera gamble. He lost. When the winners were announced, his entry wasn't even mentioned as being in the contest.

Never at a loss for influential friends and associates, Puccini, through his librettist's contacts, was invited to play the piano at the salon of Marco Sala, a wealthy Milanese patron of the arts, and he shrewdly used this opportunity to showcase his recent work. His pianistic and vocal accomplishments were appreciated to the tune of funding a staging of *Le Willis,* with Ricordi offering to publish the libretto free of charge. That's some piano playing. No wonder he liked to play in the brothels of Milan.

It opened at the Teatro dal Verme on a triple bill, sandwiched between Marchetti's popular *Ruy-Blas* and a "grand ballet" *The Countess of Egmont.* Puccini's "opera-ballet" was a smash. The critics couldn't find enough praise for the twenty-six-year-old composer: "one of the most brilliant and most promising hopes of art," "we seem to have before us not a young student but a Bizet or a Massenet," and "we sincerely believe that in Puccini we may have the composer whom Italy has long been waiting for." Pretty good notices for a loser. Ricordi had such faith in this "promising hope" that he offered a contract to Puccini for the world rights if he'd reshape the work, and then commissioned a second opera from him. Puccini was flying high indeed. Unfortunately, the re-christened, two-act *Le Villi* had her spectral wings clipped by the Turin audience and was hissed at La Scala. Subsequent performances in Brescia, Buenos Aires, Hamburg, Warsaw, Manchester, and the American premiere at the Met (1908), conducted by Toscanini with Alda, Amato, and Bonci, failed to arouse the public.

Le Villi is definite Puccini, only younger and shorter. His revised two-act version, needed by Ricordi so he could offer the larger houses a single work, was basically the original one-act neatly chopped in half with the addition of an intermission. Because the story is minimal, the original version would certainly play better these days without the unnecessary interruption. If you take the ballet *Giselle,* cut the Mother, add a Father, a chorus, and a speaking part to read two eight-line poems before the Act II *interludes,* and set it to some neo-Puccinian music, you'd have *Le Villi*. The dance music is tasty, the love-duet—repeated in the second act—could have been telephoned in from *Madama Butterfly*, while the Father's aria and Roberto's extended *scena*, both in Act II, are highly dramatic and powerfully lyric in that inimitable style only Puccini could carry off. If you cut the intermission, the whole thing is over in an hour, and you'd have time for *Gianni Schicchi*. Now that's our idea of a double-bill!

Richard Strauss's first opera child *Guntram* (1894) had a rough delivery—it took five years—and upon birth, his parentage was immediately suspect. Oh, he was beautiful, no doubt about that, but rather large for his age and had a curious resemblance to Wagner. Musically speaking, he could only have been Strauss's, but that story! The face of Wagner kept bopping in and out like a carnival's target game. Overawed by the Master's secure place in music history, a reluctant Strauss was pushed into writing an opera based upon Wagnerian principles by Alexander Ritter, a steadfast acolyte of R. W., who supplied Strauss with an appropriate story idea culled from an article in Vienna's *Neue freie Presse*. Wagner would have loved it.

A secret society of Love's Champions has sent Guntram to the evil court of Duke Robert, heir apparent, to change his cruel and profligate ways. Violence and rebellion are eschewed; only through kindness and music can the reforms be accomplished. En route, this Xerox copy of a Parsifal saves the disconsolate wife of the Duke from suicide. Freihild and Guntram fall passionately in love, but their Straussian love duet is cut short when Guntram remembers that there's work to do. Sing now, play later. At the "Triumphal Feast" in the Ducal palace, Guntram woos the court with his singing à la Tannhäuser, but Robert will have none of this prissy nonsense. Rashly he draws his sword against the saintly knight. Never having seen a Wagner opera, he is unaware of how powerful these wimps really are. Guntram slays him with one blow. The doddering Old Duke, trumpeting like King Mark, imprisons this lyre-strumming Rambo, but the dewy Freihild, knowing a good thing when she sees it, packs her suitcase, bribes the guards, and opens wide the jail doors. Who should now appear in the keep's dungeon but that musty Master of the Champions, Friedhold, who has come to take Guntram back to be judged for his violent disobedience to the code. Guntram will have none of this sanctity, tears up his membership card, and boots the old goat back into the forest. Freihild is ecstatic; now they are both free to go off, hand in hand, and play. Not so, says the suddenly contrite Guntram. In a very long aria, he tells her that he is leaving alone so that his renunciation of her will atone for his sin. She must stay here, be brave, and rule the kingdom. Before she can utter a note, he's gone in a radiant blaze of light. Resigned, with a look on her face that says, Huh?, she watches the curtain fall.

Except for that switch at the end where the Wagnerian redemption-through-love theme is turned on its head, this libretto is pure Bayreuth with its static, lengthy monologues espousing weighty thoughts and matters of art. Fortunately, what saves this garbage is Strauss's sublime music. Never has trash sounded so sweet. Richard II's lavish orchestration, those spanning melodies you could build a suspension bridge on, those impassioned duets with their unsuppressed, lyrical ebb and flow are his traits alone. Wagner never sounded like this.

Guntram premiered in Weimar on 10 May 1894 with Strauss's future wife Pauline de Ahna as Freihild. It was damned as either not enough Wagner or too much Wagner; no one seemed concerned that it was just enough Strauss. Even during rehearsals he had the same problem. Strauss reprimanded one of the cellists for not playing a passage accurately. "But, Maestro," the musician replied, "we never get that right in *Tristan*, either." A smattering of performances followed, and *Guntram* dropped out of sight. As a first child though, he was ever in Strauss's thoughts. As late as 1940, Richard was still tinkering with his beloved son in hopes of a stage redemption. He cut away some thirty minutes of music, lightened the orchestration, and clarified the stodgy text. After performances of this version in Weimar and Berlin, it, too, dropped out of sight. New York finally heard a concert version in 1983, conducted by Eve Queller, who has single-handedly resurrected many discarded operatic works. Hats off to you, Eve!

When the first run of *Guntram* was over and the prospects for revival were nil, Strauss erected a plaque in the gardens of his villa at Garmisch:

Here rests
the honorable and virtuous youth
Guntram
a singer of love songs
who by the symphonic
orchestra of his own
father was cruelly
stricken down
Rest in Peace!

Let's unearth this guy, once and for all. He may be a minor, and encumbered with some hoary conventions, but that music he sings defies entombment.

Verismo turned the operatic world from tragic tales of the nobles to melodramas of the peasants. Kings, princes, fairies, haunted groves, bellowing priestesses, doddering dons, and other unnatural personages and places were banished and, henceforth, to be duly replaced by unhappy peasants, pregnant, unwed mothers, randy circus performers, ordinary trees, and bellowing boatmen. Real life: the mundane, the commonplace, things closer to home. The fires of blood-and-guts continued to rage for years. Fighting this blaze at the turn of the century was Ermanno Wolf-Ferrari, reviving the Italian school of *opera buffa* which had burned out all by itself by 1850. Though Italian, he was an eclectic composer, combining the lyricism of his native country's vocal tradition with a Germanic orchestral style.

Eclecticism marked the attitude of the public too. Wolf-Ferrari was more popular with Germans and Americans than with his native Italians, for whom he intended his works. His first publicly performed opera, *Cenerentola,* given at Venice's La Fenice in 1900, was a stormy fiasco recalling earlier failures in that same theater, and for years thereafter he premiered his works in Germany. His career was a roller coaster of great adulation and defeat, and when he died in 1948 even the Americans had all but abandoned him. *Time* magazine's crude epitaph reported, "Died: Ermanno Wolf-Ferrari . . . heavyweight Italian composer of lightweight opera."

Lightness is the very essence of *opera buffa,* and Wolf-Ferrari's works are delightful, elegant, and entertaining. They are lighter than air but as substantial as a dirigible. And what a relief they are from all the overdone theatrics of the verismo. The only opera he composed in that genre was *Jewels of the Madonna,* a sleazy story of Neapolitan crime and sex, with a sluttish heroine, an on-stage incestuous seduction, and two suicides. His friends claimed he wrote the opera to make money, and that is exactly what happened.

Wolf-Ferrari was born in 1876 to wealthy parents: August Wolf, a Bavarian painter, and Emilia Ferrari, a Venetian beauty. As a boy he exhibited exceptional musical talent, memorizing a piano work with a single playing. He also wrote comic and dramatic sketches and composed incidental music to go with them. As relaxation he drew and painted, but when he attended performances at Bayreuth of *Tristan, Parsifal,* and *Meistersinger* at the age of thirteen, he fell completely under the spell of opera, to the dismay of his father, who wanted his son to follow him in the visual arts. August Wolf forbade all mention of music.

Young Ermanno was as precocious in the pursuit of women as he was in the arts, and he was dispatched to Germany to avoid a scandal in Rome. At Bonn's Artschule, he constantly wrote music instead of painting, sneaking manuscript paper between the sheets of his drawing tablets. Finally, with his father's consent, he entered the Munich Conservatory, but still remained a renegade. A brilliant student, he could sight-read the most difficult works and deftly handle counterpoint and harmony. On one exam he was asked to compose a fugue in four voices. Instead, he audaciously composed a double fugue in eight voices with an original first subject using the teacher's given theme as a second subject. His professor was not amused. The confines of the conservatory became too restricting, and Wolf-Ferrari left after three years, returning to Venice and the musical breezes of the Italianate school.

Unable to find a hearing for his first opera, *Irene,* his oratorio *La Sulamite* was presented in Venice (1899), just one year before the unsuccessful premiere of *Cenerentola* in his home town. After that rocky start in Italy, he returned to Germany where a revised *Cenerentola,* or *Aschenbrödel* in translation, was warmly received in Bremen. His entire life was split between the two countries, but Germany continued to present his operas while Italy ignored them. *Le Donne Curiose* was given in Munich's Residenztheater (1902), the first of his works based on a comedy by the eighteenth-century Italian playwright Carolo Goldoni, whose plays supplied librettos for Vivaldi, Haydn, Scarlatti, and Mozart. Next came *I Quattro Rusteghi* (1906) and the one-act *Il Segreto di Susanna* (1909), both premiered in Munich. At the same time, the Venetians awarded him with the directorship of the Liceo Benedetto Marcello where he arranged a bicentenary festival honoring Goldoni, but his operas still weren't being performed in Italy.

Ironically, it was in America under the baton of Arturo Toscanini that the first performance in Italian of *Le Donne Curiose* was given on 3 January 1912, with a cast that included Geraldine Farrar and Antonio Scotti. Wolf-Ferrari said that he never knew "what was in his opera" until he heard Toscanini conduct it. The same trio gave the Metropolitan its first performance of *The Secret of Susanna.* Unfortunately it was revived in only one other Metropolitan season, this time for Lucrezia Bori. This one-act opera with its two singers, a jealous husband and young wife, is a perfect example of the eternally youthful work of this neglected composer. The story is simple: husband suspects the worst of his wife, who is hiding something. She insists on her innocence but also on her privacy. Susanna's secret, which almost destroys their marriage, is that Susanna smokes—cigarettes, at that! The work provides both singers with juicy roles, requiring superb comic talents, which many opera houses can more easily produce than heroic voices. But it also offers handsome melodic vocal lines throughout and a glorious final duet. And it has that sparkling, effervescent overture.

Wolf-Ferrari's other comic operas based on his beloved Goldoni were *L'Amore Medico* (The Love Doctor) which premiered in Dresden (1913), *La Vedova Scaltra* (The Wily Widow) which premiered in Rome (1931), and *Il Campiello* (The Little Square) which premiered in Venice (1936). After his American success, the Italian theaters began performing the works of their native son, beginning with *I Quattro Rusteghi* in Rome in 1920. This work was also performed at the New York City Opera in 1951 and was revived at La Scala in 1954, but Wolf-Ferrari's works have seldom been heard in the latter half of the twentieth century. He's out of style today, and it's a pity. His comic operas have a gorgeous flow of melodic line, a reverence and flair for true *opera buffa,* and a refinement of style that is both elegant and likeable. They're a little like Puccini high on champagne; they bubble along and make us giddy with their lilting music.

In Scene 6 of Berlioz's *Béatrice et Bénédict,* the *Epithalame Grotesque,* the Kapellmeister Somarone instructs his charges, "Ladies and gentlemen, the trifle which has befallen you to perform is a masterpiece. Begin!" Very true, indeed.

We can thank Edouard Benazet for the commission of Berlioz's last opera. As manager of the Casino at Baden-Baden, Monsieur Benazet was a devoted admirer of Berlioz's music and, at his own expense, inaugurated an annual festival of Berlioz's works. Every August from 1856 to 1861, a specially formed orchestra, led by Berlioz, was housed and fed at the famed spa. "He has let me have everything I could possibly want," Berlioz wrote. "His munificence in this respect has far surpassed anything ever done for me." Given carte blanche, Berlioz could engage whomever he wanted and at whatever prices he deemed suitable. Benazet agreed to all terms in advance. Benazet's spectacular munificence, however, reached its zenith when he asked Berlioz for an opera for his new theater at Baden, the Theater der Stadt.

Depressed over his continued rebuff by the Paris Opera in staging *Troyens* and with his hopes for French recognition growing dimmer, Berlioz put away his laudanum and turned out the *opéra comique* bauble of *Béatrice.* This "caprice written with the point of a needle" shows not the slightest hint of disgruntlement or gloom; it's a fresh, witty adaptation of Shakespeare's *Much Ado About Nothing*—a delightful musical equivalent. Berlioz was as much taken by his work as were the subsequent audiences in Baden and Weimar: "To my mind it is one of the liveliest and most original things I have done." The music is quintessential Berlioz, full of that impetuous rhythmic drive, spirited harmonic adventurousness, and those haunting, melting lines of melody—musical love letters that only Monsieur Berlioz seemed able to pen with such felicity and true feeling.

Since *Les Troyens* and *Benvenuto Cellini* require such massive stage resources and massive singers to do them justice, these works aren't standard repertory pieces. *Béatrice et Bénédict,* however, as Berlioz stated, "costs nothing to put on": three principals, two sets (one, if in a pinch), a standard-size orchestra augmented only by guitar and tambourine. He also realized that "the work is difficult to perform well." That it is, for it's a chamber piece that requires a delicate balance of charm and a deftness of touch from all artists involved. The Duke of Weimar summed up the quality needed, "You must have composed it by moonlight, in some romantic spot." Contemporary opera companies, especially here in the U.S., are blessed by some extremely competent singing-actors who would be more than delighted to sink their dramatic teeth into such a succulent, moonlit morsel: Malfitano, Battle, Shicoff, Domingo, von

Stade. Rare performances of his titanic *Troyens* and *Cellini* are always welcomed and appreciated, but why must our opera houses go without those fabulous, distinct Berlioz sounds when this bright little gem is around to sparkle and glimmer? The facets are there, just waiting for some polish.

Upon the premiere, 9 August 1862, the *Baden Illustration* foretold, "Monsieur Berlioz may also give himself up with greater confidence to that melodic inspiration which, as we are aware, he possesses in abundance; and which (as we learned long ago) will always be, in his case, lofty, spiritual, original, and eminently opposed to commonplace. I believe it will run, and for a long time, too." We wouldn't want to disappoint a critic, would we?

Quick, name a Dvořák opera! Gong. Time's up. O.K., not bad. Now, name a Dvořák opera you've *seen!* We'll give you a few hours to answer that one. Why is it that Mr. Bohemia's music for the theater goes unheard except in Czechoslovakia? There's nothing is his music to be ashamed of; he's from Eastern Europe, not the Lower East Side. His beloved symphonic music is played in every concert hall in the world, cellists strain their bony fingers to execute his exquisite *Cello Concerto,* his lyric string quartets are standard repertory pieces, and every child who's taken piano lessons sweats through his *Humoresques.* So why are his operatic works neglected?

We'll give opera house managers some leeway. Of his eleven operas (counting two separate versions of *The King and the Charcoal Burner*—1871 and 1874), there are some undistinguished ones. Even Dvořák didn't press for a performance of his first opera *Alfred* (1870), and concealed the fact that he had even written one from his closest friends; *Vanda* (1875) is a five-act political behemoth, which would only scare the audience away; and *Armida* (1903) is one of those pseudo-mystical, pagan-versus-Christian crusader-type stews that is something like Parsifal and Tannhäuser using the Magic Flute meet Esclarmonde in the Seraglio. Ummm . . . never mind. *Dimitrij* (1882) and *Jacobin* (1888) would be worthy contenders for revival, since they are favorites of the Prague audiences, but we in the West have recently been surfeited with Russian operatic things, so *Dimitrij*, for the time being, would only suffer comparison to Mussorgsky's insufferable rituals; while *Jacobin*, a paean to Czech music and musicians, like Tut's tomb, remains buried, its melodic treasures unheard. Although slight, there's the charming one-act *The Stubborn Peasants* (1874), a Romeo and Juliet in reverse, in which the young lovers remain adamant in not declaring their love since their parents are so much in favor of it; the comic *The Scheming Farmer* (1877), where Dvořák's voice can finally be heard with its characteristic fluidity, melodic ease, and orchestral suavity; and the folk-inspired, Weberesque *The King and the Charcoal Burner*, in its much-improved 1874 rewriting. These all seem destined to go unproduced. That leaves two, and in our mind the two undisputed Dvořák masterpieces: *The Devil and Kate* (1899) and *Rusalka* (1900). There is no reason on earth why they should not be staged, and staged often.

Delightfully silly is an apt description for *The Devil and Kate*. This rambunctious comedy with its resourceful "happy" peasants, incompetent devils, and a contrite Princess has a beguiling folksiness. Dvořák has been blessed with a captivating libretto by Adolf Wenig that radiates sunshine and inspired the Czech master to outdo himself in luminous melodies. How could he go wrong with a garrulous, overweight heroine who, when mocked and ignored at the village dance, boasts that she'd dance with the Devil himself and, before you can say Beelzebub, one of Lucifer's minions immediately appears to woo her into Hell. Of course, once there, she drives poor Marbuel out of his mind with her complaining and carping, and eventually she's tricked into dancing right back out of the gates by her Orpheus of a peasant lad who's followed her into the depths to secure her rescue. Kate then saves the Princess from her hellish fate by frightening away the devil who's been sent there to atone for his mix-up in bringing Kate below. All ends happily: Kate, talkative as ever, is granted a fine mansion and is assured of a surfeit of suitors to turn down now that she's

[224]

rich; the peasants couldn't be more cheerful; and the Princess falls in love.

It's a delightful romp, filled with catchy dance tunes for the humans, catchier ones for the cloven-footed, and a stunning aria for the Princess in Act III. It's a fun-filled opera that really is for "children of all ages." *Hansël und Gretel* is great, and one of our favorites, but why not stage *The Devil and Kate* for the holiday season also? It's just as tuneful, has as many special effects, and is mercifully free of "cute" stage children precociously running around and making us yearn for the birch rod. Sing it in English, and we'd all be as merry as Middle European rustics.

Rusalka is a fairy tale for grown-ups, dealing with the separate-but-equal worlds between man and nature. Under a witch's spell to achieve full mortal dimensions, the water nymph Rusalka must remain dumb while her human lover remains constant. This is not to be. The Prince wearies of his silent but beautiful Esther Williams and falls for a neighborhood Princess. Rueing his choice of a gabby heiress, the Prince rushes back to the river to make amends for his waywardness. Rusalka speaks—in an exquisite aria—the Prince dies, and the sprite sinks beneath the waves, unrequited in her desire to become human.

This bittersweet tale, with interpolations from Hans Christian Andersen's *The Little Mermaid,* the French stories of Mélusine, and the *Undine* operas of Hoffmann and Lortzing, is set to Dvořák's most ravishing music. The fantastic undersea world is more charmed than the abode of the Rhine Maidens and seems so much more real than the prince's mundane world that we long to return to its spell even if he tragically waits too long. Dvořák's masterly depiction of nature and supernatural elements: forests, moonlight, rivers, elves, water goblins—would bring smiles to Weber and a familiar clap on Antonin's back from the German romantic.

Dvořák had his greatest operatic success with his water sprite. It's his only opera to be truly known in Europe and given any chance of catching on with the audience. In America, however, she's as dry as a mummy and just about as romantic. A 1976 San Diego Opera production was the sprite's American debut, and this staging was scheduled to come to the New York City Opera. But this was not to be. Like a misguided salmon, she just can't find that water route in which to spawn, and we are deprived of Dvořák's sad, but fabulous aquacade. Is there a company out there with an innertube?

Max Steiner, Alex North, Victor Young, Bernard Herrmann, and Alfred Newman will forgive us if we present the Academy Award for Best Film Composer to Erich Wolfgang Korngold. His eighteen original scores, nowhere near Max's or Victor's output, stand alone at the summit of cinematic music. Their harmonic scope, depth of invention, orchestral coloring, and sheer wealth of melody are the quintessence of that dream-romanticism that Hollywood created and skillfully promoted throughout the world. Korngold called his Hollywood scores "operas without singing," and indeed, under his master's hand, these movies owe much of their distinctive freshness and vibrant life to his musical settings. Can we even think of Errol Flynn without hearing those jaunty, swaggering marches and fanfares in *The Adventures of Robin Hood* (1938), or Bette Davis, pinned in a shimmering shaft of light, going mad to the sound of celeste and harp in *Juarez* (1939), or Ronald Reagan in *King's Row* (1942) awakening from the needless operation to find his legs amputated, the scene punctuated by knife-like dissonances, or Paul Henreid playing his virtuosic *Cello Concerto* in counterpoint against Miss Davis shooting her jealous paramoor Claude Rains in *Deception* (1946)?

Hollywood was blessed by its abundance of great musicians during its "golden age," and each one brought a unique sound to the screen, but Korngold brought a lush, chromatic emotionalism that would set the "Hollywood" style and whose influence is heard today most forcefully, and imitatively, in John Williams *(Star Wars, Superman, Close Encounters of the Third Kind).* Korngold's voice is his alone, though; one phrase is all that's needed to recognize the sweeping melody, the glittering orchestration, the muscular drive behind it. He does not lay on music in a great wash as does Steiner, nor does he point out each nuance or effect in a scene, what in Hollywood patois is called "Mickey Mousing," nor does he anticipate the action or tell the audience what to think. In his movie music, the dialogue is the libretto to an unsung opera. What the characters say determines his musical line, enhancing the underlying emotions and, at the same time, conveying the pictorial meaning of the shots. The film becomes an entity; the music has not been added on but has become integral.

Korngold was a natural for the movies. His lyricism, grand themes, and dramatic instincts were just what Hollywood needed. He gave it class. In return, he found a haven from Nazi-dominated Europe. Here, his immense talents were appreciated and lucratively rewarded. Hollywood allowed him the freedom to continue to compose, and neither his style nor his music suffered because of the movies. He was not compromised or prostituted by the twentieth-century's art form. It is because of his film music that his neglected earlier works are being resurrected and appreciated.

At the age of nineteen, when his two one-act operas *Der Ring des Polykrates* and *Violanta* were premiered in Munich (1916), Korngold's style had already formulated, and it never varied, because it didn't need to. It arose full-born. Whether writing movie scores, string quartets, lieder, or operas, Korngold's intelligent melodic voice never falters. It has a satisfying, singable, mysterious beauty that is elegant and immensely expressive. He was a *wunderkind* in Vienna and had been acclaimed "a genius" by Gustav Mahler; his "sheer unbelievable talent" amazed the conductor Arthur Nikisch; Bruno Walter called him "a modern Verdi"; and Puccini said he wished he had written *Marietta's Lute Song* from *Die Tote Stadt* (1920), which had its world premiere in Hamburg and Cologne simultaneously. His lyric and mystical *Das Wunder der Heliane* (1927) competed in Vienna against Křenek's jazzy and scandalous *Jonny Spielt Auf* (1927), going so far as to inspire rival cigarette manufacturers to offer two different products: "Jonny," a tough little number, or "Heliane," gilt-tipped, expensive, and slim. *Heliane*'s sensational Act I prison scene in which Heliane "out of pity" strips before the incarcerated stranger, even incited Albert Einstein to become a critic: "a text of an unnatural, revoltingly romantic mysticism . . . it is still more opera than mystery. With all this, there is much music in it, much solid composition which will travel to many German stages and which should be heard before very long at the Met."

Answering the call of Max Reinhardt in Hollywood, Korngold came to the United States to arrange and adapt Mendelssohn's music for the Warner Brothers film A *Midsummer Night's Dream* (1935). He so impressed Harry, Sam, and Jack with his professionalism, speed, and results (he conducted the actors while listening to the recorded score so their rhythm matched the music) that he was immediately offered the opportunity to write an original score for the debut film of their new discovery, Errol Flynn. *Captain Blood* (1935) became the prototypical swashbuckler-movie, catapulted both Flynn and Olivia de Haviland to stardom, and set a new standard for cinematic music. Returning briefly to Austria, he completed *Die Kathrin* (1937), his last opera, and returned to America to flee the encroaching Nazis.

Die Tote Stadt is Korngold's most known opera, having had a successful Metropolitan premiere in 1921, starring Maria Jeritza, who had chosen her "dear Eritscho's" work as her Met debut. The New York City Opera's premiere of the work (1975) acquainted a new generation with Korngold's achingly beautiful score, even if the multimedia production by Frank Cosaro kept getting in the way of the music. *Der Ring des Polykrates* and *Violanta* have had recent performances in New York, but they, too, deserve to be firmly placed in the repertoire. Must we be forever cursed with yet another production of *Cavalleria* or *Pagliacci?* Why not the powerful, dramatic and highly romantic Venetian world of *Violanta* or the comic and lyrical *Polykrates?* And the sumptuous *Heliane* and the folk-song inspired *Kathrin* cry out for revival.

Opera houses are sorely in need of new product. Not much

is being written these days that can even repay its commission fee by filling the theaters. Here, at least, are some already done. Managers have produced a lot worse in their choices of modern repertoire; they couldn't do much better than to choose the glimmering Korngold.

Curtain Call

———————— • •————————

A little girl, whose sister was taking singing lessons from Gioacchino Rossini, once asked him why he didn't write any new music. The maestro replied, "A waste of time, my dear girl. It's impossible for the singers to perform what I've already written."

Curtain Call

———————— • • ————————

"Anything that is too stupid to be spoken is sung."

—Voltaire

Index

[235]

[241]

[243]